VINYL

THE ANALOGUE RECORD IN THE DIGITAL AGE

VINYL

Dominik Bartmanski and Ian Woodward

Bloomsbury Academic
An imprint of Bloomsbury Publishing Plc

B L O O M S B U R Y

LONDON • NEW DELHI • NEW YORK • SYDNEY

Bloomsbury Academic
An imprint of Bloomsbury Publishing Plc

50 Bedford Square
London
WC1B 3DP
UK

1385 Broadway
New York
NY 10018
USA

www.bloomsbury.com

BLOOMSBURY and the Diana logo are trademarks of Bloomsbury Publishing Plc

First published 2015
Reprinted by Bloomsbury Academic 2015

British Library Cataloguing-in-Publication Data
A catalogue record for this book is available from the British Library.

ISBN: HB: 978-0-8578-5618-0
PB: 978-0-8578-5661-6
ePDF: 978-0-8578-5731-6
ePUB: 978-0-8578-5658-6

Library of Congress Cataloging-in-Publication Data
A catalog record for this book is available from the Library of Congress.

Typeset by Fakenham Prepress Solutions, Fakenham, Norfolk NR21 8NN
Printed and bound in Great Britain

CONTENTS

ILLUSTRATIONS

ACKNOWLEDGEMENTS

A number of factors brought us together to work on this project. The first is a shared love of independent and electronic music, the vinyl medium and record digging. Second is our mutual interest in research on material culture, materiality, iconicity and the cultural dimensions of engagements with objects. Third, despite the distance separating us, we share an intellectual lineage through having Philip Smith as part of our PhD advisory team, and also a common association with Yale University's Center for Cultural Sociology (CCS) where Dominik completed his PhD between 2005 and 2011 and Ian is a Faculty Fellow.

Yale's CCS and Jeffrey Alexander's pioneering of the iconic turn in cultural sociology has been an inspiring intellectual impulse for our thinking about material culture, but we also wish to acknowledge multiple points of sociological influence provided by many contemporary social scientists, thinkers and artists. Many of these points are evident in the bibliographical selection that forms the concise background of this book. The cultural theory and ethnographic practice of Daniel Miller was particularly important for both of us. But it is also our colleagues who are worth mentioning. Many of the following people have not provided direct assistance with the current work, but have nevertheless contributed to shaping our intellectual framing of the topic, or provided intellectual reassurance along the way. In this regard we wish to thank Andy Bennett, Werner Binder, Shai Dromi, David Ellison, Joe Klett, Michael Emmison, David Inglis, Martina Löw, Raphael Nowak, Philip Smith, Jodie Taylor, Carlo Tognato and Eric Woods.

We are indebted to many people who helped us with a variety of research assistance on the project, comprising tasks such as media searches and interview transcriptions, including Ben Green, Sally Hourigan, Susan Kukucka and Raphael Nowak. For assistance with various organizational and administrative tasks, we would like to thank Christina McKinley and Kimberley Podger, staff at Griffith University's Centre for Cultural Research and Hana Czajkowska at Masaryk University. Thanks are also due to Andy Bennett, Director of the Centre for Cultural Research at Griffith, who provided financial support for the project by funding some of the research assistance mentioned above. Csaba Szalo and Radim Marada of Masaryk University provided both institutional help and intellectual reassurance for which we are grateful. Partly this work was supported by the project Employment of Newly Graduated Doctors of Science for Scientific Excellence (CZ.1.07/2.3.00/30.0009) co-financed from European Social Fund and the state budget of the Czech Republic. In addition, when the time came to submit the manuscript, the generosity of Chris Lee from Griffith's School of Humanities in allowing Ian to spend some intensive time at Masaryk University was crucial to timely delivery.

Apart from the extended stint in Berlin to work intensively on collecting interviews and ethnographic material for the book, a good deal of the ethnographic work that was carried out in global settings was undertaken while we were completing other academic duties at meetings and symposia in Buenos Aires, London, Frankfurt, Brisbane, Bogota, Melbourne, New York and Moscow. In all these places we benefited from the help and assistance of locals, but in no place more than in Moscow and Bogota. What would have been impossible to accomplish in terms of visits to key vinyl stores due to these cities' size and complexity was made easy by the generosity of friends and colleagues. In Moscow, they were Daria Khlevnyuk, Varvara Kobyshcha, Dmitry Kurakin, Alisa Maximova and Katia Pavlenko. These colleagues drove us around Moscow's suburbs, accompanied us on its subways and traipsed Moscow's streets in late winter to help us find key vinyl outlets. Not only was the company on these excursions much appreciated, the collective sociological insights generated during these multiple vinyl-related excursions were important to our work. In Bogota, Dominik benefited from the guidance of Maria Alejandra Ochoa and Carlo Tognato. Dominik was also warmly received in London where he discussed the project at its final stages and would therefore like to thank Jeremy Gilbert, Syd Jeffers and Tim Lawrence of the University of East London as well as John Harris from the *Guardian,* the DJ and producer Colleen 'Cosmo' Murphy, Chris Moffat and the Brilliant Corners crew in Dalston for the special event on 'vinyl culture' in March 2014, which helped crystallize this culture's theory and practice. Importantly we would like to acknowledge our partners, Leanne Morgan and Kathrin Schmitt, who sometimes accompanied us on our ethnographic explorations and excursions, and shared memorable moments during our work in Berlin. Their support and belief in the value of this undertaking has been reassuring.

We would also like to express our deep gratitude towards the staff at Bloomsbury Publishing in London for taking on this project. We are especially thankful for their faith in our work on the material culture of the vinyl record. We found the Bloomsbury team to be exceptional in their professionalism, competence and assistance. Thanks especially to the project's commissioning editors, Louise Butler and Jennifer Schmidt, who oversaw completion of the manuscript, and our editorial assistant at Bloomsbury, Molly Beck. We would also like to thank the two anonymous reviewers for their helpful and timely comments on the first draft of the manuscript.

Last but not least, we want to thank the many people who we interviewed for the project and the many more we talked with during our participant observations and seminars. In particular, we benefited from insightful research conversations with professionals who work directly with vinyl at various stages of its production and consumption, from store owners to pressing plant managers, and vinyl engineers and DJs. Without them sharing their experiences and perspectives the book would hardly exist as much more than predictable media and textual analysis. To the many store owners and to all who keep the vinyl alive and have hosted or guided us during our research and digging excursions, but not participated directly, we thank you.

PREFACE

Those who find beautiful meanings
in beautiful things are the cultivated.
Oscar Wilde[1]

MISE-EN-SCÈNE

It was a chilly and dark Berlin evening, one of those that make you appreciate the interiors of the city even more. Dominik was finding his way to the newly opened second location of OYE Record Store to meet for an interview with one of the owners. It is rare for an independent shop to create another outlet in the same city, a symptomatic sign of what is a central concern of this book: the resurgence of vinyl in the digital age. It was 8.00 p.m. and the store was about to close, but a few customers were still inside digging. Vinyl is a nocturnal species, and so are many of those who hunt for it. Markus Lindner, who runs this branch of the store in the 'new' bohemian neighbourhood of Neukölln, waited in the back room. Prior to the meeting we had agreed that our interview would not exceed the standard length of one hour. But it flowed so well you did not really want to stop it just because you had discussed your main questions, or because the time was up. The interview turned into a fully fledged conversation with tangential story-telling and, eventually, vinyl playing. Markus, whom we had not known personally before, had a DJ gig that night which restricted his flexibility, but it was not until 11.00 p.m. that we finally closed the store and parted our ways. His generosity was moving, especially in the light of a prosaic but ultimately profound comment that he made about vinyl during the conversation: engaging with music through vinyl today is a kind of luxury, because it requires not only comparatively greater investment of money, but above all quite some time. And time is, after all, the ultimate luxury.

We found ourselves in a similar situation while interviewing Robert Henke, a *spiritus movens* behind the iconic projects of the electronic music world, from Monolake to Ableton. Robert kindly invited us to his apartment and explicitly limited the interview time to one hour due to his tight schedule. We ended up conversing for way over three hours, 'inspiring' Robert (his words) to pull out his favourite instruments and reflect about his illustrious creative past. To be sure, we were inspired too, and more than grateful for his precious hospitality and shrewd perception of all things analogue and digital. Likewise, being invited twice to the headquarters of Berlin-based label *Ostgut Ton* meant that we were given a privileged time in the legendary place of the club Berghain to learn directly from one of the wellsprings of world-class independent vinyl production.

This generosity was a pattern repeated time and time again by many of our interviewees, although not something to be taken for granted. Had many extraordinary individuals not given us their time and attention, this book would not have been possible. Nothing culturally significant is achieved solo, and this book is no exception. This is the case not only because it has two authors but due to the fact that any study of cultural objects owes a lot to the revelations and epiphanies that only full immersion in the social field can provide. This book benefitted directly from persons whose vinyl-centred world we set out to understand and who found time for us in their accelerated and full schedules. Our gratitude for their interest in and openness to our project can hardly be exaggerated. We enjoyed this part of the research and hope that it will show in the text that follows. Although words cannot grasp all that happens between minds and bodies, language constitutes an irreplaceable medium of human life, just like records uniquely mediate the music. Vinyl and its pleasures may not be fully *describable* but it is one of those things whose features and meanings you can see and hear, and it is those *experiences* that ground our narrative and make it intelligible.

Reflecting on the distribution and mobility of the vinyl record itself, we were lucky to be able to dig for records, talk to participants in vinyl scenes, get to clubs and bars where vinyl was played, and chat to vinyl record store staff in various places on several continents. As such, the book benefits from a cosmopolitan perspective on vinyl's emplacement in cities and scenes: vinyl moves around the world, it may signify different things in different places, it contains within its grooves diverse music cultures, but it also reflects a certain continuity of cultural meanings across these places. As Michael Bull and Les Back emphasize, different 'dance music cultures – be it R&B or techno – have deeper connections with cognate scenes elsewhere in New York or Berlin than they do with the next club'.[2]

Above all, though, the bulk of the fieldwork and interviews were undertaken in the vibrant neighbourhoods of Berlin like Neukölln or Kreuzberg. This fact forms and informs an important context for our analysis that readers should take note of. To an extent only evident in a few other places we visited in the course of writing the book, Berlin is a city not only rich in vinyl, but also where vinyl – like vintage design, third wave coffee culture, bio and second-hand markets, and cutting-edge club scenes – seems to be an integral part of the city's fabric and projected self-definition. It is, in fact, something that materially symbolizes the city, from the chic vinyl boutiques, to gritty and authentic meccas, and just simply out-of-the-way gems, to the famous Sunday Mauerpark Flohmarkt, where many vinyl re-sellers recirculate the music myths of the city in vinyl form. We were particularly fortunate, then, to be able to intensively research the topic in Berlin. Our first relatively short research stay there was in December 2011, when we visited many stores and immersed ourselves in the city's musical culture, but undertook few interviews. In contrast, just after spending a month working in Brisbane and Melbourne, we undertook a final intense period of interviews and observations over the period from August 2013 through to March 2014.

Berlin, of course, hardly needs an elaborate introduction as a city that is by now one of the global centres of music, especially dance and club culture. It is mainly in this milieu that we found many a kindred and generous spirit. It was fitting that one of our first interviews in the city was undertaken with Wolfgang Voigt, the high-octane, dynamic spirit of German electronic music, and head of *Kompakt* label. Wolfgang's candid approach to the business and art of music-making set us on the path. Learning about the scene and its relation to vinyl from the likes of Phillip Sollmann *aka* Efdemin, who received Dominik in his private apartment in Berlin to conduct the interview, or Andreas Baumecker and Jenus Baumecker-Kahmke, who made the first-hand experiences with *Ostgut Ton*'s work possible, were priceless personal experiences replete with informative conversations. Working on a symbolically charged topic, we felt a part of an iconic and nourishing environment. It can hardly get better than that. But there are also more specific reasons why researching the vinyl record and vinyl culture led us to pay special attention to what Berliners steeped in electronic dance music have to say.

First of all, these are the people for whom vinyl has never gone away. They do not 'return' to it because they have never left it. They are certainly not vinyl idealists who blindly follow this object, but nevertheless Berlin is a late modern scene perhaps most intimately connected to the thing. These producers, DJs, label and store owners have been with vinyl through thick and thin, stuck to it when the mainstream consigned it to the dustbin of history. For the most part, they are the people who keep vinyl alive, or at least the ones who have an authoritative say on what has happened to it. Things might be changing now once again, but the aura with which DJ and club culture has endowed vinyl during the last three decades remains in place, as we tried to show in our article published in 2013 in *Journal of Consumer Culture*.[3] All of our interviewees embrace cutting-edge digital technologies as they produce, play, sell and buy vinyl. They are not nostalgic purists. Instead, they combine media and take each on its own terms, whereby artistic and technological developments are revealed to be non-linear and additive, rather than mutually exclusive.

This leads us to emphasize related rationale for our focused choice of interviewees. The people connected to independent electronic dance music milieu in Germany produced, used and appreciated the analogue record when the general industry simply abandoned it in the name of technological 'progress' and greater profit. Interestingly enough, they were treating it – in Wolfgang Voigt's unabashed words – as 'the king format', even though they often embraced new electronic technologies perhaps faster than other musical milieus. In fact, new devices such as samplers formed a uniquely symbiotic relation with analogue records and lent signature feel to a great deal of underground electronic music. Working behind their turntables, the house and techno producers and DJs quite literally turned the tables of international music in the 1990s. They indeed were 'revolutionaries'.[4] As they changed the face of music, they contributed to rapidly changing culture more generally and achieved that running partly against the grain of the digital transformation. In this way, many participants in these interviews are exceptionally well placed to consider complex questions of the uses and meanings of the digital and analogue.

In other words, the artists, engineers, and store and club managers we interviewed are not only committed professionals and knowledgeable insiders of vinyl culture: they are dedicated scene-makers for whom music is a socially shared passion as much as business, and for whom the sound and the form are as important as the beat and harmonic content. Quite understandably, for some of them a tinge of sheer nostalgia may also have played a role in keeping the vinyl alive. For others, there are commercial decisions and investments behind the making and selling of vinyl. However, often their attachment to vinyl was a specific pragmatic and aesthetic/artistic decision. We find that it is precisely this range of factors that drive a good deal of the current 'revival' of vinyl. Calculation of the limitations of vinyl as thing and medium were part and parcel of assessing its relevance and uses. Endorsements of the medium were due to a combination of factors related to social commitments and personal interests, matters of aesthetics and style, investments in communal rituals and awareness of the cultural statements vinyl makes. Because they were technicians, artists and businesspeople who worked with vinyl as medium, thing and commodity, connected to particular social milieux, the people we interviewed are shrewd professionals who would drop vinyl if it weren't so important to them, to their histories and the current scenes in which they are immersed. The fact that they haven't and the reasons for it are partly what we set out to explain in this book.

As we shall show, vinyl's comparative success today becomes much clearer as we culturally reconstruct the backdrop of the wholesale digitalization of late modern culture and the sociocultural distinctions that it affords. Sociologists tend to see such a relational contextualization as one of the principles of meaning-making. This is as true of objects as it is of attitudes and values. Material things indeed work together with people to establish such meanings. These themes of context and cultural reference repeatedly surfaced in our conversations. But clearly it is the case that not all things analogue have lasting appeal just because our cultural reality got digitalized. Obviously there is more to the vinyl's enduring attractiveness. Having talked to both producers and consumers of analogue records, we believe vinyl's survival and revival to stem from a series of genuine cultural and sensual motivations nested alongside the material features of the object itself, rather than from an ephemeral retro mania inspired by a digital ennui. We find that being into vinyl means a particular lifeworld, a taste for certain experiences, and an embedded lifestyle, not a mere vintage fashion or nostalgic craze, and – as Michael Mayer once said – it is so beautiful a culture it is hard to imagine it gone.

Here we run into yet another justification to interrogate the dance and club cultures of house and techno music in Berlin and other German cities: they are exactly that – fully fledged cultures with a rich history of vinyl use, not just 'subcultures' or stylistic vogues as some may have seen them back in the day. Writing about this evolution through their study of Berlin techno scene, Felix Denk and Sven von Thülen see electronic music spinned by DJs as 'the soundtrack' to the epochal changes of *Wende*, the fall of the Wall in 1989, the 'velvet revolutions' in the region and the major transformation that ensued, including the reunification of Germany and gradually reclaiming Berlin's status as a cosmopolitan cultural metropolis. Even if difficult and uncertain, these have been truly momentous and euphoric times imbued with the *Zeitgeist* of new freedom and musical experimentation of which vinyl was an integral part. For Dominik, whose childhood was drawing to a close in 1989 in neighbouring Poland and who subsequently discovered electronic music and underground club cultures, researching the meanings of vinyl in Berlin had a special value added. From the first visits to the city and initial encounters with *Basic Channel* tracks in the mid-1990s to later academic sojourns and discovery of Shed's releases on *Ostgut Ton* in the late 2000s, his fascination with both Berlin and electronic music was incessantly deepening, and with it the passion for vinyl. Being on leave in Berlin during the academic year 2008–9 to research his doctoral thesis made Dominik familiar with the city that would soon become the fieldwork for another project. For Ian, who grew up in Australia listening to the pioneering sounds of electronic acts such as Kraftwerk and buying his first LPs on vinyl during the early 1980s, the Berlin vinyl scene was a brilliant combination of cutting-edge electronica combined with huge stocks of heritage vinyl. By our own calculations, there are over 40 vinyl stores in the city and we made many of them our ethnographic sites.

MEDIUM'S MEDIATORS: THE VINYL PLAYERS, THEIR STORIES AND BOOK WRITING

Cities, institutions and scenes are people shaping things shaping people. These things are cultural mediums. You are about to read a story of such a medium, the thing popularly called vinyl, whose multiple social lives indicate that 'mediation is a zigzag'[5] rather than a straight line. Media stem from human ideas and desires and then hone or warp them in turn. As such, media show us that culture undergoes changes through a never-ending chain of complex feedbacks between mind, body and matter, not through the fiats of technological and economic determination. The vinyl's cultural transitions and strengths bring this point to our attention, just like a DJ's mix insinuates on us the unsuspected force of individual tracks by blending and juxtaposing them in a single musical narrative.

The Berlin-based and vinyl-dedicated studios like *Dubplates & Mastering* or *Calyx*, shops like Hardwax, Rotation or Spacehall, labels like *B-Pitch Control* or *Ostgut Ton*, and clubs like Tresor and Berghain/Panorama Bar – they all have established themselves as significant players on the cultural map of the city and, by extension, reached an international recognition and status of exemplary institutions of vinyl culture. But we only begin to understand their social meanings and profundity of their cultural impact as promoters of underground records in the globalized digital era. One way of advancing our knowledge is talking to the movers and shakers behind them and reflecting more systematically on how these people approach vinyl. It is for this reason that we have decided to introduce our interviewees here as *dramatis personae* of sorts, rather than positioning them in passing in the actual narrative. We are well aware of the social and cultural locatedness of our account and our interviewees. Clearly, we cannot claim to have written the final word on vinyl. What makes our contribution unique, however, is precisely its location within particular listening and playing communities. While these communities draw on more widely held generic tropes about vinyl, the reader will find that most of the people in our study are electronic music lovers and male. More on these matters in our conclusion to the current work. Nevertheless, describing here in greater detail who they are and how we talked about the topic helps to make our story both more transparent and more human. Before we do that, a further word of sociological reflection.

In her book about romantic relationships entitled *Talk of Love*[6] the American cultural sociologist Ann Swidler cautions that 'institutions, codes, and contexts that leave their traces in talk can be hard to extract from talk itself'. We are well aware of that. We think Swidler has a point when, reflecting on her own research, she observes that 'the pragmatics of the interview situation are important, for good and ill, to the kind of evidence [a sociologist] obtains'. Certainly, there is also a danger of what sociologists and anthropologists call the 'ethnographic fallacy' – a proclivity to take the field data at face value. We have found a practical guide in Mitchell Duneier's ethnography of New York street vendors, *Sidewalk*, who recognized the pitfall of getting exceedingly 'caught up in the details' of the field. Like him, we admit that 'the scholar who wishes to avoid ethnographic fallacy must sometimes ask the reader to make a leap of faith'.[7] We believe this is true in meaningful life and art no less than in good social science. While trying to be meticulous about narrating vinyl, we attempted not to overload it with all we knew about it or learned through our research. Rather, we make it a point to organize and present what we consider significant within our new conceptual web, as well as with reference to older established understandings.

To offset the potential bias, we also analyse a range of international media materials on vinyl and refer to the extant literature on the topic. That said, we do not believe that a culture or object is fully assimilable into language. There is a degree of alterity to things and words, and it is also for this reason that participant observation on the researcher's side and an empathic leap of faith on the reader's side are jointly required. Reflecting on the 'magic of mechanical reproduction', the Australian anthropologist Michael Taussig claims that 'in the West this magic is inarticulable and is understood as the technological substance of civilized identity formation'.[8] Michael Bull and Les Back similarly conclude that 'we simply don't have the words to transpose the alchemy of sound'.[9] Musicians and DJs themselves share this reflection. In an essay symptomatically entitled 'We Breathe Rhythm', the British DJ and writer Bill Brewster reflected on this very problem. What he says about the rhythm is broadly applicable to vinyl too – the medium transmitting the rhythms of music. As he observes, 'the problem with a lot of rhythmic music and why it still lacks the language in which we can articulate what we feel is because it's not about what it is but what it does … Rhythm is about effect and it's this that I find endlessly fascinating because it's something that is almost impossible to nail down.'[10]

However, making a point about the ineffable valence to such phenomena as musical record already creatively transcends the putative limits of language and implicitly endows it with special meaning. Otherwise few books would ever have been written. While never perfectly satisfying and ridden with 'tugging of unstated sensibilities',[11] this reflexivity gives a certain sense of depth and adequacy to the said and the written vis-à-vis the concrete substances and surfaces of culture. For this reason, not unlike Taussig, Bull and Back, in writing this book about vinyl we have engaged in the process of reconstructing a 'particular story of the senses', a dimension of 'auditory culture', i.e. we were writing with a keen awareness of straddling the worlds of the senses and the mind. As we look at 'what vinyl does' we inevitably find ourselves asking *how* it does what it does, which in turn leads us to an understanding of what it is. Choosing the right words matters here. They crucially mediate culture, not unlike records, books or electronic files. David Howes put it well when he said that while 'the limitations of language are unavoidable so long as language is the medium of communication, what it is possible to avoid is the expansion of language into a structural model that dictates all cultural and personal experience and expression'.[12]

Of course, there is a difference between the difficulties of talk and difficulties of turning our finds into a narrative text. We recognize it when we interview people, then while working with them on what they had said and establishing what they meant, and finally by trying to couch the key meanings in the most fitting language. Having seen and experienced things yourself becomes as salient in this respect as a training in becoming a good writer. Therefore researching this book often relied on other, unobtrusive measures of observational studies in addition to discursive analysis,[13] and it has helped that we are both vinyl lovers as well, personally immersed in the scenes we have researched.

To aid our analysis, we used photography not only to document what we saw, which was not always possible or permissible, but also in its capacity of what Duneier calls a 'diagnostic tool' that gradually helps to derive ideas from the things seen and heard out in the field.[14] We treated words and images jointly, as mutually reinforcing elements of culture.[15] Again, due to practical limitations, only some of these images accompany our narrative here. Importantly, actual records and their covers repeatedly proved an invaluable source of discursive and sensory information, and provided us with a plethora of evidence for how independent vinyl culture represents and imagines itself, as well as how records used to be framed by the general music industry in the past. If vinyl lovers form what sociologists call an 'imagined community', then analogue record is its 'imagined commodity' – an iconic representation with sensual form and cultural impact, not just a music product.

In short, *writing* about singular cultural objects that inspire so much collective feeling of an ineffable kind in order to produce a whole *book* may run the risk of committing a kind of sacrilege and being a kind of luddite, in this case doubly so – a physical *book* about an analogue *disc*! But we think vinyl deserves a publication that frames it at once more comprehensively and more intimately. This is when talking to people behind independent vinyl enterprises and 'regular' vinyl lovers becomes again indispensable. In the end, our book is about a love, too. It may not be as complex or deep as romantic love between humans, but there is evidence that it is one nonetheless.

Having said all that, here we present finally the main players in our vinyl story, many attached to key independent institutions related to vinyl production and release, presented in alphabetical order.

Andreas Baumecker. Andreas is a renowned DJ and producer who releases records on the acclaimed Berlin-based label, *Ostgut Ton*, closely associated with the iconic Berlin club Berghain. He is also a booker and one of the resident DJs known as *nd_baumecker* at the Berghain/Panorama Bar in Berlin. Andreas can be described as an avid record collector and vinyl lover but not a purist. His collection includes tens of thousands of records, the exact number being so big as to elude the owner. Dominik interviewed Andreas at the office spaces directly above the Berghain club in November 2013. Andreas is German and in his forties, and originally from the Frankfurt metropolitan area where the electronic scene of the 1990s was particularly strong, on a par with that of Berlin. As part of the creative techno duo *Barker and Baumecker*, Andreas released a slew of 12-inch records and the critically acclaimed album *Transsektoral* in 2012, all on *Ostgut Ton*.

Jenus Baumecker-Kahmke. Jenus is the label manager at the renowned *Ostgut Ton* label in Berlin. We interviewed Jenus in November 2013, also atop the formidable building which houses Berghain in Berlin's Friedrichshain district. Jenus is a German who spent the 1990s in London, working as a master goldsmith, and moved to Berlin in the 2000s, delving into what by then was an international music scene in full swing. His extraordinarily meticulous attitude to the creative projects he is involved in aided our work on this book and shed light on what makes *Ostgut Ton* vinyl releases the high quality products they are.

Domenico Cipriani aka **Lucretio, and Alberto Marini** aka **Marieu,** are producers and DJs, who as a duo form *The Analogue Cops* and together with Steffi work under the moniker *Third Side* that contributed remixes to other labels, including Barker and Baumecker's *Remixes* on *Ostgut Ton*. They are co-owners and managers of *Restoration Records*, a label based in Berlin and are strongly committed to vinyl. In October 2013, Ian and Dominik interviewed Domenico and his label partner, Alberto, in a small Italian restaurant in a dimly lit street running through Berlin's Kreuzberg district, enjoying fresh handmade pasta, pesto and German beers. We were originally put in touch with Domenico and Alberto by Borut Cvajner, a Croatian DJ and dedicated vinyl lover himself. The two-and-a-half-hour meeting was punctuated not just by the noise of passers-by on the street, but the cheery interventions of the restaurant's chef who delivered a range of handmade delicacies. Both men are Italian and in their thirties, share a love of underground techno, and like many of their compatriots and other underground artists from Mediterranean Europe, have found a home in Berlin.

Lawrence English is a musician, producer, curator and multi-platform artist who works out of Brisbane, Australia. Lawrence founded, curates and runs the esteemed experimental label *Room 40*, which releases experimental and ambient music from Australia and around the world on all release platforms, including vinyl. As a composer Lawrence has released some sublime albums based around drones, rich tonal and electronic experimentation, and field recordings. Dominik and Ian met with Lawrence at a garage-cum-café in the Brisbane suburb of Milton, in July 2013.

Robert Henke. Robert's take on vinyl is one informed by many years of making, producing and engineering sound, not only for his own music but others also, especially as a former master cutter at the Berlin-based studio *Dubplates & Mastering*.[16] He has a keen interest in sound design and engineering. Robert was educated at Technische Universität Berlin, and he remains faithful to his background, additionally supported by the family legacy of several generations of Siemens employees. Living in Berlin since 1990, he not only understands Berlin's electronic music scenes but devotes his professional and personal efforts to creative sound engineering and pushing club performance into new directions. As well as releasing a series of influential records under the name *Monolake*, Henke was one of the developers of the groundbreaking electronic music composition and performance software package, *Ableton*. In the music website *Resident Advisor*, he describes his music as being 'about the exploration of sound, rhythm and structure, about the interaction between a sonic event and the space in which it happens'. Ian and Dominik interviewed Robert in September 2013, in his apartment in Kreuzberg, Berlin.

Michael aka ***Puresque***. Although Swiss by passport, Michael has been a citizen of Berlin for many years, and is currently living in Colombia. Despite having been deeply immersed in the Berlin techno scene, Michael is far from being enamoured with it, though the music he released as part of the duo *Puresque* is sharp and highly innovative. Being an insider for many years, he is well aware of its downsides and learned the game the hard way. Still, his love of vinyl and music is undiminished. Dominik and Ian met Michael at a quiet hour in a Japanese restaurant on Bergmann Strasse, not far from the famous record store *Spacehall*, in Berlin's Kreuzberg, where Dominik and Michael originally met witnessing a set by the legendary DJ Andre Galuzzi at one of the record store's parties.

Markus Lindner. Markus is the co-owner and manager of the well-established Berlin record store, OYE, now at two different locations, the main one at Oderbergerstrasse in Prenzlauer Berg, and a smaller outlet in the up-and-coming bohemian neighbourhood of Neukölln. Markus also performs regularly as a DJ. German and in his thirties, Markus grew up on hip-hop, notable because it was a genre whose attachment to vinyl as the key medium in the 1990s was also crucial. While still interested in hip-hop, Markus – as consumer and DJ – has decidedly moved towards dance genres, everything from disco and house to techno. This is reflected in the stock of OYE records, one of the most versatile in the Berlin electronic dance scene.

Andreas Lubich aka **Lupo** or **Loop-O**. Andreas is an internationally known and experienced vinyl mastering engineer, working in the industry since 1995. In the course of nearly two decades of state-of-the-art vinyl production in electronic music and beyond, Lupo has surely become an icon of a master cutter. Formerly spending many years at Berlin's renowned *Dubplates & Mastering*, Andreas has recently moved to *Calyx Mastering*, also one of the world's best-known mastering studios based in Berlin. Dominik interviewed Lupo at *Calyx* studios located in Kreuzberg in February 2014. The visit gave an invaluable opportunity to witness an entire cutting procedure and to see the main studio that brilliantly showcases how the analogue and the digital can coexist rather than compete with each other.

Dr Peter Runge. Peter is the general manager at pressing plant Optimal Media in Röbel, Germany, roughly an hour's drive north from Berlin. As doctor of engineering and maintenance sciences by education, and pressing plant chief supervisor by profession since 1996, Peter perfectly understands both the physics of production and economics of the trade. German and in his forties, he is by no means a vinyl purist but he appreciates it enormously. During Dominik's interview with Peter at the Optimal headquarters, he expressed his identification with and paid homage to the ethics of his independent clients who remained faithful to the format, placing passion before profit. Peter is also sensitive to what we call in this book the poetics of vinyl – the unique aesthetics and tactile appeal of the format. It is these aspects that kept popping up in our conversation and convinced us that, more than a sound carrier, vinyl is a sensual and reliable object.

Nikolaus Schäfer. Nikolaus is owner and founder of *Rotation Boutique*, located at the border of Prenzlauer Berg and Mitte districts of Berlin. The store is widely acknowledged for its superbly curated and fine selection of techno and house labels, friendly service and also much visited because of its fantastic location along the pretty Weinbergsweg. *Rotation* started out as a record-only store, but now, as is reflected in its name change, it is a broader lifestyle-oriented 'boutique' selling clothing, books and magazines, which go well with Berlin's music and youth cultures. The store, however, is founded and based around vinyl and Berlin's dance and club culture, and is therefore popular with locals and tourists alike. Nikolaus is a friendly and accommodating local whose knowledge of the Berlin vinyl scene is remarkably good. We interviewed Nikolaus in September 2013, in a café on Weinbergsweg, a few stores up from *Rotation*.

Phillip Sollmann aka **Efdemin.** Phillip is a musician and producer associated with the Hamburg-based well-regarded *Dial Records*, and resident DJ at Berghain's Panorama Bar. Like *Ostgut Ton*, *Dial*'s releases are famous for their carefully designed visual identity and minimal yet melodic approach to house and techno, often exploring their more melancholy sides. Phillip has released a slew of 12-inch singles and three albums of sophisticated techno under the name Efdemin, the most recent being 'Decay', which was written and produced during Phillip's stay in Japan in the fall of 2013 and reached the market in April 2014. Dominik and Phillip met at Phillip's apartment in Berlin in February 2014. The meeting was made possible by Niko Schäfer who acted as an invaluable liaison and recommended Phillip, whose knowledge and sensitive observations indeed proved very helpful. The way one fruitful encounter led to another illustrates the point we develop in Chapters 2 and 5, namely how vinyl culture forges tightly knit communities and ever-expanding social networks based on trust and commonality of style. Being one of the last conversations, Phillip's generous engagement with the topic and broad reflected approach effectively crystallized various themes of the book. It was a great pleasure to hear the artist talk – the artist whose music one knew and enjoyed for years but obviously never met in person.

Mieko Suzuki. Mieko is a DJ and artist, born in Yokohama but now living and based in Berlin. We met with Mieko at the Fuchsbau café in Berlin's Kreuzberg district, in November 2013. Mieko is in her thirties and works in a number of underground art and music scenes. She is also an expat – like a *flaneur* in Walter Benjamin's time – roaming the spaces of Berlin, and asserts the role of females in the cultural landscapes in which vinyl players were until recently mostly men.

Wolfgang Voigt. Wolfgang is a renowned and pioneering producer and musician, and co-owner of *Kompakt* records in Cologne, Germany. Wolfgang is well known for his seminal releases as the artist Gas, playing in a style lauded for blending minimal techno, modernist composition and the deep sounds of the kick drum with the spirit of German minimalist composition. In the 1990s, Wolfgang was a leader in the acid house, via his well-remembered Mike Ink persona. Dominik and Ian interviewed Wolfgang in August 2013 on the occasion of the 20th Anniversary Kompakt Event in Berlin, co-organized by Ableton and held at their studios in Prenzlauer Berg. With the live sets of *Kompakt* and *Ostgut Ton* artists banging just a few rooms away, Wolfgang gave us an interview laced with wit, insight and business acumen.

Needless to say, not all the valuable insights we received from our interviewees and only a fraction of our other recorded observations and experiences could be woven into the textual fabric of this book. Each interview amounted to dozens of pages of transcribed material that later underwent necessary revisions and additions which we did together with our interlocutors. Limitations of space and time as well as structural requirements of this book meant that we culled out an array of illuminating quotes and exchanges rather than all the important statements. For various reasons, every book – like every record – is a selection. And yet the entirety of our conversations and perceptions created an intellectual and emotional space without which a nourishing context for our work could not be created and sustained. Over the course of the last few years we have talked to and exchanged emails with many people involved in vinyl culture as amateurs and professionals, informal collectors, DJs, marketing specialists and label managers. There are too many to mention within the confines of the preface. Some of them, however, provided personal written accounts of how they see their engagement with vinyl as well as some more general but locally rooted reflections about vinyl's contemporary meanings. They come from such different backgrounds as Australia, Colombia, Croatia, Poland and Switzerland. We would like to thank Rafal Grobel, one of the managers of S1 label from Warsaw, who was behind bringing the International Record Store Day event to the Polish capital, as well as many of the icons of international club culture, from Moodymann and Rick Wade to Blawan and James Blake. We have learned a chunk of vinyl and music history from Ben Gosney and Yuri Gomez Morales. We found a proverbial vinyl lover in the person of Borut Cvajner from the city of Pula, who connected us to the Analogue Cops in Berlin. It is through the talks with very young people like Moritz Reisberger and Dominique Lebel that we could maintain our conviction that vinyl's international revival is not driven by nostalgic sentiment of aging baby-boomers or orchestrated by middle-aged hipster victims of vintage fashion, but by broader and deeper processes cutting across many variables in which the young cohorts that grew up with laptops and iPods also play a significant and self-conscious role.

THE BOOK'S TRAJECTORY

In this work we tell the contemporary story of the vinyl record from multiple vantage points. Though the analogue record is over 125 years old, we don't aim to simply retell or reinterpret the history of this object. Many excellent studies of the history of sound and recording are already available and this is not our primary interest. Rather, for the most part, we look to account for the recent situation of the vinyl record by exploring the range of materially mediated cultural meanings within which it is entangled. To identify and articulate these meanings we propose a series of interlocked narratives encased in separate chapters, each of which proposes a distinct set of notions and conceptual arrangements designed to illuminate different dimensions of vinyl. More specifically, we provide a heuristically structured historical background of vinyl's cultural biography (Chapter 1), and subsequently delve into different aspects of vinyl's functionality as medium (Chapter 2), vinyl's production and qualities (Chapter 3), as well as the consumption of analogue records (Chapters 4 and 5). At every stage we look to the institutional means, material affordances and properties, economic and cultural agents, and cultural-economic logics which sustain the vinyl in the current era when for all intents and purposes it should be extinct.

How could an old and apparently obsolete medium possibly withstand the tide of digital-technological revolution that effectively transforms the musical carrier from cumbersome physical object to weightless electronic information? This question reverses one foundational question posed by Regis Debray in his manifesto for social mediology, namely 'how does a novel technological object dislodge a traditional domain?'[17] The digital revolution certainly dislodged much of the analogue domain, but the analogue record has somewhat unexpectedly managed to withstand the radical turn of events.

The story of this unlikely survival is complex. This complexity resides not only in the myths and narratives surrounding the vinyl and its rich history but also in how they correspond with today's material reality and in the relational and physically mediated constitution of such pairs of meanings as old/new, authentic/contrived, original/copy, valuable/cheap or 'warm' vs 'clinical' sound. To understand the analogue record in the digital age means also to re-evaluate all these traditional dichotomies. The analogue/digital divide works here as a heuristic master trope that can stand for many contemporary processes of social distinction and symbolic classification. Our contribution to these debates and topics is to indicate that the associated boundaries and differentiations are not just arbitrary conventions but are also materially mediated, intersubjective experiences. This is a new perspective in sociology. Undoubtedly, though, using the resources of cultural and material analysis, the complexity of vinyl's appeal is discernable and traceable, precisely because such accounts innovate by bringing objects and their mediating effects into the picture. Writing histories of the senses and sociologies of sensory formations as we do in this book on vinyl culture enables us to flesh out an alternative to purely discursive idea of culture which, as George Marcus noted in his endorsement to Michael Taussig's book, 'is now threatening to reach a level of saturation and predictability'.

Working from within the relatively recent traditions of cultural sociology, but fusing it with and extending it through the intellectual resources offered by studies of objects and materiality, we aim to further advance meaning-centred analyses of material objects. We believe that this is still an innovative path to follow, especially within the mainstream currents of cultural sociology where standard intellectual training and pedigree consistently favour a focus on discourses, on narrative structure, and the uses of words to do things. We believe that this study of vinyl shows how we can benefit from adding a perspective that recognizes a series of consequential ways in which things do things as well as form human subjectivities, including our seemingly purely conventional verbalizations. As contemporary thinkers from George Lakoff and Mark Johnson to Jonathan Sterne emphasize, there is no neutral or 'innocent' language because our speech has a deeply figurative dimension. Our work contributes to a growing understanding that this dimension is in great part nested within specific regimes of materiality and concrete 'sensory formations', not just discursive formations, and that it is imbricated with our experiences with things and spaces. Thus, we also approach object–human relations as ones of deeply *felt* and tangible connections rather than just *coded* and decoded communications, based on supposedly stable abstract logics. Like records, humans remain 'analogue' and corporeal beings, the crucial point made by both Peter Runge and Robert Henke.

We found it symptomatic that Wolfgang Voigt would repeatedly refer to vinyl's sexiness, and we heard this description of vinyl's 'magic' in a number of informal conversations we had within Berlin scenes. Indeed, our evidence reveals the analogue record to be multisensory object, full of not only special sonic properties and auratic affordances but also tactile and visual qualities amenable to sensually charged uses and pleasures. There is not only unique acoustics to vinyl but crucially also an engaging haptics. Drawing on German language, we might perhaps describe it as a kind of *Gesamtkunstwerk*, a compressed multisensory performance that works both in dance/club and rock contexts. Interestingly, this is the word used on Joy Division's rare German-titled 7-inch single 'Licht und Blindheit' which was the original 1980 release of the band's famous track 'Atmosphere' and included imagery redolent of Caspar David Friedrich's romantic paintings. Limited to 1,578 copies and never reprinted, it has become one of the holy grails of independent vinyl culture, reflected in exorbitant prices of thousands of pounds for a copy in mint condition. As the book unfolds, we discuss more of such cases and present the synaesthetic impact that vinyl makes on people.

In short, vinyl is a historically iconic sound carrier. Despite being the mechanically reproduced copy, it has the 'magic' of temporality and full-blown *poetics* replete with sensual connotations and intimate necessary connections to artists and other objects like turntables that make it move and play music. In this sense vinyl is not just about mixing sounds or tracks but also about blending sensations, objects, thoughts and ideas within one package. It possesses a multisensory, poetic beauty that may be beyond perfect description, but many of our respondents did not hesitate to use the word 'magic' or 'sensual' and for them any interesting record is a kind of prize. Georges Bataille provides a crystallizing insight for these remarks: 'Poetry leads to the same place as all forms of eroticism – to the blending and fusion of separate objects.'[18]

We found the multidimensional perspective adumbrated above intuitively persuasive and feel it needs to be further elaborated. In what follows we offer this kind of elaboration about one of the enduring icons of modern material culture and along the way we unravel the attachments people have developed to it. These attachments and perceptions are worth narrating. After all, sociologists study people, their intentions and commitments, their attitudes, behaviours and values, don't they? The material turn decisively expands a scope of potential answers to this question. It enriches sociological explanation. Words do things, they make other things happen, they form boundaries, identities and collectives, but *things also do things,* they shape people, and without objects in our analytic frame we miss out on masses of relevant information.

We find it telling that one of the landmark techno albums by Jeff Mills released on the legendary Berlin label *Tresor* in 1994 contained this explicit statement: 'The need to understand others and the way they live, think and dream is a task that is nearly impossible to imagine without theory and explanation.' We aim to contribute to the task with concepts and explanations offered in this book.

CHAPTER ONE

Vinyl as Record

Several Lives of the 'King Format'

THE POWER OF THE FORM

Perhaps there is no such thing as music, only musical experiences, and these vary greatly. Listeners always seem to bring an element of 'subjectivity' with them. The physical properties of sound 'objectively' shape what we hear. These two popularly distinguished levels of understanding are actually intertwined, so that the line between them gets blurred. If we learn from our historical experiences with sound and intensive modern exposure to music, then one of the lessons indeed is the fact that 'you can take the sound out of the human, but you can take the human out of the sound only through an exercise in imagination'.[1] What remains rather clear is that musical experiences exhibit variability typical of other cultural experiences and a chief reason why they vary is that creation and transmission of music requires complex mediation. The musical medium matters, the conditions of production and reception do too.

Mediating music is a universe unto itself. There is no doubt that the technological and cultural *how* of music is as important as its melodic and rhythmic *what*. As John Cage[2] has stated, 'What people ultimately have to learn is to use records not as music, but as records'. Broadly conceived matters of form can and often do trump the issues of content. As this book seeks to show, the boundary we conventionally tend to draw between these aspects is another one that loses its sharpness as we set out to understand the life of a music format like analogue record. In fact, when it comes to vinyl we talk about multiple lives. This seems especially true when we consider the social significance of music. The question of the sound carrier and its historical trajectory belongs to this story. In real life, the music format is inseparable from the practices that it affords and contexts in which it is typically ensconced. This is true of the vinyl, equally as it is of the Walkman and the cassette,[3] or the mp3 player.[4] The practical entwinement of manifold aspects of musical experience makes it difficult to tease out how they are connected to each other and what does what. As listeners, we tend to intuitively simplify the matter by saying, 'music is all that counts'.

In this book we would like to take a more counter-intuitive path and show that, however useful, 'music' is a simplifying figure of speech, an elision of everyday language that may gloss over many obvious and less obvious conditions that make it such a powerful social force. These conditions are historically dynamic, technologically contextualized and materially mediated, and as such they count for more than we would normally care to admit. In short, there is more to music than meets the casual ear.

At least since E. H. Gombrich, we know that the frame contributes to making its content. Marshall McLuhan famously insisted that the medium is the message. The American historian Hayden White argued that, even when it comes to writing non-fiction, the form of representation constitutes its content. In more general terms, the 'outside' defines the 'inside'. The *way* we do *things* co-constitutes these things and us too, although there has been a bias to downplay this insight as mere technicality or 'surface' of social life in favour of society's putative latent functions, generative codes, 'deep plays' or simply its 'depth'. However, the surface and depth are intimately related, one recalling the other through practical engagements. In fact, the two frequently become indistinguishable in practice. And, precisely because of this intimate relationship between surface and depth, the issue of the material form or format of things keeps returning in social sciences. Daniel Miller strikes a compelling note when he suggests that the historical contexts of materiality constitute our collective unconscious. But this may be particularly true of professional scholars and intellectuals conditioned – to be sure – by their own contexts of production and interpretation. In what may be called lay communities, *materiality* and framing is not so much suppressed; instead, it is taken for granted or acknowledged in non-discursive ways. It also tends to get conflated with the idea of a *materialistic* approach to things that economize everything, reducing aesthetics to mere decoration, and framing to packaging. The thing is that both styles of thinking – the materialistic reductive one and the abstract discursive one – miss the point of material form being something special and co-productive of even our deepest sentiments. This is the general idea behind some specific tasks of this book such as treating the analogue record not only as a musical record but also as a record of culture (in the current chapter), seeing the analogue medium *itself* as a cultural message (in Chapter 2) and experiencing 'deep stuff' in the concrete surfaces of the thing (Chapter 3).

The vinyl-centred trajectory of mainstream producers, publishers and consumers of musical works is an illustrative record of modern aesthetic developments. This trajectory has somewhat erratic character. As we shall see, vinyl's cultural biography has been a transformation of something presented as irreplaceable, that 'can't get obsolete', to something that gets discarded as soon as more profitable and convenient stuff comes our way. But there is also another parallel dimension to this story, one that is surprising and that offsets the putative power of the mainstream. It sensitizes us to the independent force of mediums and the mediating power of independent cultures. It is about vinyl's own resilience and what it has come to mean to different communities and pockets of the market which picked up the pieces where the mainstream left off. And it is about what social scientists and our interviewees alike call the aura of art objects, or the 'magic of things', or the 'power of appearances'. These are not mere esoteric metaphors, although metaphors too do count for more than we typically grant them.[5] These descriptions refer to real experiences.

To assert that there is no such thing as music, only historically specific social experiences of music, goes hand-in-hand with an understanding that there are no 'immaterial' cultural phenomena. The world of human culture is the world of sensual bodies, concrete objects and complex mediations. Perhaps it is the overpowering extent to which our culture is nowadays mediated that sometimes gives rise to certain romantic ideas of 'direct' contact with art or belief in 'pure' aesthetic substance. But there has never been a way out of material mediation. What changes is the *kind* of medium we adopt. Key questions are how and why media change, and why some happen to resist change. The persistence of the analogue record in the digital age offers a track record of a medium that refused to go despite being marginalized and that therefore gives us a fresh angle on the importance of the medium in general. Continuity despite massive irresistible transformations – that is the issue at stake when we talk of vinyl's lasting and resurgence in the digital age.

In his book *How Music Works*, David Byrne kicks off with a reflection congenial to ours. He writes about creation: 'Context largely determines what is written, painted, sculpted, sung and performed. That doesn't sound like much of an insight, but it is actually the opposite of conventional wisdom.'[6] We concur. The story of vinyl we narrate in this chapter and flesh out in greater detail in the subsequent parts of our book is a specific variation on this general theme. In particular, what we learn from the case of the survival and revival of the analogue in the digital context is that even if the context does not *determine* cultural phenomena, it actively shapes our interpretation of what is created, and how we establish the value of things. The wholesale digitalization of culture, not just of music, made us sensitive both to what we have gained and to what we have lost, or may be losing, as we are rushed to embrace perennially upgradeable technologies. Often times, things once taken for granted reveal their value only when they are displaced. We will talk more about it in Chapter 3, which is devoted to the 'thingness' of vinyl, its qualities and entanglements.

A given cultural experience makes more sense or feels unique or compelling especially in contrast to a different variation on this experience. What it means is that we need to connect the thing and its context at the level of embodied experiences, not only abstract 'processes' and 'structures' that historians and sociologists tend to foreground. As we put things in historical perspective, bringing in new circumstances and current developments is as important as recognizing the 'roots' and past developments. And to make both the past and the present alive in our words, we have to account for what things meant in practice, how they changed sensual experience, what they made possible aesthetically and socially, why they move our bodies and souls. As cultural objects do these things over time, some of them change history. We learn all this from the career of vinyl. We just have to approach it holistically, not only with 'reason' but also with 'heart', to use Blaise Pascal's old distinction.[7] As Constance Classen writes in her book *The Deepest Sense: A Cultural History of Touch*: 'The intention is to explore how the corporeal practices of any particular period relate to the cultural context of the time, and how this relationship changes under the influence of new factors'.[8]

In other words, while vinyl demands attention as a neglected and rediscovered cultural agent whose inherent properties will be scrutinized here, it would be unfair not to realize that the context of digital revolution made us aware of more than one thing about analogue records and other pre-digital media. When it first entered the world, the digital seemed to be the kiss of death to the analogue. Nowadays the idea of the 'analogue' record makes sense again, and it is not *despite* but partly *because of* digitalization. Sometimes displacement does not mean being replaced but relocated to a new, perhaps more advantageous position.

While this is a paradigmatic unintended consequence, it is not random either. Digitalization sheds new light on analogue technology. It is easier to see vinyl as the 'sacred' format when virtual files become the mundane 'everyday' format. Moreover, as our use and understanding of 'virtual reality' has proliferated and deepened, we are in a position to realize that what we face is more of an 'augmented reality' than anything else. This is 'more like adding a layer of digital content to the existing world'.[9] Under such circumstances, it is easier to see vinyl and other 'analogue' media as a base for the digital, or as one of the strands of the 'real' that grounds the digital. Adding even more complex layers of electronic stuff to our experience may blur the traditional contours of 'reality' but – and here comes an important point – it may nowadays be more of an intellectual than bodily/experiential effect. As Steven Levy notes, 'it's interesting that "virtual reality" never really caught on all that much. I guess people don't really want their senses completely hijacked.'[10] Robert Henke shares this sensibility, and we will return to it in Chapter 4, where we unravel the meaning of the 'good physical commodity' vinyl exemplifies.

To the extent that the radical digitalization initially turned vinyl into endangered species of cultural and technological evolution, it seems to be one of those Nietzschean forces that make vinyl stronger rather than weaker. The truth is, nevertheless, that few cared at all about the hastily abandoned vinyl until sales numbers 'proved' that it *can be* 'successful' and when the hip showed that it *is*, well, hip. Vinyl's cause needed its committed carrier groups who would act upon its objective and relational powers when few believed in their relevance anymore. Without such groups, their dedication, passion and sacrifice, the *social value* of a thing is merely potential. Importantly, for the lovers of music on vinyl, like the ones we interviewed for this book, numbers did not matter then and they do not really matter now, even if some of them happen to make more money out of vinyl than only five years ago. It takes such dedication to command respect and create cultural meaning, although even these may not be sufficient conditions of successful cultural performance. In the face of massive systemic top-down changes, it is the unflinching commitment of the representatives of these dedicated independent carrier groups that establishes them as credible in our eyes and effective in their respective domains. Still, we always have to keep one eye on the broader context and ask why vinyl would have to go through the bumpy mainstream technological dialectics of triumph, downfall and renaissance? All this within the span of half a century.

THE ARC OF 'PROGRESS': THE RISE AND FALL OF PHYSICAL RECORDS IN THE MAINSTREAM

The analogue record stores tones and tunes. It gives tactile form to the ephemeral temporality of music in a double sense: as a fixed durable playback device whose lasting enables us to return to it at any given time, and as continual sonic wave etched in vinyl whose form is the concrete image of a musical piece unfolding in time. In the former capacity it resembles the book. In the latter capacity it is akin to traditional photography. As such the analogue record is one of the landmark elements of the modern mediascape, an icon of recording that thanks to its remarkable affordances came to sit at the core of great cultural transformations of the twentieth century.

In a nutshell, vinyl was a high-modern sound carrier. Connecting artists and their audiences via the work of other artists and engineers, vinyl materialized what at first glance seemed immaterial: feelings, thoughts, ideas and ideals. It captured the abstraction of music, it fixed sonic waves in the tangible form of a record. Lawrence English put it succinctly when he told us: 'composing music is intangible, vinyl makes it tangible'. When the people of The Vinyl Factory produced a short documentary about the art of vinyl mastering, it was tellingly entitled 'Sculpting Sound'. While records are like books and photographs in their capacity to create cultural archives, they may also be artistic objects in their own right. They resemble sculptures and pictures. You do not only hear music, you are in direct visual contact with music as the tone arm 'reads' the sound message of a revolving record. That's part of an analogue musical experience.

As early as 1935, Marcel Duchamp created a series of so-called 'rotoreliefs' – discs that resemble contemporary slip mats and feature special graphic designs. Observing them rotate on a turntable creates all kinds of mesmerizing visual effects. In keeping with his idea of opposing what he dubbed 'retinal art', Duchamp's rotoreliefs presciently pointed to the artistic valence of records as readymades. Today not only picture disc or centre label may play a similar aesthetic role, but also a special kind of cut or aforementioned slip mat.

In this context it is quite easy to see why the analogue record may be approached as a kind of *Gesamtkunstwerk* – a total piece of art. And yet, before the tsunami of digitalization hit, we took the synaesthetic character of vinyl for granted, just as we have done with many other miraculous marriages of technology and culture. It is therefore useful to unlearn our blasé approach to common technologies like vinyl. Michael Taussig phrased it well when he wrote that 'Westerners would do well to be reminded of the magic of sound-reproduction in their recent histories – their fascination with the introduction of transistor cassette recorders in their lifetimes, and beyond that the effect of the first sound recorders and reproducers in the United States'.[11] Today we indeed need the analysis of a social scientist or the sensitivity of an artist to be reminded of these facts and appreciate what made so many of our aesthetic delights possible in the first place.

Mesmerized by the deceptively effortless pragmatics of the digital world, we have for a time become detached from the poetics of physical media, as well as their politics and historical importance. We seem to have forgotten that the analogue record was to sound and music what the book was to word and literature. This is an enduring legacy of vinyl, one that does not automatically cease to exist when a new thing comes, just like theatre hardly gets 'replaced' by cinema. Each outstanding medium is capable of generating its own culture, and every culture sustains its iconic objects. Vinyl is a case in point, underscoring a principle of objectification once articulated by Regis Debray: 'No tradition has come about without being an invention or recirculation of expressive marks and gestures ... and no new dimension of subjectivity has formed without using new material objects.'[12] When introduced in its current modern form of the 12-inch vinyl LP in the late 1940s, the analogue record embarked on a new path of changing both the subjectivity and objectivity of cultural life. As we shall see, it has created conditions for blurring the boundary between the two. By the time it was technologically honed and made widely accessible in the late 1950s, vinyl began to change culture forever.

Sociologically, it meant two things above all: (1) music and sound could now be transmitted not only in space but also in time; and (2) music entered the household. Music is thus fixed through a tangible and durable form of records, and as such it is a giant – and unprecedented – step in democratization of access to musical experience, recorded voice and other sounds. Not only is it a giant step, it is truly revolutionary event that has irreversibly altered the scale and depth of the reception of musical aesthetic and other audio content. Now, once recorded and disseminated, records are in principle available to anyone. It is a truly public medium for private use.

Because music is both an entertainment factor and a matter of knowledge, the implications of introducing records to the world were far-reaching. Vinyl was spreading knowledge in various senses of this word: it exposed people to music and thus made them aware of what is out there and what other people are capable of doing with voice and instruments. It enabled people to learn the musical forms from hearing without socially privileged and costly formal training, it made them aware of themselves as they reacted to music, and opened up the world of cultural multiplicity and musical tradition. This is a privilege in a pre-recording world and cannot be taken for granted. It is hardly a random occurrence that giant pop legends of our time like Sinatra, Miles Davis, the Beatles, the Rolling Stones or the artists of Motown emerged and inspired incredibly intense response at the time when records entered the market as socially available modern products. Consider this statement from Keith Richards' autobiography:

> I've learned everything I know off of records. Being able to replay something immediately without all that terrible stricture of written music, the prison of those bars, those five lines ... Being able to hear recorded music freed up loads of musicians that couldn't necessarily afford to learn to read or write music, like me ... With recording it was emancipation of the people. As long as you or somebody around you could afford a machine, suddenly you could hear music made by people, not set-up rigs and symphony orchestras. You could actually

> listen to what people were saying, almost off the cuff. Some of it can be a lot of rubbish, but some of it was really good. It was the emancipation of music.[13]

You would expect records to forever occupy a venerable place in the cultural landscape, if not in the big music industry. As music continues to be an ostensibly heavyweight player in global civilization, so could records continue their historic mission and aesthetic appeal. In 2007 the analogue double-sided disc became 120 years old. A year later the world could join Columbia Records to celebrate the 60th anniversary of its flagship product – the 12-inch vinyl record as we know it today. But no spectacular festivities ensued. No special releases and high-profile debates preceded those historical dates. On the contrary, the mid-2000s was the time when vinyl's presence on the market reached its all-time nadir, both in the mainstream and in the club scene. Overlapping with that was the sharp decline of CDs that repeated the life cycle of vinyl at a significantly faster rate, additionally accelerated by the steep improvements in electronic formats. Consequently, big music outlets and smaller independent stores, especially in the United States, were closing fast, since the *raison d'être* of their physical existence seemed to be called into question.

Few cared about this silent downfall as the digital revolution has come to triumphant completion. Then it was the Apple iPod that iconized the decade and *sound* seemed to matter only insofar as it could *move* along with people and things.[14] Mobility and the designed personal object seemed to have overridden other considerations. Therefore, even fewer expected that the upcoming years would bring a sense of vinyl's renewal evidenced by skyrocketing sales and ensuing media buzz. In half a decade between 2009 and 2014, the analogue record had its breakthrough, or it seemed to have broken one more record – it gained a new commercial life and unexpected publicity. Although some of this unexpected media attention looked like paying long overdue lip service, the phenomenon appeared to have undeniable appeal of a cultural anomaly in the paradigmatically homogenized late modern music market.

BECOMING ICONIC: THE GOLDEN AGE OF THE VINYL LP

Like other technological objects, vinyl is both a child and a victim of 'progress', and thus – ultimately – can be seen a mere step in the chain of technical and economic evolution. It is all the more effortless to buy into the notion of an inevitable succession of formats and irreversible replaceability of media when almost every aspect of our key technologies gets constantly 'updated', whether it is pragmatically necessary or not. Despite some initial enunciations to the contrary, in time it became clear that the analogue record was destined to repeat the life cycle of its kind – just like it replaced preceding formats, it would in turn be replaced by new ones. It did not come out of the blue. Its birth meant superseding the earlier forms such as shellac records, with life expectancy strictly dependent on the coming of the next species of technical evolution driven by quest for improvement. Comparatively, vinyl had a long run and undisputedly ruled the music world for quite some time. It definitely had the proverbial '15 minutes of fame'. Interestingly, it largely overlapped with the lifework of pop art master Andy Warhol who coined the phrase.

Vinyl rose spectacularly in the mid-1950s only to quite abruptly exit the mainstream in the mid-1980s. However, because music records are not *just* the transitory *products* of technology and economy but furnish the world of culture and aesthetics too, they have remained responsive to non-capitalist and non-rationalistic logic of the human sensorium and social meanings. Such 'cultural logic' is not necessarily linear, and not necessarily logical in the strict sense either. But it retains a certain autonomy, strong enough to withstand pressures of money and power, to explain counter-intuitive phenomena and to question and critique seemingly 'natural' or 'inexorable' trends of the social life of this object. The arc of vinyl's story provides us precisely with such a denouement. In particular, vinyl's unlikely survival and perhaps even more surprising revival charts a sociocultural path that questions supposedly normal, inevitable and totalizing effects of progress. It shows us what can transpire instead, suggesting alternatives and pointing to non-standard, hybrid practices of an 'augmented' rather than 'virtualized' reality. Let us glance over this historical drama.

While the 12-inch vinyl really hit the market only from the 1950s on, the double-sided black analogue record had entered the mediascape of modern society much earlier. Throughout the first half of the twentieth century, records were made of different materials but the one made of a shellac resin became predominant. It revolved at a speed of 78 revolutions per minute (rpm), which meant 4 to 5 minutes of audio material per side for the 12-inch record and only about 3 minutes for another popular format of 10-inch. Even if a relatively elite object in the preceding decades, the shellac record slowly but surely permeated the domestic spaces and collective consciousness of Europeans and Americans, and certainly provided the early experiences of delight and magical fascination with the recorded music that Taussig mentioned.

By the time Germany plunged Europe into the abyss of Nazi terror putting the powers of modernity to its darkest uses, the analogue record had become a paradigmatically modern cultural medium there and beyond. During the dire wartime, records might have provided a spark of normality and hope on both sides of the barricades. That was the case in Berlin too, which only a decade earlier experienced an unprecedented creative boom in many domains of art and technology and that 'was never a natural constituency for the Nazis' due to its left-wing traditions and cosmopolitan elites who generated 'more opposition to the Nazis than any other German city'.[15] We find a kind of record of that in the oeuvre of the German painter Karl Hofer (1878–1955), a chronicler of the social life in Berlin during WWII who was considered a 'degenerate' artist by the Nazis due to his involvement in the movements of expressionism and so called new or 'magical' objectivity. In 1934 he was dismissed from his professorship of art and until 1945 had to create under a work and exhibition ban. One of the paintings that survived the bleak era hints at the analogue record's potential as diversion. Created during the war in 1941, two years before his studio got destroyed in a bombing raid, the painting 'Mädchen mit Schallplatte' (Girl with Record) foregrounds the iconic look of the 12-inch

FIGURE 1.1: 'Mädchen mit Schallplatte' (Girl with Record), Karl Hofer, 1941. With thanks to the Albertina Museum, Vienna.

analogue record held by a half-naked young woman, while another, smaller disc and a gramophone are placed on the table nearby. While the dominant background palette matches the girl's lackadaisical and sad countenance, the stark red and purple round labels of the records stand out. The Vienna-based Albertina Museum used the caption which explains the presence of records as an act of 'integrating the elements of modern life' portrayed against the background of 'listlessness and resignation of the picture's protagonist'.

Interestingly, the war contingently occasioned the appearance of the vinyl record. As the introductory information of Yale University Music and Sound Recording Cataloging states, 'during and after World War II when shellac supplies were extremely limited, some 78 rpm records were pressed in vinyl instead of shellac (wax), particularly the six-minute 12″ 78 rpm records produced by V-Disc for distribution to US troops in World War II'.[16] The shellac discs produced between 1925 and 1947 employed electrical rather than earlier, strictly acoustic and mechanical recording techniques that provided decent fidelity but were monophonic and brittle. Moreover, due to the high revolution speed they utilized, not much musical material could be squeezed onto them.

With Europe ravaged by the war, the record industry first thrives especially in the Americas and it is in the United States where the 12-inch and 7-inch vinyl records were pioneered and commercially launched to a great success. Introducing the so-called microgroove that contained sound data to be played at significantly slower speed of 33⅓ enabled the industry to pack much more sound on the by then familiar format of a 12-inch (30cm) disc. The birth dates for the 12-inch album and 7-inch single discs are 1948 and 1949, respectively. But these inventions were not just a direct consequence of the wartime material economy. Aesthetic motivations were at play too. They took the forms of individual vision, collective feelings and the feedbacks between them. Goddard Lieberson of Columbia Records was one of the industry executives whose aesthetic taste and business decisions proved visionary. As Clive Davis recalls, it is Lieberson who 'is widely credited with introducing the LP format – the vinyl, 33⅓ "long player" that replaced 78s, which held far less music – to the American public. Not coincidentally, the more expansive LP was ideally suited to the classical music and original-cast recordings that Goddard loved.'[17] The incredible potential of the new sound carrier was lost neither on Columbia nor on anyone else in the industry.

As a result, the 1950s was the decade that quickly and firmly established vinyl as the dominant modern analogue format. In 1957 stereophonic vinyl became available. An unprecedented quantity of music was then made available in unprecedentedly high quality. Quantity and quality went more or less hand-in-hand, a true feat of civilizational change. Increased production and availability overlapped with dynamic technical enhancements. Columbia not only collaborated with such institutions as the New York Philharmonic and Leonard Bernstein to release the classical repertoire and whatever then passed for 'high culture', but used the expertise of artists like Bernstein to promote new, avant-garde or dance-oriented musical forms through the new sound format. Jazz was a perfect genre to promote, as it encompassed vibrant avant-garde and dance cultures. Here the cutting-edge musical genre of progressive cultural potential matched the cutting-edge industry and its vision of progress. The inventive company very self-consciously advertised not only such genres and their ambitious, often black representatives like Miles Davis, who debuted on Columbia in 1956, but also its own educational role in developing the new signature product, the long-playing vinyl album. Records were the source of knowledge and cultural competence, both aesthetically and technically. Leonard Bernstein's 1956 educational record *What is Jazz* is an epitome of how vinyl was at once the perfect medium for new music as well as an element of acquiring a new lifestyle and new competence offered by corporate innovation and standardization. Released the same year, Erroll Garner's *Plays for Dancing* is another example. The back cover contained instruction on how to properly use the turntable's needles: '"Permanent" needles may cause permanent damage.' Customers were advised to 'play safe' and consult their Columbia dealers.

Many other albums released at that time included all kinds of commercial and technical information, one particularly common being: 'Columbia, the greatest name in sound, is the originator of the modern "LP" record. Your dealer can demonstrate a varied line of Columbia phonographs, styled to enhance the decorative scheme of your home. See him today for the pleasure of your life.' For quite some time the sleeves of Columbia LPs featured carefully curated covers and special notes explaining the cutting-edge production process and the technique of providing 'the true spectrum of high fidelity'. Importantly, they invariably evoked the authority of science and technological progress to establish its cultural legitimacy and ultimate technical perfection, a strategy that three decades later would be turned against vinyl itself. Symptomatically, Miles Davis's 1958 album *Jazz Track* had not only standard musical liner notes but also the information about the vinyl format itself that read: 'This Columbia High Fidelity recording is scientifically designed to play with the highest quality of reproduction on the phonograph of your choice, new or old. If you are the owner of a new stereophonic system, this record will play with even more brilliant true-to-life fidelity. In short, you can purchase this record with no fear of its becoming obsolete in the future.'

As we shall show, the industry changed its mind as soon as a prospect of increased profit became apparent, but it required a change in the discursive presentation of progress too: the ideal of *true-to-life high fidelity* was gradually replaced by *high-end clean* sound. Before that happened, however, vinyl happily enjoyed its golden age. Between 1956 when Miles Davis released his Columbia debut *Round about Midnight* and the iconic 1959 *Kind of Blue*, Lieberson doubled Columbia's sales to $50 million. The 1960s saw the triumph of the album format when pop and rock and roll bands like the Beatles and the Rolling Stones became the soundtrack of the decade.

Taking the pioneering experiences of Columbia as a benchmark of mainstream developments, one can clearly see the magnitude of change, responding to and in turn inspiring the changes in culture. Explaining this condition in monetary terms, Clive Davis, who assumed the presidency of Columbia in 1967, recalls that in 1965 'Columbia's pretax profits were about $3 million, roughly 3% of sales ... By 1970 our market share was 22%, after tax profits had risen to $6.7 million in 1968, then to $10 million in 1969, and, incredibly, to more than $15 million in 1970. The record division had jumped from a tiny fraction of CBS's overall profits to about one-third of its bottom line. It was a sensationally good period.'[18]

Indeed, taken together the two decades of 1950s and 1960s turned the tables of not just music world but entire cultural universe the way that the two previous decades of 1930s and 1940s couldn't despite moments of historical prosperity, for example in the aforementioned American jazz world. The US market was not the only one in the Western hemisphere that was gradually embracing the analogue record, although it may well have been the most enthusiastic. Interestingly, analogue record's reception was by no means unanimously celebratory in South America upon its introduction to the mass market. While records and gramophones were becoming huge there too, notably in the blooming market of Brazil, their success was initially bemoaned by some renowned Brazilian critics and musicians. One of the more remarkable examples is Luciano Gallet who complained in the 1930s: 'pianos are no longer sold; the creation of serious music is extremely weak, and so people are throwing themselves to records and dance music.' A complaint was voiced that musicians were becoming unemployed 'due to the popularity of gramophone'.[19] To some music-loving Brazilians, records came to be associated with the 'ominous, absorbing empire of the gramophone'.[20] Although rather undemocratic in their spirit and critical about new forms and hybrid genres like bossa nova inspired by international cross-fertilization and jazz influences, they understood the power of records as something potentially threatening to the entire system of social privileges and cultural hierarchies. Slowly but surely, the spread of records meant not only increased profits for big record companies but also spreading knowledge, awareness and emancipatory sentiments, especially among subaltern groups that from the late 1960s on would revolutionize the music world. From globally renowned *Motown* and reggae labels to tellingly named house and techno labels like *Underground Resistance*, vinyl remained the hopeful medium for the subaltern peoples in the Americas, even if initially it was a relatively pricey commodity. Comparatively weaker but similar effects occurred in Eastern Europe, behind the Iron Curtain in the 1950s. In a rather unlikely way, jazz was considered pernicious there and thus targeted by the communist state propaganda as subversive, particularly in Poland and Czechoslovakia where underground groups were relatively strong. Vinyl records from the West were rare cultural objects but – as renowned Polish trumpeter Tomasz Stańko recalls – the fact that jazz was a 'forbidden fruit' was significant for the formation of modern musical avant-garde there which later gave rise to the now iconic and internationally sampled vinyl series 'Polish Jazz'.[21]

The generational change was inevitable everywhere, and as the stereo record-cutting process had been perfected by the end of the 1950s, vinyl effectively conquered the hearts of the listening public and hence the market. To understand the significance of the change and appreciate the profundity of its social and cultural meanings, let us turn again to Keith Richards, a representative of a cohort that benefitted from the vinyl revolution directly and that subsequently transformed international culture at a hitherto unheard of rate. There are few artists more qualified to reflect on the relevant effects of recording from the 1960s onwards than Keith Richards. It is the case not only because of his crucial role in creating and maintaining one of the greatest and longest-lasting music acts of the modern era, the Rolling Stones, but also because he is now regarded as the unquestionable bearer of the band's authenticity and a genuine guardian of the cultural tradition it stands for.[22] Richards made an important point when he emphasized:

> It surely can't be any coincidence that jazz and blues started to take over the world the minute recording started, within a few years, just like that ... It was like opening the audio curtains. And available, and cheap. It's not just locked into one community here and one community there and the twain shall never meet. And of course that breeds another totally different kind of musician, in a generation.[23]

In his book *Kansas City Lightning: The Rise and Times of Charlie Parker*, Stanley Crouch portrays one such momentous generation of new musicians epitomized by the lifework of Parker. He points out that 'they would learn from the mass technology of print, from the phonograph record', and cites Ralph Ellison, who recognized that new musical phenomena were about cultural change, not just a shift in the entertainment business.[24] This cultural change meant – among many significant things – projecting previously marginalized black artists into the national and international limelight. The career of Miles Davis, who refused to be perceived as mere entertainer and insisted on using his albums for the purpose of making artistic statements, is a well-known case in point. Although Parker himself, who died in 1955, was not able to see his influence come to full fruition, the cohort of musicians he nourished and inspired, like Miles Davis, utilized the vinyl format perfectly and it is hard to imagine the cultural ascendancy of such icons without the analogue LP. Keith Richards shares this view and likewise emphasizes the social and cultural impact that recorded music made in the mid-twentieth century, comparing it to the cultural power of printed words:

> What I found about the blues and music, tracing things back, was that nothing came from itself. As great as it is, this is not one stroke of genius ... And so you suddenly realize that everybody's connected here. This is not just that he's fantastic and the rest are crap; they're all interconnected. And the further you went back into music and time, you think thank God for recording. It's the best thing that's happened to us since writing.[25]

The productive reciprocal feedbacks between new music now widely accessible on records and the collective social effervescence of the 1960s gradually made vinyl a kind of 'charismatic' cultural object that spliced new aesthetic sensibilities with nearly revolutionary political awakening. Importantly, it had then become a relatively inexpensive cultural object. As David Byrne noted, it was 'cheaper than a concert ticket'. Today it is particularly true of performances by bands like the Rolling Stones – their *Sweet Summer Sun – Hyde Park Live* may not be seen as exactly cheap but it is roughly ten times less expensive than a Rolling Stones concert. The disproportion may not be so pronounced in other cases, but it is going to be there. Records are cheaper and they stay. Not much has changed in this respect since vinyl's formative decade of the 1950s. But it was then that vinyl became the big bang of mass music market, the first and only format of high quality called 'high fidelity'. It had a truly transformative effect as the format with democratic features and aristocratic properties. Records enabled music to travel globally just like commercial planes made global modern tourism a genuine social phenomenon, at least for certain chunks of Western middle classes. As David Byrne observes:

> Not only could recordings bring distant musical cultures in touch with one another, they also had the effect of disseminating the work and performances of singers, orchestras, and performers *within* a culture. As I suspect has happened to all of us at some point, hearing a new and strange piece of music for the first time often opens a door that you didn't even know was there.

In other words, during the first two decades of their commercial career, long-playing vinyl records opened the new doors of aesthetic perception, just like the culture of the 1960s did socially, taking quite literally Aldous Huxley's famous spiritual quest first spelled out in his iconic 1954 book, *The Doors of Perception*. The aesthetic and the social seemed intertwined. Buying and exchanging vinyl symbolized the new cultural awareness, new networks of learning and teaching. Records were milestones of cultural development and different releases punctuated social time no less than great books, literally becoming *instant* classics, reaching millions of people across all social and racial divisions, not only reflecting but directly inspiring change.

Such records carried musical, visual, sensual and political messages, and the medium itself was an integral part of it. As the swelling currents of modern pop and dance music emerged in the 1950s and subsequently defined the revolutionary, 'swinging' decade of the 1960s through the sound of rock and soul, vinyl records became inseparable part of that story. Think about the musical and broader cultural impact of such records as Jimi Hendrix's *Electric Ladyland* (1968), James Brown's *I'm Black and I'm Proud* (1969) or Janis Joplin's *Pearl* (1970). They were then new and fun things to observe and own, and 'by the early 1970s, no matter where you were, the record store was the coolest place on the block'.[26]

Interestingly, the late 1960s was also the time when beneath the surface of thriving popular analogue culture new tendencies began to form. One such tendency particularly important for this book was the gradual emergence of electronic music. An unusual harbinger of the electronic revolution to come, both in aesthetic and technical terms, can be found on the 1968 spoken word record of Glenn Gould released by Columbia Masterworks. Entitled *Concert Drop Out: Glenn Gould in Conversation with John McClure,* this vinyl features the legendary classical pianist covering a variety of topics related to the performance and recording of music. Asked by McClure how he feels about electronic music, Gould symptomatically responded:

> I'm inclined to think that it's the future, very much the future. I feel rather optimistic, not about what's been done up till now but what can be done with electronic music. I think that a lot of doors are going to be opened there, especially if we get very good technicians involved with it.[27]

As we shall show in greater detail below and in the subsequent chapters, electronic music became a particularly relevant musical phenomenon, not only because it has indeed come to signify futuristic sensibilities, but also because it greatly helped to save vinyl when it declined in the mainstream and because of the crucial role that the technicians did play in the process of advancing electronic music by experimenting with the analogue medium. Robert Henke, whose experiences and perspective we relay throughout this book, is one such exemplary figure connecting the technical with the aesthetic and expanding our notion of what 'good technician' means.

Before all that happened, however, vinyl records had been enjoying their undisturbed 'golden age' as they witnessed and contributed to the effervescent transformations of the mid-twentieth-century world. They created new consumption patterns along with new kinds of aesthetic competence, technical knowledge and cultural anticipation. Proliferation of records became the undisputed social fact. Partly for these reasons, vinyl stores began to form real modern archives on a par with big libraries and as we show in Chapter 5 equally worthy of attention. Miles Davis's biographer John Szwed tellingly observed that 'record stores are also libraries of a sort'.[28] Moreover, many records had the aura of cool that only few books can ever achieve.

THE PREMATURE DECLINE: SHORT END OF LONG PLAY

Notwithstanding all sacred overtones, every charisma is prone to be routinized, at least in the eyes of the lay audience. Already by the late 1970s the analogue records could be seen as sliding into ordinariness, or at least as increasingly quotidian when one considered the consumers of the maturing pop scene. Christian Marclay recalls that time in his American experience:

> Coming from Switzerland to the United States in the 1970s, I noticed that change in attitudes towards objects. I would see records on the streets, in the gutter. I would see thousands of records in thrift shops that nobody wanted, that nobody cared about.[29]

Vinyl certainly had not lost its importance and aura to the artists though, especially those committed to the ethos of new independent scenes such as punk in the UK and Europe. It is telling – and moving – to read Peter Hook's recollection of his early band Joy Division's struggle to legitimize their existence by releasing a 7-inch vinyl and the poignant moments of anticipation and exasperation upon initial playing of the first self-produced record of Joy Division *An Ideal for Living* in 1978: 'Now I was going to play *my own* record. Excited doesn't cover it: I was nearly wetting myself. I put on the record to play. It sounded awful.'[30] Joy Division members, committed but under-informed and penniless working-class men, were devastated to have discovered that they had requested what could not possibly bring good results – four tracks packed on a 7-inch single that can contain only 3 or 4 minutes of properly sounding music on each side. As Hook admits, 'in the end we were just giving them away, and weeks after delivery we still had hundreds left over. God knows what became of them – they're worth a mint now, of course. *An Ideal for Living* is probably our most bootlegged item.'[31] Indeed, today one must be prepared to pay anything between $1,000 and $5,000 for one of a thousand original copies.

This anecdote indicates not only how important records still were in the late 1970s, especially for young and independent artists, but also what could go really wrong with the format given its limitations and specificities. Vinyl required expertise, knowledge, competence and care, not only from producers but also consumers. It was a demanding medium. The inherent potential of frustration among artists and audiences could be decreased by the next cycle of inventions that imperceptibly travelled from laboratories to studios and then stores and homes, swiftly becoming a *fait accompli* of much-vaunted technological development. Specifically, at the turn of the 1970s and 1980s a new sound revolution was under way: *digitalization* of the recording process. By 1982 when the Compact Disc (CD) was introduced, it was clear that this new step offered exactly what the vinyl LP promised some three decades earlier: more music on a single disc.

This technology and its effects were not just introduced to the public but advertised as an improvement that would eventually supersede the existing records completely. An improvement in sound quality needed to match quantity of sound content of a given disc, just like the previous leaps of progress did. For this reason the CD had to deliver a *better* audio experience. This involved summoning scientific discourses that hardly mattered in everyday listening practice. The very first commercially available digital recording was Ry Cooder's album *Bop Till You Drop* released in 1979 by Warner Bros Records, which then meant that it was still a vinyl release. Like the groundbreaking records of the 1950s, the back cover of this album featured a little explanatory note about digital sampling. It is instructive to analyse the narrative presented on that occasion by the industry on each and every copy of this pop LP: 'Digital equipment can encode and play back from 20 cycles to over 20,000 cycles without noise and harmonic distortion produced by analog recordings. No generation loss, noise build-up, or loss of presence occurs with this form of recording through mixdown and tape transfers. The result is that music sounds cleaner, brighter and more dimensional.'

Despite official enunciations, the reception of the album seemed less enthusiastic, if not directly contradicting the asserted improvement of a new technology, reportedly even in the artist's own opinion. In the *Allmusic* review, Brett Hartenbach wrote: 'Something must have gotten lost in translation from what was played to what came across on the recording. There's a thinness to the tracks that undermines the performances, which according to Cooder is due to the digital recording.'[32] Clearly, certain qualities seemed to evaporate. The perfect coverage of the frequency spectrum that the new medium was promised to deliver could hardly help. As Jonathan Sterne explains, although in principle human hearing has exactly the range of 20 to 20,000 cycles mentioned by the note on Cooder's record, 'in practice most adults in industrial society cannot hear either end of that range'.[33]

Still, the nascent digitalism revealed the possibility of delivering a remarkably 'cleaner' sound, one free of any unwanted sounds and imperfections of vinyl when delivered on CD. Doing away with the vinyl meant, however, that the characteristic 'warmth' of analogue sound was gone too. The digital solution resembled throwing out the baby with the bath water. But the narrative of clinically perfect sound combined with convenience of a truly long-playing device overrode other considerations and helped the industry to convince nearly the entire buying audience to purchase their favourite music again!

The 1980s was still the time when 'digitally remastered' versions of many classic albums would be released on vinyl, for example Columbia Jazz Masterpieces series. The series was described as a next generation project that 'signifies a complete dedication to bringing the listener the finest sound quality possible. All recordings in the series have been digitally remastered from the original analogue tapes, using state-of-the-art equipment.' By doing that Columbia contradicted its own, once explicitly stated promise that records could not possibly become obsolete, indicating that they do belong to culture, not just to technology. It was a kind of recycling of the old catalogue that offered a middle way that nevertheless proved to be a *cul de sac*. Today the original releases are often considered more valuable than those remastered versions. Yet, to be fair, it took the experience of the digital phase and its experimentation to make this difference fully apparent and embodied. It is now that the 'cleaner' digital sound can be coded as 'too clinical' in all its guises, and thus inauthentically removed from the original source recordings. It also takes the reputation, integrity and critical acumen of senior stars like Richards and younger like-minded artists like Jack White of the White Stripes, who persistently uphold vinyl through a narrative of simplicity that keeps music and technology at a healthy remove from each other. Here, the analogue is good enough to capture the ineffable qualities of music creation, its soul and its warmth. It is also very good at literally capturing and materializing the creative moment for others to enjoy. Richards's approach comes in handy one more time:

> I always felt that I was actually fighting technology, that it was no help at all ... You can't get these indefinable things by stripping it apart. The enthusiasm, the spirit, the soul, whatever you want to call it, where's the microphone for that? The records could have been a lot better in the '80s if we had not been led by the nose by technology.

Indeed, at the turn of the 1970s and 1980s when new digital recordings and remasters were introduced as a solution to the perceived noise- and distortion-related 'drawbacks' of the analogue technology, different special techniques like Direct Metal Mastering (DMM) or audiophile pressings were being released. They too provided explanatory notes suggesting that these new, carefully crafted analogue productions were in fact as perfect as it gets. Consider the liner notes from Cat Stevens's *Teaser and the Firecat* LP released in the Canadian Audiophile Series: 'The Audiophile process produces a superb master from which this record is manufactured on the purest possible anti-static vinyl. The cutting of the master from the original stereo tapes is performed at half the normal speed, the velocity of the cutting stylus being dramatically reduced results in a more faithful cutting of heavily modulated passages and the general extension of the frequency range. A&M Records' Audiophile Series provides extremely high fidelity sound reproduction, remarkably clear and distinct, virtually free of surface and background noise.' Similarly, Miles Davis's Blue Note release *Volume 1* came in 1984 as an audiophile DMM cut, digitally remastered and designed to be 'eliminating the volatile nature of lacquer pressings and faithfully reproducing the intended sound with absolute accuracy'.

However, the die-hard fans of the old tried and tested vinyl complained about DMM's perceived overemphasis on high frequencies. Was 'absolute accuracy' ever the dream of the mass audience created by the record in the first place? Was not 'high fidelity' faithful enough? For the then young independent musicians like Peter Hook of Joy Division, the superiority of the analogue recording is out of question: a valve recorder that makes music 'really warm- and fat-sounding' is 'the best recording medium that you can ever use. Sounds immense.'[34] If anything, the new 'digitally remastered' vinyl releases proved the analogue format's flexibility. Its full compatibility with digital technology was debatable but not excluded. The fans of the new, however, seemed fed up with some practical nuisances and 'dirty' aspects of vinyl. Crucially, what once made vinyl win and even gave it its very name, Long Play, now could be relativized to the point of obsolescence. As a result of an intense marketing reorientation, within a decade analogue records were supplanted by the CD, a physical digital format that was smaller but longer-playing, potentially too shrill sounding, but 'cleaner' and more portable.

A remarkable fact about those explanatory notes attached to records released during the first wave of digitalization was not only the reiterated claim to aural perfection but the very idea that the buying public cared or needed to care about it. Thirty years after the first educational actions, the big labels started talking again, dwelling on a scientific parlance and acoustic facts. The music industry clearly did not believe that its sonic product could speak – or sound – for itself. On the contrary, one is under the impression that music was badly in need of professional spokespersons in the 1980s. The seemingly self-evident power of progress nevertheless needed its articulate industrial avant-garde. Recorded sound became the site of corporate technological debate and associated discursive struggle showing one more time that music is not just about music.

In the end, the decision had predictably been made in favour of the new, if only for the sake of trying it out, and the industry simply switched gears one more time and went into a promisingly profitable direction, eventually leaving the buying public with little choice and unwittingly proving that new bottles *do* make the old wine seem to taste 'better' even if it had been quite delicious already. For example, the LP's share in the US market of pre-recorded music dropped roughly from 40 per cent to 1 per cent in the ten years following the full-scale commercial launch of the CD in 1983.[35] Consigned to oblivion by the corporate agents of technological progress, the analogue record became an endangered species of the late modern mass media.

Peter Runge reminds us of the root motivation for this dramatic digital shift on the side of the producing industry. According to him, the production of CDs is roughly eight times cheaper than the analogue record. At the same time, however, the prices of CDs have never been comparatively lower. The discs remained relatively expensive well into the 1990s when it was still possible to buy most of the second-hand pop rock canon on vinyl for far less money. Robert Henke makes the market consequences of this situation plain:

> CD was basically the golden age for the music industry because the cost of the CD went very, very quickly all the way down and the price stayed very, very high for a very long time. I believe that what happened in the music industry in the last 40 years was a very abnormal, historically unique singularity because it was just able to make a lot of money with very little effort. The amount of money you could make with a CD release is insane … an unhealthy amount of money, an unjustified amount of money.

In short, while the golden age of vinyl meant a giant leap of popular music, it was the shift to the digital that meant the golden age for the popular music industry. However, from the consumers' point of view, CDs *did* take less space and attention, the considerations that played an important role even for some committed collectors we interviewed like Ben Gosney, shaping their buying practices in favour of the CD. On top of that, the digital compact disc offered remarkable pragmatic gains in line with the Zeitgeist of the 1980s – the sometimes unfairly parodied decade of excess, plastic chic and easy listening.

While the CD revolution was originally presented as a sound revolution, it was primarily a convenient advancement with no ambition to create a democratizing effect similar to the original impact of the LP, however imperfect. More than anything else, it was a profitable novel commodity that tapped into popular desires of lightness, ease, perfection and cleanliness. Only the introduction of digital mp3 files achieved a truly new level of democratization. Yet this time the sound was severely compromised. Music lovers were encouraged to purchase their favourite catalogue the third time in order to make music more portable than ever. Amazingly, quite a few did spend money again. However, this time it seemed more about *mobility* of music than music itself. Specifically, you were buying the excitement of 24/7 access and portability. You could take your whole personal collection of recorded music to the next party, 'plug in and play', as some iPod parties encouraged. The swiftness with which the CD was jettisoned and superseded with initially sonically inferior, new digital format suggests that as far as the mainstream market is concerned music and its sound does not necessarily come first.

Both generations of the digital wave, CD and mp3, meant progressively easier listening and material streamlining of music formats, but it also created an unprecedented excess of sounds and files so that depreciation of the musical commodity observed by Marclay was further exacerbated. As our interviewees admit, from teenage DJs to icons of new electronic music, today no one can hope to impress anyone with tens of thousands of files. There's no glory or merit to having your iPod stuffed with millions of electronically cloned files because no serious sacrifice stands behind obtaining them. There is no serious selection factor involved if a young person boasts of having hundreds or thousands of albums. And there is little sense of adventure either. As Jack White says, 'there's no romance in a mouse click'.[36] As object, music reduced to computer data becomes practically indistinguishable from bureaucratic folders.

The relative depreciation created by otherwise useful computers applied to CDs too, at least from a certain point on. As soon as personal computers rendered CDs perfectly and cheaply replicable objects, their meaning changed and they came to be interpreted as mundane objects even quicker than records did before them. Acceleration of technology led to acceleration in transformative interpretive processes too. In fact, it was CDs that just 20 years after their invention became a paradigmatic 'cheap plastic', to evoke Marclay again. This created a new dynamic context in which analogue records could be seen as a comparatively valuable and stable format, the only physical sound carrier that made sense precisely because it was *not* digital.

Furthermore, the ever-increasing ease with which music as virtual file could be copied, transferred and exchanged meant putting the traditional idea of buying to own on the slippery slope of anachronism. Cultural meaninglessness was promptly revealed as the flipside of perfect convenience. As a result, vinyl could emerge as not only the authentic and uniquely sounding format but also the *only* music carrier worth owning and collecting in the strict sense of the term. This phenomenon suggests that there are limits to economy of convenience and that a modicum of non-economical values and a minimum of traditional notions of materiality and continuity retain meaning.

Although all this may not be exactly surprising to sociologists and cultural analysts, it took years for the general public to realize it and act accordingly. As far as sociology is concerned, already in 1900 Georg Simmel clearly articulated the mechanism of value that is created through the relative difficulty in producing or getting a given cultural object:

> There is a series of cases in which the sacrifice not merely raises the value of the aim but even produces it. It is the joy of exertion, of overcoming difficulties, frequently indeed that of contradiction, which expresses itself in this process. The necessary detour to the attainment of certain things is often the occasion, often also the cause, of regarding them as valuable.[37]

Then and now, the passage of time is required to make the shifting conditions of life obvious to the point of general visibility. Only then can socially significant and economically palpable reorientation occur. A series of practical experiences must make themselves manifest as well, so that contrasts and differences that produce conditions of cultural re-evaluation become embodied and observed rather than merely theorized and understood. This is partly why vinyl re-emerged as a valuable counterpoint to the new mainstream only after some time. Jenus Baumecker-Kahmke makes a related observation:

> I think it just took a really long time for people to understand that they neglected vinyl and I think that it's definitely here to stay now, at this relatively healthy level. I'm kind of surprised how long it took, but it's a natural kind of process. I think that people started to realize that CDs are not what the industry promised them. People put in a CD that they bought in '88 and it doesn't play any more, so I think that this is a kind of awakening to that fact that vinyl is actually quality product, that's how people understand it now.

GOING UNDERGROUND AND THE REBIRTH OF THE COOL: THE 'SECOND LIFE' OF VINYL DURING THE FIRST WAVE OF DIGITALIZATION

Before vinyl could be rediscovered, fully re-experienced and economically revived, it first needed to *survive* the systematic neglect of the industry and maintain dynamism capable of supporting the last remaining pressing plants and mastering studios. By the late 1980s analogue records were effectively banished from the mainstream. Most pressing factories ceased to be viable enterprises. There were, however, firms that decided to buy well-maintained equipment at relatively low prices from those who decided to get rid of what now appeared to be 'relics'. The limited supply of records that did appear on the market despite the slump in vinyl sales in turn attained the status of a rare good, at least in terms of quantity if not always quality. The radical redirecting of industry's attention to the new digital technology meant that from the mid-1980s on, no special advances in analogue production were proposed. As Peter Runge recalls, 'there was no further development in vinyl recording technology after 1984'. Subsequently, and unsurprisingly, the craft of pressing records experienced a sort of crisis in the 1990s when many professional plants simply stopped operating. Institutional learning processes got interrupted, infrastructure eroded or got concentrated in fewer hands, not all of which were able. As a whole, the world of analogue production gradually sank to a lower or sometimes even sub-par level. Jenus diagnosed this situation in the following way:

> Now there are a lot of labels that put a lot of effort into the quality of their productions the way we do. I think the pressings, overall, have gotten a lot better than they were ten years ago. Ten years ago there were still shit pressing plants operating, and people would go there because it was cheap and they would get a record that sounded shit. That's all been weeded out a little bit and the pressing plants that are successful make really good quality products, so when you buy a record now, usually the production is good.

Vinyl culture may have seemed abandoned and impoverished, or even downright moribund by the time the 12-inch vinyl record became 40 years old. And it may have been effectively dead by the mid-1990s, were it not for the purposeful dedication and spectacular rise of another musical universe – the new underground dance cultures such as house, techno and drum'n'bass. Just as the mainstream producers and consumers ditched vinyl like an antiquated toy, an urban avant-garde of club music embraced it as its medium of choice. The vitality of that culture gave vinyl the breath of life at a critical point. Even if not always of high technical quality, analogue records kept being pressed and thus present in various niches of the music market. They were the key tools of DJs and, through them, stayed on the radar of young generations accustomed to CDs. Bill Brewster and Frank Broughton are certainly right when they wrote that the DJ saved the life of many a club-goer and music lover. By reinventing the performative charisma from behind the turntables, countless selectors from Frankie Knuckles to Nina Kraviz not only saved vinyl but made it cool and sensual, perhaps cooler than ever. As far as vinyl is concerned, the late 1980s and early 1990s meant a musical revolution done by a reinvention of the single – now just one track would take the entire side of 12-inch disc, often played at 45 rpm, which proved more suitable to loud cuts and club-oriented bass music whose low frequencies required more vinyl space.

This reinvention was of a special kind and meant new, sometimes extreme or 'abnormal' uses of the analogue technology and it gave a chance to experiment with other people who shared the DIY, punk-infused attitude. Robert Henke traces this connection between punk and techno in Berlin around 1989 and how they may have had more in common than we now assume. Basing the emerging techno culture on analogue records was a crucial ingredient of the independent and experimental spirit that corresponded so well with the Zeitgeist in that part of the world. Vinyl meant being able to do the old thing in a new way by freeing your mind and exposing yourself to serendipity and spontaneity of a creative process uniquely framed by technological and political revolutions.

> As a matter of fact, no one was experienced … there was actually no experience apart from the understanding of the basic process. As a matter of fact, no one even thought about it, and in retrospective, this is really interesting … So, we were really experimenting.

The juicy irony of that remarkable cultural process is that it was propelled precisely by those explicitly committed to advancing *electronic* music connected to new digital devices. Thereby they proved that, instead of pitting the digital against and the analogue, new hybrid forms of symbiotic coexistence of technologies can be central to ongoing creative musical developments and new musical experiences. It was a rather open approach at a time which was just enamoured with the digitalia of the rising electronic age more than anything else. In the mainstream the first wave of digitalization was something fresh and it meant some genuine practical ameliorations. But because it did *not* mean obliterating the physical, discrete items of musical pieces called albums and singles, it did not inspire a backlash that we would observe a few decades down the line when turning music into files pushed digitalization into its second, 'virtual' phase. Buying albums and singles still meant collecting the actual discs and some people would keep buying both kinds. What Antoine Hennion called 'discomorphosis' remained firmly in place throughout the 1980s and 1990s.

During much of these two turbulent decades vinyl went underground and remained healthy there, carrying remarkable momentum into the early 2000s. What may have been inconvenient for the general public proved practical for DJs. The alternative electronic dance music was always about computer innovation and digital sound but vinyl remained central in all its divisions. In particular, it was the use of 12-inch 45 rpm singles that kept visually identical but functionally different records alive. To use the concise words by Matt Black and Jonathan More of Coldcut from the description of their 1997 track 'More Beats + Pieces', 'the best interface for DJs is still direct vinyl manipulation'. One more time, vinyl records gave rise to a new kind of musician, one dabbling in 'sounds that are itchin' for a scratch', a *bricoleur* who samples and rearranges them, sometimes beyond recognition, as another producer of the British *Ninja Tune* label Amon Tobin evocatively showed with his *Bricolage* LP released the same year. Other vinylists like DJ Shadow and Madlib may have been less experimental but they crucially revealed the richness of analogue archives and creatively showed an enormous extent to which they can be reappropriated, sampled and juxtaposed. They have connected the past to the future with vinyl being the key link. It was a recontextualization of the analogue that clearly indicated the additive not mutually exclusive relation between the main mediums. But this potential for hybridization was first overlooked. In 2012, nearly a decade after his seminal album of remixed Blue Note classics *Shades of Blue*, Madlib stated in a conversation with Thomas Fehlmann that going through the archives of the iconic label 'was fun' and that 'they have way too much stuff they should have released. The best records are still in the vaults.'[38] It is the skills, knowledge and integrity of those producers, diggers, turntablists and remixers that earned them critical acclaim and significantly contributed to the rebirth of vinyl's cool and esteem.

Of course, these creative uses of vinyl were not entirely new. Already in his 1937 essay 'The Future of Music: Credo', John Cage anticipated the potential of the turntable as a musical instrument.[39] 'With a phonograph it is now possible to control any one of these sounds and give to it rhythms within or beyond the reach of imagination. Given four phonographs we can compose and perform a quartet for explosive motor, wind, heartbeat and landslide.'[40] This is a techno revolution foretold. But prior to that, in the late 1970s, US American DJs such as Jamaica-born Kool Herc, Grand Wizard Theodore or Grandmaster Flash developed a series of techniques of mixing, scratching, backspinning and cutting that later became the standard repertoire of hip-hop and house performers. Importantly, for all these artistic circles turntablism was 'more than just dragging a record back and forth under a stylus, or segueing two tracks together nice and smooth. Hip-hop is very much like the British class system: it's not so much what you say that matters, but how you say it. This is as true of the DJ as it is of the MC and graffiti tagger. Thus, turntablism recognises that the best music is a complete triumph of style over substance.'[41] While the question whether one could define the best music in such radical terms may be debatable, the trajectory of vinyl in the digital age indicates that matters of *style* in music consumption and production is a key issue. Vinyl as a medium and a practice is an element of style in the music world.

For DJs and producers in the underground electronic music vinyl was the source and the medium, an instrument to play and a sound to use. Certainly it was not an antiquated toy. On the contrary, there were enough artists for whom vinyl became connected to both the exuberance of partying and the seriousness of heritage protection. The development of samplers crucially boosted both aspects of vinyl's importance and aided the creative rearticulation of its cultural worth at the time when it was being marginalized as something 'obsolete', ostensibly in the name of digital progress. Paul Miller, aka DJ Spooky, may have been more convincing as a writer than a musician when he used his 1996 LP *Songs of a Dead Dreamer* as a manifesto of the new DJ culture. His words still stand as a symptomatic statement of purpose of a generation that embraced the old format of the past for the sake of a new future:

> DJ culture – urban youth culture – is all about recombinant potential. It has as a central feature a eugenics of the imagination. Each and every source sample is fragmented and bereft of prior meaning – kind of like a future without a past. The samples are given meaning only when represented in the assemblage of the mix. In this way the DJ acts as the cybernetic inheritor of the improvisational tradition of jazz, where various motifs would be used and recycled by the various musicians of the genres, in this case, however, the records become the notes.

It is hardly a coincidence that many DJ pioneers and stars of electronic music drew on jazz, from experimental excursions of Amon Tobin and Bill Laswell to master house DJs like Danny Tenaglia, Ashley Beedle or the German DJ-collective Jazzanova to producers like Ludovic Navarre aka St Germain, or Garza and Hilton of Thievery Corporation. As their artistic profile rose in the 1990s, vinyl-dedicated *underground* quite literally became a *groundbreaking* force in music, doing what any bohemian culture can do well: challenging and undermining mainstream sensibilities and industrialized officialdom by simply following its own independent vision. The underground electronic music culture was rarely explicitly political or critical the way rock artists could be in the past. Again, there was rather an elective affinity with more aesthetically driven avant-garde and dance traditions of jazz. However, even in the hedonistic sphere of the 1990s techno culture, releasing and playing vinyl retained an element of cultural mission and socially relevant intervention. In the wake of DJ Spooky's pronouncements, the US American techno star Jeff Mills used the back cover of his 1997 Tresor release *Waveform Transmission* for the message whose core we have already cited at the opening of this book and which is worth quoting again in full: 'As barriers fall around the world, the need to understand others and the way they live, think and dream is a task that is nearly impossible to imagine without theory and explanation. And as we approach the next century with hope and prosperity, this need soon becomes a necessity rather than a recreational urge.' The German producer Hendrik Weber aka Pantha du Prince describes his attraction to techno in a concrete way that complements Mills': 'what fascinates me in techno is the idea of endlessness. The idea that something constantly emits the pulse. People of different social backgrounds can simply dock to this pulse.'[42] Recognizing a similar socially uniting potential in other kinds of electronic music, Thievery Corporation emphasized music's critical and awareness-raising role and gradually developed its outspoken anti-capitalist attitude. More examples could be given. If anything, these more culturally or even politically conscious attitudes within new independent genres grew over time. Writing in the new 2006 preface to their classic history of the disc jockey, Brewster and Broughton observed that many DJs learned to keep their distance to the pitfalls of stardom and that 'most people now understand that DJing is more about collecting great music than doing supernatural things with a mixer'. The DJ is a respectable artistic figure when he or she refers to values of knowledge and authenticity besides doing their regular job of musical entertainers. Importantly, independent labels kept pressing vinyl and thus disavowed the conviction that analogue record culture was inexorably destined to expire in the digital era.

Perhaps most crucially, vinyl remained healthy during the lean years of the 1990s by association with what turned out to be one of the most dynamic new incarnations of hipness and youth energy. Being the medium for new party music, the seemingly old-fashioned vinyl found itself at the core of cutting-edge developments and intensely effervescent rituals of club culture. It was this paradoxical juxtaposition that ensured not only the economic survival but also cultural resignification of analogue records. Vinyl had been endowed with the edginess and coolness of the flourishing 1990s electronic music underground. It was 'rejuvenated' because those were rather new sounds and a novel approach to musical experience championed by the generations that grew up listening to rock, soul and disco, often already on CDs, but wanted to push the boundaries further without jettisoning the heritage. Keeping vinyl alive was the intuitive way to go. Vinyl appeared in considerable quantities in new record shops where one could see the structure of fresh genre differentiation that stood for the stylistic dynamism of the electronic underground. If many of these productions were parts of the independent micro-trade, they also introduced a whole range of micro-genre classification in addition to the apparently complete analogue canons of pop and rock. The new vinyl stores were full of jungle, trance, ambient, breakbeat, progressive house, glitch and all kinds of crossovers between these styles. Those who resented specific genre-categorization used other kinds of labelling, for example place-related such as Detroit techno or Chicago house. One way or the other, these signifiers were the symptoms of underground dynamism that used vinyl as a totem. The stronger the underground grew during the 1990s, the healthier vinyl culture was. As some DJs began to outgrow their humble niches, vinyl gained a modicum of global public visibility again. The hip media presence of various DJs, from the star producers and remixers like Norman Cook aka Fatboy Slim and Paul Oakenfold to drum'n'bass icons like Roni Size and LTJ Bukem meant that vinyl too could appear hip, or at least curiously useful and directly connected to high musical standards to which these alternative artists held themselves. Finally, there were those who maintained somewhat lower profiles but high standing within broadly conceived electronic dance music, and those were often the undisputed champions of vinyl, often running their own independent labels: Moodymann, Theo Parrish, Mike Huckaby, Carl Craig, Sven Väth, DJ Krush and many more.

In short, this new underground culture supported the vinyl when corporate labels basically gave up on it in the name of 'progress' and the pop- and rock-buying public deemed it a dead or funny relic. While the CD was a customer-friendly money-making machine, vinyl became the DJ-friendly party-making machine. It was also the treasure trove of the musical traditions. This saved it from the vulnerable fate of obscure collector's item or audiophile's elite product, the stuff of old musty basement stores or expensive sound salons. If industry could pride itself on being technologically 'progressive' and economically skilful, it was culturally and aesthetically blinkered. The drum'n'bass producer Darren Jay noticed – and explicitly stated on his own vinyl release – that certain 'corporate record companies jumped on the bandwagon' in the second half of the 1990s. Still, the mainstream needed more than two decades to reconsider vinyl and apparently did it only when risk-free profit and social hipness of vinyl was made obvious by persistence and dynamism of various independent sections of the market. For this reason DJs indeed were the true musical 'revolutionaries', to use Brewster and Broughton's phrase, especially in the last two decades of the twentieth century. Nowadays, however, the situation gets more complex and fluid again.

THE GENERAL REVIVAL: THE 'THIRD LIFE' OF VINYL IN THE SECOND WAVE OF DIGITALIZATION

Today it is safe to conjecture that if vinyl culture remained confined to underground electronic music, it would not experience a substantial revival. Even if this sphere of musical production grew to permeate larger sections of the listening public, it would still be a stretch to claim that vinyl has experienced an international renaissance. In fact, the ever-expanding virtual universe and the 'magic' of its continual improvements on all fronts forged a situation in which many DJs either downscaled their professional use of vinyl or were convinced to suspend it altogether. Outside countries with strong club and vinyl cultures like Germany, Holland, UK or Japan, one cannot assume that dance venues would provide professional turntable systems. As we show in Chapter 5, dynamic vinyl-related electronic music club scenes exist only in certain urban environments. Meanwhile, house and techno have entered the sphere of bigger entertainment business and DJs in demand often find SD (Secure Digital) cards more DJ-friendly than records. This means that even the vinyl-buying communities of professional musicians do not necessarily demand as much as they used to when vinyl was undisputedly 'the best interface for DJs'. This circumstance contributed to vinyl's comparatively stagnant or even downward market performance in the mid-2000s.

Toward the end of the 2000s, however, attitudes began to shift within the broader independent sphere, especially among everyday listeners of all ages for whom matters of *style* not only in music but also in more generally understood aesthetic consumption are as important as any 'substantive' issues. Just like stylistic innovations of DJs in the 1970s and 1980s connoted creativity, subversion and respect for skills and effort in dealing with tradition, so did the commitment to vinyl by the new groups of aficionados who wished to critically distinguish themselves in a fully saturated musical world, now technologically 'augmented' to the point of being overblown. The second wave of digitalization meant unprecedented convenience and thus turned music into a low hanging fruit. In such a context the line between legitimate convenience and inauthentic and facile shortcutting may become rather thin and that much harder to navigate. Vinyl and its by now firmly entrenched underground cachet made it a tool of authenticity to the committed for whom musical experiences are about purposeful cultivation of broader aesthetic sensibilities and identities. To be sure, there were then more opportunities to capitalize on these tendencies and stores and pressing plants registered steeply increasing sales.

The mainstream followed suit within a couple of years. In 2007–8 both the independent and mainstream registered a certain upward tendency that did not abate. On the contrary, it never stopped growing, reaching long-time unheard of dynamism within a couple of years. Between 2008 and 2012, and only according to the mainstream Nielsen SoundScan data, over 15 million analogue records were sold internationally, which amounted to more than the entire sales between 1993 and 2007.

In the UK, data compiled by the BPI (a body representing the UK's recorded music industry) stated that sales of vinyl rose by 43.7 per cent over 2011, representing what it called a 'modest resurgence'.[43] In the USA, the mainstream rock and pop magazine *Rolling Stone* recently ran with the headline 'Vinyl Sales Increase Despite Industry Slump', reporting Nielsen SoundScan data which showed that 'though overall album sales dropped by 13 percent in 2010, sales of vinyl increased by 14 percent over the previous year, with around 2.8 million units sold'. The magazine report continues with the comment that 'this is a new record for vinyl sales since 1991, when the format had all but disappeared in the wake of the CD boom'.[44] Further evidence of the current remarketization of vinyl comes from the *Wall Street Journal*, which in early 2012 proclaimed in a headline, 'It's alive! Vinyl makes a comeback', and reported that:

> The digital revolution was supposed to do away with a lot of fusty old relics. First compact discs took their toll on the long-playing (and long-played) vinyl record; then iPods and digital downloads began doing the same to CDs. But long after the eulogies had been delivered, the vinyl LP has been revived. The LP still represents just a sliver of music sales. But last year, according to Nielsen SoundScan data, while CD sales fell by more than 5 per cent, vinyl record sales grew more than 36 per cent.[45]

The trend continues. In June 2014 CBS News ran a report entitled 'Vinyl's Resurrection: Sales at a Record High'.[46] Although impressive, these mainstream reports paint an incomplete picture that suffers from a typical shortcoming of the big industry perspective and a broad brush vision of general media outlets: it barely registers what occurs below the official corporate radar. This is a problem because in a post-Fordist world much is happening in the independent spheres and secondary vinyl markets. Peter Runge observes that his pressing plant Optimal alone sold over 25 million records between 2008 and 2012, which represents a significant increase, as the entire period between 1999 and 2007 only sold nearly 40 million records. How could it be? Optimal has been selling mostly to independent clients who ordered then and continue to buy now. A story would be different without them and it is the broad spectrum of those clients, from punk rock to techno, that helps understand the resilience and eventual rebound of the format. A simple visual chart of Optimal's average sales over the course of the 2000s supports the general sense of relatively dramatic resurgence that began half way through the 2000s and exploded at the beginning of the next decade.

Between October 2013 and February 2014 alone, nearly every month more than a million records left the plant. The story of Optimal's success tells you more than the mainstream reports because it makes explicit the role of the independents. Roughly during that time, around 10,000 separate orders were made and independent clients from around the world placed approximately 80 per cent of them, receiving approximately 60 per cent of the total number of records then produced. This leaves little doubt about the continued leadership of non-mainstream agents of

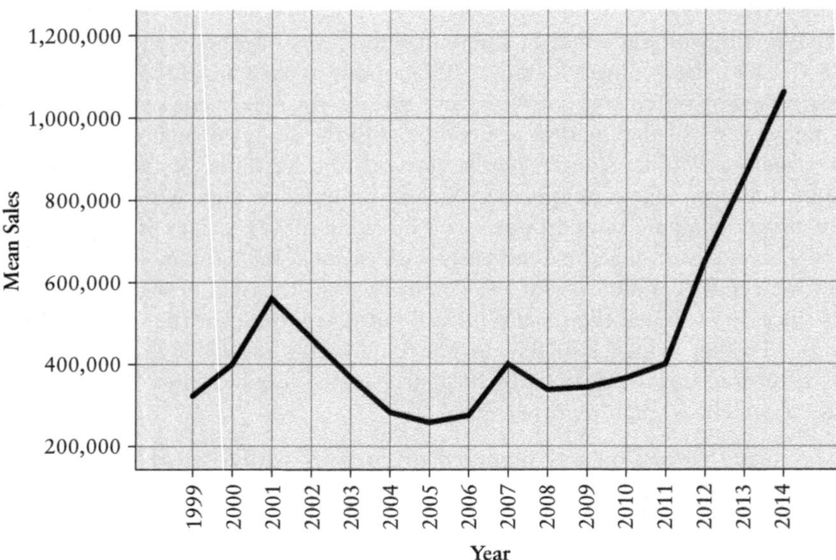

FIGURE 1.2: Average vinyl production between 1999–2014 at the Optimal pressing plant, Germany. (DB, with thanks to Peter Runge)

vinyl culture. According to Peter, who has been running the business since the beginning of vinyl production, major labels merely try not to miss out on emerging profitable opportunities, trying to capitalize on rather than stimulate new trends. Vinyl's energy comes from outside the mainstream but its responsiveness, however ambiguous, certainly adds to the swelling tide.

Undoubtedly, then, vinyl has been given a third life. It seems to have come to stay, if only as a healthy, incrementally growing niche. In the club scene its presence, although reduced, continues to play the same role it had before – it is a signifier of underground authenticity. Despite its cumbersome features whose limited practicality is made obvious by outstanding convenience of virtual tools, it remains an old-school awe-inspiring medium, still championed by the most renowned DJs and iconic clubs concerned with sound quality and traditional skills, for example in the Berlin-based Berghain/Panorama Bar. Importantly, few among those who keep DJing with vinyl are purists. They are far from endorsing any kind of myopic cultural reactionism. If cultures learn, then the underground electronic music milieu seems to have absorbed the lesson of the past by advocating hybrid arrangements and aural uniqueness of vinyl rather than its 'objective' superiority or 'absolute' value. Love does not have to be blind, even if it appears blindingly passionate. This is perhaps a message that emerges out of the conversations we have enjoyed with our vinyl-loving interviewees in those venues. Whether fans of electronic beats or indie rock, the vinyl lovers we spoke to tend not to be vintage fashion victims, snobbish retro maniacs or fetishistic fanatical collectors. Likewise, few, if any,

FIGURE 1.3: Hybrid media arrangements: Vinyl-CD DJ setup. Nick Höppner mixing tracks and media at the 20th anniversary of Kompakt in Berlin, August 2013. (DB)

traces of sentimental nostalgia came to the fore in our talks. Rather, vinyl signifies a commitment to a particular *style* and *experience* that do not have to be mutually exclusive with other types of experience but has enough uniqueness and autonomy to withstand the competitive pressure of other media.

To return to music on vinyl is a way of retaining a possibility of irreducible physical experiences. Instead of symbolizing knee-jerk conservatism, the vinyl revival shows a resistance to progress based on an idea of linear chain of replacement. Its survival of the lean years within the haven of underground club cultures indicates that progressive attitude embraces plurality rather than any kind of exclusive mainstreaming. The persistent commitment to vinyl, even if still a relatively niche phenomenon, shows that seeking particular pleasures may be as important as searching for very convenient and profitable solutions. Style and ritual may appear as important as the 'substance' or even question the very idea of separately taken 'substance' and its role for human enjoyment and well-being. It does not seem accidental that vinyl culture typically gets associated with meanings of sensuality, warmth and sexy features. Indeed, in the experience of playing vinyl, not unlike in sexual experience, *reproductive function* recedes in the face of *pleasureable act*. We do not merely reproduce previously created music, we also derive particular pleasure as we give it a form of a particular, repeatable experience. Drawing a revealing comparison to eating, Wolfgang Voigt brought the message home when he quipped in our conversation that you don't want to download your food. He also offered an ultimate perspective on vinyl's multifaceted value when he said:

> [Vinyl] has the most sexual credibility, if you like, it's touchy, it's warm, it has the biggest, warmest and most impressive history in pop music. CD has not that much history and as for mp3, I think it will never have a history, not for me. So vinyl is the 'king format'. I can't think of another way of saying it.

THE 'KING FORMAT': BEGINNING TO MAKE SENSE OF VINYL'S REVIVAL

Vinyl may indeed be the king of contemporary musical culture: it does not rule, but it reigns. How does this work?

Records are unlikely to be the 'ruling' format in the environment effectively run and dominated by convenient and versatile digital devices that make most things happen in virtual reality. But as long as performance of playing and listening occurs in real spaces on actual objects, vinyl retains attractiveness as a tactile definitive thing and thus it retains a possibility of intimate connection with humans. It is an 'organic' object in a world increasingly facilitated by all kinds of artificial intelligence. As long as private domestic sphere and public club sphere remain the loci of actual ritualistic performances of music, there is a chance for vinyl to stay meaningful, just like theatre remained meaningful after cinema had taken over the collective imagination.

Moreover, if music is something uniquely abstract and seemingly immaterial because it is invisible, then vinyl comes possibly the closest to materializing music in a directly palpable and observable way. A record revolving on a turntable is music materialized, visualized, sculpted. Not only can we see tracks and their structure in the micro-architecture of the groove. We can also touch it. Music on vinyl is eminently tactile. As Constance Classen has reminded us, being 'the deepest' and perhaps the most taken-for-granted sense, touch gives us sensuous access to reality which is at once fundamental and somewhat overlooked. Nevertheless, it is precisely the haptics of analogue records that distinguishes them today more than ever. It is the haptics that makes analogue pragmatics so different and unique when compared with digital interfaces.

While vinyl lovers and DJs have good intuitive and practical understandings of vinyl's attractive tangibility, it is instructive to collate them with Hegel's conception of aesthetics and music that had been created before sound recording became possible. In Hegel's view 'sound in contrast to the material of the visual arts is wholly abstract'. His presentation of music points to one of its unique dimensions as an immaterial art that 'cancels' space and seems to exist, so to speak, outside fixed spatial contexts, forever invisible, ephemeral, untouchable. To make this point Hegel offers insightful comparisons of music and visual arts:

> Unlike the visual arts, [music] does not permit the manifestation in which it flourishes to become free and independent and reach an existence self-reposing and persistent but, on the contrary, cancels it as objective and does not allow the external to assume in our eyes a fixed existence as something external.[47]

Records have altered the perception of this situation, at least to a certain extent. They gave fixed tactile form to music, seeming to turn it into an external object and a material manifestation that we can return to each time we want, just like we can look at the painting again and again. Hegel seems to have been keenly aware of this human urge or desire to somehow fix or reproduce music when he reflected on the meaning of musical notes: 'Unlike buildings, statues, and paintings, the notes have in themselves no permanent subsistence as objects; on the contrary, with their fleeting passage they vanish again and therefore the musical composition needs a continually repeated reproduction.'[48] Again, records offered a form of reproduction, a way of dealing with music's evanescence. Thus, in the 1950s, when the world obtained relatively long-playing high-quality records that could be kept at home, a truly new era of musical experience commenced. Moreover, this fact added a completely new kind of practice to the world of music – playing records. Eventually, a separate culture of mixing and DJing emerged, showing what imaginative and creative handling of records can do to music and to human beings themselves. Today cultural theorists do not shy from acknowledging the deeply transformative character of objects. In the words of Andreas Reckwitz:

> The central issue then is that certain things or artifacts provide more than just objects of knowledge, but necessary irreplaceable components of certain social practices, that their significance does not only consist in their being 'interpreted' in certain ways, but also in their being 'handled' in certain ways and in being constitutive, effective elements of social practices.[49]

High modernity of the mid-twentieth century made people accustomed to this condition but it is important to recognize it for what it is – a genuinely groundbreaking transformation of arts and culture more generally. Records played their distinguished part in this transformative process. We have tried to show that as they became 'routinized' and later largely surpassed by the next generation of recording technology, the objectification of music became largely a subconscious fact. The subsequent digital objectification removed music a step away from the world of haptics and vision. Stripping a piece of music down to its sonic data and making it one with electronic devices may have made it as 'pure' and 'clean' as it gets. But by becoming weightless and virtual, music disappeared in machines, its material existence dissolved, as it were, in the existence of electronic devices.

In the case of portable machines, musical experience certainly became our nearly perfect companion. The danger may be that listening to music starts to belong everywhere, that is – *nowhere*. In case of personal computers that over time began to store thousands if not millions of musical and other files, music got integrated with everything that the computer is designed to perform, which nowadays practically means – *everything*. Turning cultural products into files is a convenient reduction, but a reduction nonetheless, one curiously compatible with the hyper-accelerated culture of 'progress'. If the vinyl *re-vival* retains an element of simple *re-action*, it is the element that makes it interpretable as a perfect antidote medium to a culture stuck on fast-forward mode. Vinyl offers 'slow listening' at home and adds value to club performance.

In this context vinyl becomes the epitome of 'warm' and 'humane' materialization of music, a perfect mode of making elusive music tactile, friendly and more 'sacred' again. The digital and the virtual brought music somewhat closer to its abstract 'pure' state. Vinyl, on the other hand, grounds it in our concrete experiences, in actual spaces of our existence. This is not to say that computers are inherently incapable of achieving that. They may do so too, but in a very different manner. Features of records can be simulated in virtual reality, but so far experiences provided by the actual handling and playing of vinyl simply cannot be replaced. Vinyl may be seen as a strange medium by a future generation but it can hardly be dismissed as replaceable. It is with this example that we can discern the fact that 'progress' is not perfectly linear. Rather, as a cultural and human fact, technological development has a multi-track character, a social movement with lateral moves and parallel trends.

The career of vinyl as we have narrated it here indicates not only the fact that there are limits to the seemingly hegemonic rule of linear progress, but also that there are limits to our standard cultural criticism of it. If the capitalist notion of creative destruction is exactly that, a cultural *notion* rather than an exceptionless social law, then the disenchanted vision of artefact advocated by Walter Benjamin and replicated by his followers should also be approached precisely as such, i.e. not as an axiom of sociology but a *critical vision*. Among other things, our research indicates that by itself technological reproducibility does not rid cultural objects of aura. Many other, more salient conditions must be *jointly* fulfilled for this to be the case. Conversely, a whole constellation of cultural factors must come into play to make increase in value and recognition possible and lasting. The binary logics and relational structure of meaningfulness form one set of such conditions. Another set of factors consists of various aspects of materiality of a given object in relation to its environment and human sensorium. By an ironic turn of events, the late modern revival and iconic consecration of mechanically reproduced analogue records neatly contradicted Benjamin's vision. His was an ideological rather than strictly theoretical work. Understandably, he responded primarily to what he saw were the critical demands of his day and pressing sentiments of his heart. A price to pay for such an approach, however sensitive, is not negligible, for it consists in misconstruing the complexity of culture and its irreducible material entanglements.

Considering the cultural trajectory charted by vinyl, a much more fine-grained understanding of cultural meaning and its transformations is required if we are to make sense of it. As material context relativizes nearly every act of value creation, historical developments in such technology-dependent artistic domains as electronic music easily went far beyond Benjamin's vision. As one analyst argues, 'with electronic music, the artwork moves from the era of mechanical or "technical reproducibility" to the era of digital hyper-reproducibility – to an extent that even Benjamin himself might not have dared to imagine. Henceforth, there is no longer any question of an original. Everything takes place through duplication. The computer and the network have merely accelerated a process that has been underway for some fifty years.'[50] The presence of the analogue record in the digital age points to the necessity of relativizing our understanding of such notions as duplication, reproducibility, acceleration and meaning. As all cultural designations, these are hardly absolute entities. Authenticity resides in multiple webs of meanings and things, not in a singular notion of originality. The career of vinyl also shifts our basic understanding of what counts as an oxymoron or contradiction in terms, showing that there indeed is such thing as a 'unique copy'. In his critique of Benjamin's 'erroneous prophecy', Jacques Rancière concisely settles the score:

> From Romantic fragmentation to the contemporary practices of *deejaying*, sampling and remixing, which multiply the 'unique copies' created by the artisans of reproduction, via the development of the industry that deals with conserving heritage and obliges its constant broadening and 'rejuvenation', it is possible to trace an empirically erratic but theoretically coherent line.[51]

In this opening chapter we have attempted to draw such a line or trajectory, if only provisionally. It is in this empirical and conceptual context that we now wish to present a series of close up views of vinyl's multifaceted eminence. Besides being the kingly interface of the most abstract of arts, vinyl and its associated objects form a holistic artwork that uncannily materializes and synthesizes the sensual appeal of music concert, sculpture, picture and book. It is an ordinary medium that is an extraordinary message, a thing whose form defines its content, a commodity that redefines fetish, and a totem for modern tribes called music scenes.

CHAPTER TWO

Medium

Handling and Hearing

The medium is something which serves as a focus point.
It's a singular thing that accumulates.
Robert Henke

FORM AND FUNCTION

Ours is a world of multiple media in which form tends to follow function. This helps explain the range of cultural phenomena, including the relentless modern quest for change and never-ending updates commonly understood as 'progress'. But as cultural anthropologists point out, the reverse tendencies have also been the case: function follows form, and our formal arrangements respond as much to utilitarian novelty seeking as to keeping certain aesthetic and sensual comfort zones intact.

The matters of form matter. As Marshall McLuhan[1] observed, 'societies have always been shaped more by the nature of the media than by the content of the communication'. It *is* good when a medium is instrumentally effective but it *feels* good when it is aesthetically satisfying and reassuringly familiar as well. The observation regarding the role of aesthetic sensibility seems particularly true when it comes to cultural media, from magazine design to the look and feel of Apple products, whose utility and economic profitability are hardly separable from the experiential pleasures they can and do afford. Successful cultural tools do their job but each one entails also a specific set of more deeply satisfying experiences. We know that some modernist objects 'formed entirely on the basis of utility have proved singularly unattractive'.[2] That is an ironic malfunction of modernity. We also know that late modernity is partly understood as an era of intensive aestheticization of everyday commodities.

Media work for us but they also form us, often imperceptibly. Records, as the name indicates, represent cultural data but they are more than data. They are a part of a lifeworld. In other words, there is a phenomenology to every technology, and a mythology to every medium. While deeply intertwined, these spheres also respond to different sets of social imperatives and individual desires, so that what may be an improvement regarding the user's convenience does not necessarily mean the same regarding the user's experience. An imperfection may be an asset, perfection may seem sterile. This is the case because media are not just instruments but also messages full of meanings. Medium is a culturalized thing, and this is how it comes to sociological perception first.

Media's formal and functional meanings are relationally defined rather than simply given. We assess them by comparison, juxtaposition, trial and error. The universe of music formats is no different. Vinyl in particular is at once a mythology and technology, a signifier and a tool, a form and function. As we shall show, vinyl, and especially its revival in the digital age, certainly fits the concept of cultural myth in that it is a distinctive, relationally established mode of signification, a form of listening and playing that matters and makes it unique beyond its obvious utility. However, it is also the case that this special way of representing things is partly due to the very properties of the medium itself and the experiences it affords. In other words, while contingent and by no means obvious, the continued relevance of vinyl does not seem random, trivial or artificially contrived by industries of mass entertainment. In fact, we have shown in the previous chapter how rather the opposite has been the case. There is a dramatic biographical arc to the analogue record that reveals it as a medium resilient enough to retain aesthetic and pragmatic allure.

In this and subsequent chapters we present vinyl as an object that generates worlds of knowledge and sensuality, conducive to cultural archaeology and irreducible aesthetic experiences. We now know that whether a medium is physical or virtual, analogue or digital, complex or simple, matters a great deal. This is so both in terms utility and beauty, sense and sensibility, for the professionals and the amateurs.

Moreover, it is precisely these binary distinctions that make us more aware of the fact that each medium has its own world of praxis unlike others, even if in the end the commercial recording technologies seem to be about one and the same thing – music. As we indicated in the previous chapter and explore in greater detail here, music is not a purely natural fact. That it could be is a myth in a negative sense of the term. Likewise, there is no medium that can easily be isolated as a function and reduced to the technical issue of its 'format' whereby this or that sound carrier is turned into pure scientific case. Even seemingly 'immaterial' virtual files imply specific practices and engagement with physical devices.

In short, music is a necessarily and intricately mediated experience. Media, in turn, relate to ways of life. They have specific affordances that facilitate certain social effects rather than others, invite this use and make that one unfeasible. They feed on each other. Above all, different media occasion distinct forms of consumption and different relations to space, time and other humans. They have different life expectancy, imperfections and unique 'health issues' associated with their relatively vulnerable constitution. For example, as Roger Silverstone established regarding the materiality of another common media object, the television serves an important transitioning function related to fixing rituals, routines, spatial and temporal demarcations and the emotional textures of daily life.[3]

In this chapter we wish to reflect on all those issues, particularly on the way people acquire, listen to and hear, handle, play and care for analogue records. We believe it is crucial for informing their understanding of vinyl as a specific music medium. Again, as a medium, vinyl is also a message. This message – concerning its cultural qualities which various user groups venerate as warm, credible and critical – is not just narrated but experienced through the various ways vinyl is acquired, physically handled and the particular sound characteristics vinyl offers. The practices involved in, and involved by, physical handling – the feel and weight of vinyl, the way it plays and sounds, its cover and packaging – provide information and feedback. In this way the multiple meanings of vinyl are realized and reinforced through modes of engagement that the analogue record affords. However, engagement with the medium is not just discursively framed intentional commitment on the part of humans but rather a complex set of interactions between the potentialities of objects, cultural codes and the human sensorium. This is why we talk about vinyl's *affordances* while discussing it as a medium. American cultural sociologist Terence McDonnell clarifies the concept of affordances, asserting that 'the latent set of possible actions that environments and objects enable are relationally tied to the capabilities of the person interacting with that object'. This definition enables us to analytically distinguish 'affordances' of media from qualities of things that are inherent and independent characteristics,[4] discussed mainly but not exclusively in this and the following chapter, respectively.

We begin with exploring the way vinyl can be – and has typically been – obtained through practices of crate digging, before moving to consider the way people describe the way they play and hear vinyl. As an objectual medium, vinyl is distributed across space and time. That is, vinyl moves about physically. Unlike in other domains such as financial markets where the screen becomes the key unit of analysis and interpretation,[5] locating and buying vinyl is largely not an element of virtual sociality. The objectual quality of analogue copy – its key feature as a medium – means it needs to be sourced, selected, carried, shipped and dealt with physically. It is this physicality that contributes to vinyl's status as a discrete medium. It is true that online markets such as Discogs and virtual digging apps like 'iCrates' make this easier, but in the end the emplacement of vinyl is 'on the ground', discovered through the city and neighbourhoods, stores and warehouses, through the feet, through the fingers, and through corporeal immersion within vinyl marketplaces.[6] Importantly, this pertains to the key issue of playing too. Vinyl engages your hands in a different way than electronic devices. In fact, as we shall show, it orchestrates and activates much of the body of the handler and requires particular procedures of playing and caring that are conducive to ritualization rather than routinization.

Whether it is about acquiring or playing, the analogue medium profoundly shapes the respective practices. In line with the work of George Lakoff and Mark Johnson on metaphors in everyday speech,[7] this gets reflected by how we casually speak about music-related practices. Specifically, there is a series of clear linguistic distinctions that expose experiential differences between the analogue and digital formats: digging vs surfing, picking up vs downloading, spinning vs clicking, etc. Behind these phrases stand embodied experiences; they are not arbitrary conventions. Indeed, they are 'metaphors we live by', to use Lakoff and Johnson's catchy phrase. Also, as a physical medium, vinyl is always located *somewhere*, rather than just online, which increasingly feels like *nowhere* due to the omnipresent and dissipated networks of mobility. This *somewhere* matters because it is culturally and concretely located – in cities and neighbourhoods, interiors and streets, as we discuss more fully in Chapter 5. In short, vinyl is not only a mode of mediating sound and music but also – and crucially – it mediates human relationships as well as relations between humans and other associated objects and settings, to use Ian Hodder's apt formulation. The sum of these relationships creates what he calls 'sticky entrapments', a term that enables us to see media as nested rather than arbitrary.[8] Some of the associated effects that we explore below may seem obvious or banal, but as Regis Debray reminds us in his sociological manifesto of mediology, 'the trivial, peripheral or basely material incidentals of how any given message, doctrine or idea is put across' are every bit as important to the 'mediologist' as the content of such cultural entities.[9]

DIGGING AS SOUND ARCHAEOLOGY

The marketized practices of buying, trading and selling vinyl records tell us a lot about the meanings and mythologies of vinyl as a medium. In particular, the iconic vinyl-related practice of what is called 'digging' or 'crate digging' for vinyl establishes a portrayal of vinyl buying which reverberates through the imaginations, representations and practices of vinyl-loving listeners. To understand digging – a term referring to practices related to searching for and browsing through stacks of vinyl records, especially second-hand records – we must reflect briefly on what it means to do leisure in late-modern culture.

Having fun can be a serious business. In late-modern societies, leisure, hobbies and having fun require time, money, knowledge, various forms of physical effort and emotional investment. What people do in their free time can be related to matters of lifestyle, to the acquisition of skills and knowledge, to the tallying of experiences as prized possessions, to the refinement and shaping of self-identity, and ultimately to forms of cultural capital or social distinction. How we spend our free time points to our personal values and also our cultural identifications. Within any field of leisure activity people learn to become, to varying degrees, expert in their chosen leisure activity. What exactly is counted as expert and authentic knowledge by participants of a certain form of leisure activity relates to mastering and displaying the key values of practice; for example, learning to read the break of the surf, understanding the play of a court or pitch, being able to read and understand the imprinted symbols on old silver cutlery, knowing how to trim a sail. As Chris Rojek[10] characterizes it, leisure is often a matter of acquiring and displaying emotional intelligence, of participating in various forms of labour which increase competence, knowledge and ultimately allow the acquisition of skills which somehow pay off for a individual.

In other words, leisure can be and often is work. Getting into a hobby is not always just about having fun, but it can also be a rewarding – even if demanding – learning process that involves willingness to embark on a path of mastering something. This necessarily means time, effort and money investment. The distinctive affordances of vinyl that we have described above make it amenable to becoming a medium around which this kind of leisurely activity revolves. And, because labour and mastery confer value to things and activities, vinyl has the special affordance of being able to appreciate and constitute a meaningful pursuit. This is what we call passion, which is connected to such values as persisent devotion, accumulated effort, deferred gratification, serendipity and social collaboration.

Given this understanding of the work of leisure, and also the personal and cultural returns associated with forms of leisure, the notion that some practices of buying vinyl are commonly understood through the archaeological metaphor of 'digging' can begin to make sense. In the mythical form, digging refers to the practice of searching through stocks of second-hand vinyl. Although it can also apply to stores that have stocks of new vinyl, it commonly refers to expeditions to places with large, mixed, old, possibly unsorted stocks of mixed quality second-hand vinyl. Vinyl diggers are normally, although not necessarily, dedicated to digging vinyl as either a hobby or a professional practice. Like any leisure practice, regular engagement and dedication to the task pays off through increasing skill, knowledge and ultimately acquisition of vinyl. Although a one-off, infrequent dig will often yield surprising finds of vinyl, diggers tend to be highly knowledgeable about their digging patches, or at least that is an ideal they aspire to. While serendipity of digging makes it an attractive cultural adventure of sorts, it is systematicity that distinguishes it as an authentic practice that commands respect. The former offers the excitement of *finding*, whereas the latter makes it a genuine *search* in the time when searching has been reduced to running virtual engines and thus relatively trivialized.

A broad familiarity with the stock of a store allows the digger practical authority over a store's collection, allowing efficient surveillance of new additions to the vinyl stock of any store. But there is still broader familiarity involved, one that stems from knowledge about genres, styles, artists and labels as well as fluctuating prices and value of older records. This knowledge is typically acquired only over years of continuous and attentive involvement with music culture, just like taste is an incrementally acquired disposition or gradually formed performative engagement rather than a big bang of personal revelation. In short, obtaining music on vinyl is typically harder than acquiring electronic files. Because it requires more attention and effort, there is a value added to any collection acquired through digging.

The archaeological metaphor inherent in the term digging emphasizes the mythological aspects of digging practices and is accompanied by a series of interrelated narratives: the idea of going on digging expeditions, the search for rare, spectacular and hidden gems which are uncovered through the dig, the negotiation of hard or difficult conditions for the dig, the feeling of being lost in new, complex and large archives with difficult-to-search stock, the feeling that one is dealing with a collection that is relatively untouched or undiscovered, negotiating the dirt and grime that collects on long-stored vinyl, and the way rare or exceptional finds are displayed and shared to interested friends and wider communities. As Shuker[11] has pointed out in his study of record collecting, mythological ideas about 'the find' and 'the bargain' are important discursive frames for digging. Additionally, the way analogue medium engages the digger points to the fact that it lends itself to constitute archives that demand manual browsing and checking, just like we do with books or documents. Going through such archives may be tedious and could require the use of particular techniques. But it is exactly this condition that makes running into a valuable record special or even ecstatic.

If you have access to huge vinyl stores or warehouses, the serendipity factor and sheer luck become more pronounced. If supply is low or what you are interested in is released only as a limited run, which often happens in these days of small-batch production, then you enter an equally thrilling game of 'hunting' for rare pieces. Both situations may generate a degree of frustration normally absent in the digital sphere of the internet. But, by the same token, because it involves an investment of time and energy based on modes of cultural participation and leisure identities, it can be that much more exciting and meaningful. As in many other domains such as fashion or any kind of collecting, the magic stems from the hunt.

In their book about the Berlin techno scene, Felix Denk and Sven von Thülen give a telling example of it, while reflecting on the scene's early days at the end of the 1980s when there were only two stores in Berlin with cutting-edge American house and techno records. The local DJs recall the state of the scene as 'comparatively poor'; they had to quite literally 'hunt' for vinyl. In the end, when combined, the excitement about new hard-to-get music and the frustration connected to the lack of contact with those who produced and released the new music inspired locals to make records more available. This is how the now legendary store Hardwax was established. At that time vinyl was already being pushed aside by the CD, but, as we have explained in the first chapter, for club DJs it remained the key format. Today both availability of music and electronic mixing technology make the work of DJs different, certainly easier in many ways. Analogue records are not indispensable anymore. However, while devoid of the earlier difficulties that now may seem prehistoric, the world of perfectly available digital medium loses all the aura typically associated with hard-to-get media and digging practices. This is one of the reasons why Hardwax remains a temple of a store even as it provides the set of electronic interfaces to its collection.

As the important mode of acquiring music on vinyl, crate digging is a manual labour in its own right. Needless to say, even the vinyl purists choose to purchase certain records online, sometimes it can be the only way. Likewise, successful DJs in demand have less time to dig regularly or spend hours browsing the crates and here the technology comes in handy. Andreas Baumecker's perspective is exemplary in this case:

> I definitely have less time to go to record shops and dig … I order online quite a lot of records that I heard snippets of on the internet and fortunately I found a shop where I can hear those records the next day, around the corner of my house.

Still, it has been precisely the DJ culture that supported and continues to support digging as an essential part of the *craft*. In special cases, it gets elevated to the status of *art* in its own right.

In its basic form, digging as an art of music consumption is most strongly associated with musical genres that are beat- and sound-driven, namely hip-hop, techno, house, disco, funk and soul. It is from DJs within these genres who take their search for obscure and cool beats very seriously that the heroic figures of digging emerged. The artist DJ Shadow is one such exemplary figure in the digging community whose fame rests upon his extensive and specialist knowledge of even the most obscure vinyl releases and above all his legendary dedication to finding new music through the practice of digging. While being a groundbreaking and popular DJ best known for his debut LP *Endtroducing*[12] released in 1996 and now a classic within instrumental hip-hop and DJ genres, Shadow also stands as a type of iconic vinyl digger. Famously, and notably, *Endtroducing* is composed almost entirely of samples taken from Shadow's personal collection of vinyl LPs. Eliot Wilder, writing on *Entroducing* for the Bloomsbury series '33$^1/_3$' which commemorates, explains and mythologizes important albums, quotes William Burroughs's statement that 'you cut up the past to find the future' as an appropriate epigraph for this record. Wilder's guide to *Entroducing* begins in this way:

> When it was released in 1996, *Endtroducing* … sounded like nothing before or since – an album of beats, beauty and chaos, a sound that cuts to the very blue flame of the heart. Looking back, no other record, to my mind, better summarizes the end of the last century. Josh Davis, alias DJ Shadow, took elements of hip-hop, funk, rock, ambient, psychedelia as well as found sounds, oddball spoken-word clips and cut-out bin nuggets – a literal sweep of sounds that exist on planet earth – and then wrote the ultimate lesson. All this from a suburban kid who grew up in Davis, California – a small, out of the way college town. But Josh as a suburban kid with a passion – an obsession, really – for vinyl. Davis spent a good chunk of his life scavenging through what most dismiss as ephemera: the records that reside in those musty and dark used record stores. To many of us, they are meaningless. But to Josh David, they are lost souls. And, as their rescuer, he has done them an honor. Because these souls have a home on *Endtroducing* …

Endtroducing was reissued in 2011 on deluxe, heavyweight double LP vinyl package as part of Universal Records' 'Back to Black' series. It is widely regarded as the album that actually initiated and defined the genre of instrumental hip-hop. The album is so influential in its creativity and style that in reviewing the deluxe reissue of the album the music website Pitchfork says that many subsequent records obviously inspired by *Endtroducing* will be called 'Shadowesque'. In some ways, the album is a perfect expression of a postmodern sentiment in music-making: few real instruments are played, the artist has no musical training except for his personal taste, extensive musical knowledge and unique listening ear, the music is 'played' on turntables, and what we hear as recorded music is actually an artful reconstruction of samples artfully selected and compiled in the style of the ultimate musical bricoleur. *Endtroducing*, however, is not evidence of a spectral form of emptied-out postmodernism – a signal of the end of musical creativity – but what Scott Lash once called 'organic postmodernism', relying on tropes of extensive musical knowledge and pop cultural referentiality combined with a mood of warmth, critical celebration and political reinvention. In short, it is a record entirely (re)composed of snippets and selections of others' recorded music. Crucially, this reconstruction cannot be afforded without the knowledge that DJ Shadow makes his composition selections from his apparently very large personal stock of vinyl – he reportedly owns up to 60,000 vinyl LPs[13] – that he has amassed over many years of visiting record stores. The cover of *Endtroducing* is itself instructive on the centrality of digging to vinyl culture, featuring two vinyl diggers in a scene from the vinyl record store 'Records' in Sacramento, California, where Shadow is said to have acquired much of his collection. The photo makes the store a mythological sacred space for collectors and fans. 'Records' says on its website that it is:

> One of the largest record stores in Northern California. We have 5,000 square feet of floor space (mostly vinyl) and over 5,000 square feet of storage space (our basement). We have many rare and collectible records. We also have many records that can be used for sampling/music production. We have old albums with breaks, sound effect albums, spoken word records, instructional records, and DJ albums.[14]

This statement helps us visualize the stock of sonic sources of *Endtroducing* and assists us to understand how Shadow used a unique history and archive of vinyl to make something completely fresh. Featured in the film about hip-hop culture and DJing, *Scratch*, and quoted by Wilder, DJ Shadow is called by the artist Cut Chemist 'the king of digging'. Wilder describes him this way: 'Not only a master sampler and turntablist supreme, he is also a serious archaeologist with a world-thirsty passion for seeking out, uncovering and then ripping apart the discarded graces of some other generation.' DJ Shadow enhances his mythical reputation as a digger at 'Records' and helps us understand his conviction for digging vinyl by incorporating some of his own interview material on the alternate version of his song 'Best Foot Forward', the first track of his *Endtroducing … Excessive Ephemera* album, voiced over the final 30 seconds of the track: 'When I'm not making music, I'm shopping for music, whether it's new music, old music, and when I get home it all just ends up in one big stack.' Shown in the film *Scratch* sitting among vast stacks of old records in the basement of 'Records', Shadow reflects upon the store where he went on digging expeditions:

> This is my little nirvana. Being a DJ, I take the art of digging seriously, and this is a place I've been going to for eleven years. It's an incredible archive of music culture, and there's the promise in these stacks of finding something that you're going to use. In fact, most of *Endtroducing* … was built off records pulled from here.[15]

The DJ Shadow example perfectly illustrates the fusion of labour and work with hobby and love. In this case, effort and passion are fixed on the material object of the vinyl record. The practice of digging is suggestive of work, but is more likely to be associated with the desire for practical mastery and forms of cultural authority. Digging as a cultural practice requires commitment, and takes investment of various kinds. It rewards materially through the acquisition of the physical object, but culturally via the acquisition of expertise. Whichever accomplishment or status it attains, it is never achieved alone. For this reason, we need to consider the social dimension of digging and the construction of digging communities.

THE SOCIAL ELEMENTS OF DIGGING

There are a number of interrelated things that make digging such an enjoyable pastime for buying music. The first, to use Claude Lévi-Strauss's maxim, is that objects are *bonnes à penser*, or 'good to think with'. The record store, especially the type of store DJ Shadow refers to above, is a historical stock of vinyl that functions like an archive, often categorizing genres, and thus allowing browsers to look at and listen to the key musical works in many genres. Here the physical nature of vinyl and the information typically attached to it contribute greatly to its archival capacity in a double sense. It is a durable record capable of long-term and safe storage with relatively little fuss and technological maintenance. Moreover, once objectified as a physical medium replete with production data inseparable from it, the analogue record is a record of more than just music, in that it represents a particular label and artist, genre and style, production year and specific pressing, albums and singles, etc. As such it is amenable to all kinds of classification. If *music* itself tends to defy easy categorization, vinyl at the very least suggests some mode of categorization, and in principle enables us to give a palpable sense of order to the otherwise overwhelming universe of tunes. Being a physical medium, it imposes restrictions, making our engagement with music manageable, legible and formalized as genuine cultural legacy. Thus vinyl can be said to let customers identify with the broader culture of music production, listening and buying.

All this gets actualized through contact and communication with other people. Being located *somewhere*, vinyl brings different and otherwise dispersed persons to one place, facilitating direct contact and face-to-face interaction of like-minded people. Even if you are a lone digger, vinyl places are inevitably social spaces.

Additionally, digging introduces an exciting element of luck and chance to buying music. When done with others, these feelings of fun and joy can be directly and immediately shared. Unlike digital downloads, where the music browsing experience is often guided by automated 'suggestions' or the browser's limited musical knowledge, and where the dimensions of touch, sensuality and social engagement are necessarily excluded, digging is a social pastime where the excitement comes from picking up the unexpected, forgotten about or unusual vinyl edition, some of which can be recommended to us by others, both friends and strangers. Here, both the archaeological and social dimensions are clear: one might dig for hours or even weeks on end without uncovering anything special, unusual or rare, but occasionally a gem or forgotten classic will be unearthed, sometimes under completely unexpected circumstances. Such situations serve as a reminder that the world always holds more than meets the eye.

Last but not least, the excitement of digging comes also from the experience of getting one's hands dirty and engaging in the hard graft of sorting through stacks or bins of vinyl and periodically being rewarded with the valuable vinyl find. The reward for effort is even greater if that rarity is a bargain. In addition, the social opportunities of showing off one's rare find are rewarding too. Here, material immediacy and objectness are crucial qualities. One could probably just as easily download most albums available in-store, but possessing the material vinyl version is so much more impressive and demonstrative of the effort gone into the search. Pioneering electronic music artist, co-owner and co-founder of Kompakt records in Cologne, Wolfgang Voigt reflects on this in a revealing manner. Before it was a record label, Kompakt started out as a physical record store, so Voigt as one of the label's chiefs perfectly understands the value of the analogue medium as something requiring a physical-social space for its dissemination, circulation and exchange:

> We've got this day in our record shop in Cologne, called 'summer camp'. In summer, two or three times, there will be free beers, there will be a beer sponsor, and then we got a big party in front of the shop, and then we give 20 per cent off on every record. We made this a few weeks ago and the shop was packed the whole day. They buy everything. Sometimes you have to do this because it's an event, and then they buy all the back catalogue, and stuff like that.

The sociality connected to vinyl consumption – the listening to and learning about music through the music store as a living cultural archive and also as a social space – is something music listeners are likely to discover as teenagers. The record store and the club are often dedicated young person's spaces. Neither home, school, nor job, they are social spaces where codes of cool and hip can be observed, and a complex meaningful world of engagement with records replete with many subtleties and distinctions abounds. Michael aka Puresque reflects on this social dimension – materially evident in the club setting as much as the record store – of the origin of his own attachment to vinyl:

> *Dominik*: When did you discover vinyl for real?
>
> *Michael aka Puresque*: Vinyl for real to me came really, really late; it was like when I was maybe 16 or 17 years old, I saw Sven Väth playing on vinyl, and to me it was like, I don't know, just this massive record in his hand. Sure I had had records before, like my sister had a record collection and played records at home, but to me like playing with records in nightclub has this magic thing. And it came by watching this guy play, I don't know, 17 hours in a row on vinyl, and that was like: 'shit, that's what I want to do for my living'. I wanna be him, I want this magic! It was like from when I was 16 or 17 years old from then, I started to slowly buy records and go to record shops and I discovered the whole thing. It was so nice because talking to people, hearing other opinions, discussing records, that was like, you don't do this at home when listening to your mp3s … that's this thing for me.

The sense of community participation and solidarity to be experienced from digging is a theme many of our research participants raised. Mieko Suzuki, a Japanese Berlin-based DJ and artist, points out that digging matters for her profession because this is how she gets exposed to artists and tracks she might be unaware of and especially where staff can help guide her to tracks she should know about, and those which they know will fit with her tastes:

> There is an interesting surprising element about going to a record shop and listening to a record … By chance or recommendation … Also there are

recommendations if you want to buy. If the record shop staff recommended me something, or somehow it catches me in the listening, this is amazing. This is the only way. If you want to get it, you have to go to record shops. Yeah, tomorrow I have a gig, and I go to *Spacehall*[16] because they have such a huge history of the record and you can easily pick up anything there. This is nice, because sometimes you forget.

Robert Henke also contemplates this facet of how the physical medium of music listening affords a particular form of transient listening communities and formation of tastes during the phases of music discovery and purchase. For Robert, who tells us he listens to a lot of music these days but seldom buys, the role of the physical artefact in building solidarity and interest among customers is not to be underrated. Here, he describes the 'pre-internet' mode of buying records:

> It was completely important, absolutely. I mean, the process of record buying or listening to music was a social process too. So you went to a record store and you grabbed a new release and you put it on the record player in the shop and everyone was listening and there was an immediate discussion about this music: 'Let's flip back. Yeah that sounds better', 'But at the end of the B-side, there's a track that's better', 'Yeah, it grows on me'. A discussion within the shop about 3 or 4 pieces of music, 5, 6, or 7 people involved in it. It just happened. It's on the disc and they discuss it. It's of course a cultural and social aspect of this whole scene which definitely changed, because there are other ways of getting information about new music. This was pre-internet, what you listened to then was something that was really new, you didn't have a chance to pre-hear it on a website.

The singer and artist Björk has also reflected on the implications of the changes introduced by digitalization:

> The physical process of going to a record shop to buy a physical object has been made more or less obsolete ... But the very idea of what's physical needs to be redefined. All the record industry pessimism towards the disappearance of the physical is unwarranted, if you ask me. The meanings are merely shifting. You know, people will always hunger for physical experiences.[17]

Although the social and concrete pleasures of actual record shopping may have seemed obsolete just a handful of years ago, it is precisely for the corporeal and sensual reasons Bjork herself recognizes that record stores retain their social roles that prevent them from vanishing completely. In fact, as we shall discuss in Chapter 5, in particular contexts certain types of record stores are actually multiplying. Some of their meanings and functions may be shifting but, as the aforementioned example given by Wolfgang Voigt illustrates, the core social role retains relevance.

HEARING THE VINYL: ANALOGUE RECORD AS 'ORGANIC' AND 'WARM' MEDIUM

In order to succinctly couch the salience of medium in a broadly recognized parlance, we refer to the phrase 'medium is the message' in this book and our other published research on vinyl record culture. What we mean by this, in large part, is that for some listeners it matters not just *what* one listens to, but *how* one listens to it and how it sounds: the medium of listening is just as important as the content of the listening. The specific sensations afforded by a given form may not be replicable in another, which inevitably makes the question of medium central to the reception of music. One's music knowledge and taste can be judged not merely by what one listens to, but the visible and other sensuously mediated ways one listens to it. In this way, music listening becomes like many other skills where aesthetic-technological objects mediate the relationship one has to the object of consumption, which in this case is music and sound.

Many examples of where function is overlaid by expressive and aesthetic discourses come to mind: chefs who discuss their preferences for different brands and styles of kitchen knives; guitarists who prefer particular guitar brands, shapes, materials or strings; cyclists who discuss the pros and cons of particular gear and tyre set ups; hairdressers who discuss their preferences for using particular brands of scissors, dryers or hair product. In each case, discussions ensue about the relative value of techniques, media and skills, and opportunities for fine, boundary-marking distinctions based on specialist knowledge or taste are afforded by these discussions and the experiences made possible by different media. One of the twentieth century's finest anthropologists, Mary Douglas, has written about the meanings associated with particular modes of making coffee and grinding coffee beans. This illustration serves as a nice example of what we are talking about. Douglas and Isherwood discuss different ways to make coffee as an example of how routine, everyday acts of consuming things (coffee beans, liquid, cup, grinder) become opportunities to delineate very deep subjective debates about the inauthentic and the truthful, the good and bad. They consider the symbolic meanings of whether one chooses to grind coffee beans with a mechanical grinder, or pestle and mortar. Their suggestion is that is not just about the drink itself and its supposed utility, but about *how* the drink is prepared that matters. In the case of coffee, the artful and skilful preparation of the grind matters for appreciation of the cup of coffee:

> The grinder works mechanically, the human hand only supplies force, and electric power can easily be substituted for it; its produce is kind of dust-fine, dry and impersonal. By contrast there is an art in wielding the pestle. Bodily skills are involved, and the stuff on which they are bestowed is not hard metal, but instead the noblest of materials, wood. And out of the mortar comes not a mere dust, but a gritty powder, pointing straight to the ancient lore of alchemy and its potent brews. The choice between pounding and grinding is thus a choice between two different views of the human condition and between metaphysical judgements lying just beneath the surface of the question.[18]

The point Douglas and Isherwood make is that it is not just that one grinds coffee beans, but how it is done and the embodied way this is fused with discourses about the proper and best way to conduct the grind. This introduces plays of distinction centred upon the completion of certain technological procedures that are endowed with aesthetic qualities related to skill, style and design. That is, the way to grind coffee beans (and if one chooses to grind at all, as opposed to buying coffee powder) becomes a property not just of technology and skill, but is linked to wider symbolic meanings via aesthetic properties and the way procedures are seen to afford or emphasize such qualities. In the case described by Douglas and Isherwood, physical, embodied pounding of coffee beans with natural materials is the most ennobling way to produce a satisfactory grind. This is partly because it involves the body coming into direct contact with natural materials, which is perceived to symbolize authenticity. This assignment of value becomes especially salient given the context of digitalization and virtualization of culture, as Bill Brown notes in his treatise on thing theory: 'If the topic of things has attained a new urgency ... this may have been a response to the digitalization of our world.'[19] The process of physically producing the grind from the raw material with the aid of hand-held tools has a certain honesty to it: its transformation from bean to powder is visible and it is related to and felt directly by bodily processes.

In a similar way, we can conceptualize the meanings applied to music listening, and especially vinyl, as a way of extending the self into the material object and related technological assemblages of music consumption. By virtue of the visibility of sound reproduction – lowering the tonearm, allowing the needle to reach the groove, observing the rotating vinyl disc and so on – and the mechanical process of instituting the listening process means listeners can have more palpable contact with music. For purists, it is *the only* way to listen to music. The ritualistic aspect of this kind of engagement with the world of sound and music is allowed to come to the fore with this kind of physical medium. The character of the format engages all consumers who choose it, whether they are purists or not.

Perhaps most importantly, vinyl's affordances as an analogue medium allow for distinctively engaging listening experiences and aural sensations. What we observe is that few believe absolutely in the objective superiority of vinyl as a high-fidelity medium for reproducing sound. Although some enthusiasts of course claim it, most understand very well its capacity to evoke individual sound quality. They argue that vinyl is, after all, a 'warm' and 'rich' medium, and so understanding this character of the medium is indispensable to understanding vinyl. This discourse appears in a variety of contexts. Symptomatically, it has directly translated to the name of a Berlin-based label called 'Warm Sounds'. The centre sticker of a recent release by the artist *Raw Interpreter* includes the following information: 'Not licensed for digital broadcasting. Only vinyl release.'

There are multiple discursive resources that people call upon in order to emphasize this distinctiveness of hearing the analogue sound. Among them are those who marvel at the sound to the point of sentimentalizing the experience. Others see vinyl as a vehicle of more pure and direct contact with the music they produce or play. Finally, we can distinguish a large group of vinyl lovers who pragmatically adopt a hybrid approach that recognizes symbiotic rather than mutually exclusive relations between media and interfaces. Regardless of specific evaluative angle, vinyl aficionados and amateurs converge on the theme of vinyl's affording individual aural experience. Consider first the illustrative case of someone whose engagement with vinyl mirrors the one exhibited by the mainstream industry, rediscovering it after a long hiatus. Writing in the the *Guardian* newspaper in 2013, in a somewhat mawkish piece titled 'How I Taught My Son to Love Vinyl', Tony Myers recounts how he reconnected with his vinyl collection after 25 years of listening to CDs and mp3 digital files. After being gifted a turntable and investing in relatively inexpensive speakers, he talks about becoming reacquainted with the Impulse vinyl version of John Coltrane's celebrated jazz album, *A Love Supreme*. His story vouches for the emotional connection listeners can feel to vinyl, citing its perceived warmth, richness, intimacy and immediacy:

> I still have my jazz and blues vinyl, and reconnecting with John Coltrane's *A Love Supreme* in its original gatefold sleeve on the Impulse label was the nearest I'll come to a religious experience. Playing the record after almost 25 years I was almost moved to tears as my living room was filled with music of such warmth, fullness and richness you simply don't hear on digital. I felt I was in the studio with the band as they put the tracks down.

Even if one can sceptically ask why would someone of this deeply sentimental orientation abandon vinyl in favour of something that 'simply' cannot match it, we still can treat it as evidence of vinyl's capacity to recapture the attention and devotion of wider music-listening public. This attitude to vinyl as a particular medium finds recognition on the side of those who produce and market vinyl records too. As we discuss in greater detail in Chapter 4, this in turn gives rise to marketing discourses that centre on notions of legacy, heritage and original intention behind a given musical release. For example, *Legacy Vinyl* frames its releases in a manner that epitomizes the phenomenon of re-enchantment with the way vinyl mediates and conditions musical experience:

> Hear What You've Been Missing. Formats come and go, but nothing sounds as good and as warm as a vinyl recording. There's something about the combination of needle and groove that showcases music in its very best light. Which is why Legacy Recordings has gone to great lengths to present this classic recording exactly the way it was intended on the day it was recorded – in all its original glory, with all the warmth and nuance that only vinyl can offer.

We can see here that heritage tends to be instantiated through the experience of warmth, and concepts of authenticity and recognition of the original conditions of recording and production. These experiential and conceptual notions are presented as the ones responsible for saving vinyl from irrelevance. However, there is a group of vinyl lovers for whom vinyl never lost its status as 'vibrant matter'.[20] Most prominently, these were electronic music producers and DJs. They continued to work and play with it despite the surrounding changes. There are at least two reasons for this enduring attractiveness of vinyl. One relates to the fact that vinyl was turned into an 'organic' medium by the appearance of 'synthetic' digital formats. Moreover, digitalization provided producers with such devices as a sampler that turned the analogue heritage into a giant archive of sounds. Interestingly, being a vinyl 'purist' meant a somewhat paradoxical embrace of its 'dirty' aspects, along with high-sonic fidelity and DJ-friendly characteristics.

Discussing the formation of techno duo Puresque, the legendary Berlin-based Tresor label says that 'they met over a mutual love of vinyl and entered the studio together with the desire to create something raw, as removed as possible from the synthetic feel of purely digital production'. Puresque's sound is described on the *Resident Advisor* site in this way: 'Puresque intend upon cultivating an up-tempo and dirty sound culture that is anything but digital – analogue sound for analogue people.' The framing of Puresque's sound through ideas about rawness, dirt and realness is expressed in such a way that its relationship to analogue production and the vinyl medium is made clear. Vinyl is the format. Among many other things, Michael shares an amusing anecdote that points to the revelatory aural qualities of vinyl:

> When you are at home, you turn on the radio, it's not the same as putting on a vinyl. Also if you have a date and invite a girl over, how can you impress her? You put on a vinyl, you don't just turn on the radio, or put on a CD. It kind of brings life into your life. It's like the magic and everyone feels it, you know. A friend of mine once told me: 'Yeah it's really cool you know, I use YouTube to mp3 converter' and they download my music like that. And I was like 'Dude! what are you doing to yourself? The feeling of the whole music...', and he was like 'No, it's OK!', and I was like 'OK, you stand here now, select one of my tracks I have on vinyl and we're gonna listen to it on a proper vinyl system now'. And he was shocked! He stood there, he was like, he was almost crying about what he did to himself in the last couple of years, then he went to a shop, he bought himself a record player and since then, he goes to shops and buys records ... He wants proper sound. But you know, some people, you have to tell them, or show them. And if it's side by side, the feeling is something all different. That's what keeps it alive, it's not like digital mess ...

Ultimately, the metaphors of 'organic' or 'warm' sound point to vinyl's being perceived as an alive medium, as opposed to digital formats that tend to be experienced and verbalized as too clean or clinical. Andreas Baumecker connects this not only with the format itself but with the broader issue of analogue production process which grafts the 'deep' analogue sound onto vinyl surface. 'Records are mastered in a different way ... The sound is living, it changes. On CD it doesn't change.' Michael aka Puresque offers another spin on exactly the same point:

> *Michael*: Vinyl is something alive that can die, I mean, you can break it. It's not like a CD, I don't fucking care, I can throw it away, but a vinyl, if somebody would break a vinyl, one of my vinyl ...
>
> *Dominik*: It could kind of break your heart right?

Michael: I could kill him! [laughs] ... this keeps the industry alive because music is about this magic. And life only exists on vinyl.

Not only are there the differences between digital and analogue mastering, every vinyl release is mastered and cut differently as the record goes through several stages of human decision-making and complex production that we explore in the next chapter. Perhaps most interestingly, what is often interpreted as the 'warm' sound of vinyl can be traced back to its technical imperfections and vulnerabilities, especially different distortions imposed by the characteristics of the medium that generate the mythical warmth of vinyl.

PARADOXICAL MEDIUM: IMPERFECTIONS AND LIMITATIONS AS ASSETS

There are a variety of imperfections and limitations imposed by the analogue medium that are worth exploring. Andreas Lubich, mastering engineer of *Calyx* Studio in Berlin, tells us that the differences commonly attributed to analogue compared to digital media reference the built-in properties of the medium itself. The characteristics of the vinyl material and the cutting process introduce aural features which make it different to any other format. What matters strongly, of course, is the way these features are heard and interpreted. The magic denotation of 'warmth' happens at the intersection of objective characteristics married with subjective and contextual interpretation. This intersecting and its outcomes are not random. They are open-ended but within the bounds of possible affordances. Andreas Lubich points out that analogue record can't be described as simply better than other formats. Technically speaking, it is not, but it is precisely what counts as its technical shortcomings that afford unique, widely venerated experiences of playing and listening to vinyl. Consider this exchange with Andreas:

Dominik: What is it in particular, from the technical point of view, that actually makes analogue record worse?

Andreas Lubich: I mean, the whole discussion about the difference between digital and analogue boils down to the flaws of the analogue in comparison to the digital. So, what makes us enjoy listening to analogue media and analogue sources are mostly the flaws of the analogue technology.

Dominik: So, what kind of flaws could you name, technically speaking?

Andreas Lubich: It's about distortion, and in the best case, harmonic distortion. That's what happens with tube processing. Depending on how you treat it, that happens to tape or reel to reel, but especially to vinyl records.

This particular phenomenon endorses the point by Jonathan Sterne that the 'elusive world of sound – the sonorous, the auditory, the heard, the very density of sonic experience – emerged and became perceptible only through its exteriors'.[21] Medium and the machines that make it are such structuring exteriors. They have specific affordances that may be particularly suitable for a given kind of aesthetic effect. Some of those effects can be arrived at serendipitously – no machine can in advance prescribe all its potential uses. Still, no one sonic machine can satisfy all sonic needs. In this sense the affordances of media are bounded rather than universally opened to arbitrary applications. It is instructive to use in this context Robert Henke's description of the limitations of the analogue technology that were treated as advantages by underground electronic music artists:

> The ideal of the record how it was envisioned by Neumann and others when they built these machines was that despite the shortcomings of the medium they deliver high fidelity, which more or less implies that you go with an excellent recording into the process, and you end up with a nice translation of this recording. And there's limitations: there's noise, there's distortion – that's pretty much the two limitations you have.

Another side to these distortion-induced sonic effects is increased complexity of the signal. Robert Henke re-emphasizes the point that, in part, what one hears is a result of the imperfections of the vinyl medium, or we might say the *sonic prejudices* inherent in the physical affordances of the medium and the sensitivities of our hearing apparatus. This knowledge emerged in particular as a result of experimentation common in independent and avant-garde music production. As Robert specifies it:

> In the early electronic music culture, some of the problematic aspects of vinyl turned out to be really cool. The sounds of the old rolling drum computers are very simple, and adding distortion always adds complexity to the signal. So what happens is that you put something in which is, let's say, a clap, which is just this 5 tons of noise, it goes 'clap'! When you listen to it, and if you hear it after the vinyl is cut, especially if the cut is very loud, you get this kind of 'Tcharack'! You get much more complexity as part of this signal, and you get something that is really hard to emulate with other means, it's very specific. And there are many properties to the sound of vinyl which are just technically wrong, but from an acoustic perspective, very pleasing.

In addition, the other part of this story is that vinyl ages just like living beings. Not only does this introduce certain patinas of packaging, for example, but the vinyl groove erodes when it is being heavily used or when operated in sub-optimal conditions. This too may alter reception of the sound of vinyl. Andreas Baumecker's reflections on his extensive experience as a DJ provide additional insights into this vulnerability:

> If you use it extensively in the club, then of course it wears off and it gets scratches. It doesn't sound as good as it was at the beginning. But, I have to say, if you use the vinyl and the vinyl gets used, it really also gets an even crazier, greater sound. It does get a different sound. It loses the high frequencies. So, every time you put it on, you have to re-equalize it, but it really gets its own character. It definitely gets character. And you cannot get that character with a digital file.
>
> *Dominik*: The digital format, whether virtual file or physical CD stays the same, the same loudness, it's always the same frequency range and so

on. Whereas vinyl is a bit like a human, it changes slightly over time. It's unique.

Andreas Baumecker: It definitely changes over time. There was this launch for Theo Parish I played in the 1990s, and I just remember playing this record one time in the club and it was like ... every brain cell was like ...

Dominik: ... dancing!

Andreas Baumecker: Dancing, exactly. Then I didn't touch it for ten years and when I put it back on, it sounded so shit compared to the rest of the newer 12's I got at the time. So I was thinking, how did I do this? How was it possible that it sounded so amazing? I think it has to do with volume. You just have to blast it. It's pressed in a really crazy way, way too much bass, you think at first. As soon as you turn the volume up and make it as loud as other tracks, if it's possible without getting feedback in the club, then you can make it sound totally amazing. And that's the cool thing. Even if records wear off, you can still make them sound really cool and unique. That's what makes it not so interesting when you play the digital files in the club because it's always staying on this one specific peak that you can't get rid of. Maybe there is a kind of algorithm that could do this on the CDJs but you can't do it, as of now. Thank God.

As we can infer from this description, not only extended use but also other seemingly obvious factors such as amplification affect experience of sound. Amplification is typically taken to mean increasing the power of the signal. However, combined with the analogue sound, it may mean also changing the perception of the signal. Imperfections therefore contribute to understanding vinyl as a unique medium. Andreas reiterates this point:

Andreas Baumecker: You can make a really shit vinyl sound very good, just by putting the volume up, that's it ... There's also of course the example of the record that has been pressed 250 times and it sounds shit, because maybe the label couldn't afford to have a second master, a second pressing. But that also can make the records quite unique, because they sound so shit. That's also something very interesting – some sound shit, but maybe exactly that shit sound can be the bomb in the club.

Dominik: The imperfection of vinyl can be somehow attractive.

Andreas Baumecker: Yeah.

All these sonic features of vinyl become more pronounced and conducive to positive interpretation once the digitalization of music profoundly altered our engagement with it, leading to a new kind of music experience. Robert Henke succinctly emphasizes this point: 'Only after the CD came out, we figured out that the sound of vinyl is something that due to the specific distortions is actually cool.'

Notwithstanding imperfections, the analogue record presents users with a limited palette of possibilities. This must be considered not just in terms of the dimensions of the medium itself, but also in relation to fields of practice and devices. Vinyl production and playback is connected to analogue devices that impose their own limitation. Henke observes the way that working with such devices is bounded by fixed decisions, finite possibilities and a limited range of choices. He identifies that this boundedness might actually turn out to be a desirable thing in terms of making and procuring music, and also listening to it. It also introduces the necessity for discipline in the face of potentially costly and time-consuming production:

> In a digital world, we have unlimited access, the creative version of everything. We forever store every piece of thought we have in our head, so we create this constantly growing world of data, which in one way or the other, is also very dangerous. It doesn't enforce decision, and so there's all this revival of people working with analogue, actually. The one answer is of course the tactile interface, that's clear, the incapability of creating the same thing twice: it's always a new surprise, it's always something existing in the moment, the uniqueness and the feeling that everything that counts is the now, the present. And there's no hopping back to what I did yesterday. There's no, 'wait, compare, maybe yesterday was better' – work in the now. And you either say that now it is great, let's record it, or it's gone forever. And this is something that seems to be very appealing these

FIGURE 2.1: Robert Henke with his custom-made legendary Monodeck, Kreuzberg, Berlin. (DB)

days where you can just go back to the world of yesterday. It's another exercise of focus. Here the focus is on a limited palette of functions. Sometimes I focus on a limited point in time, which is the present, and that's something that to me feels more and more important, the more our virtual world around us supports looking at things in many, many ways. We cannot spend our time accessing everything which the media put out right this very second, which is already way too much, way more than we can handle. That's the essential question of these days. It's the big data and your small home. When do you stop inhaling of all this stuff, there's no boundary any more, there's no effort any more. And in this context, having a self-contained world which imposes boundaries and says 'no you can't go beyond that', or 'no you can't go back to yesterday', that's something I believe is really important.

Robert Henke is certainly not alone in this reflection. Consider two other takes on the same issue. Recalling the work that Joy Division did with the legendary British radio DJ John Peel, the band's bassist Peter Hook wrote:

> 'When you did a Peel session there was no messing about … You were in and out. Which suited me down to the ground. A great way to do things, if you ask me. Nowadays you're so spoiled by technology you can spend hours and days and months on the computer perfecting every tiny detail. Of course, there's some great music being made that way. But is it greater than the music being made back then? No.[22]

Brian Eno offers a similar perspective on the relative advantages of the analogue over the virtual world:

> People are often paralysed by a range of choices when they're presented to them on a silver platter with unlimited time to explore and process them. You can't forget: everybody works better with fewer possibilities. You see it over and over again that good artists end up coming back to the same ideas they've always worked with.[23]

Vinyl offers a sense of continuity and familiarity of this kind. It limits the producer who has to think about space limitations of the analogue disc and the mastering process, as well as a DJ who can come to a club only with a limited number of records. Phillip Sollman aka Efdemin tells us that he plays vinyl whenever he can, even though it can be cumbersome when he has to travel to his gigs. He reflects on the difference between the limitation of vinyl playing versus the unboundedness of computerized DJing: 'It's such a big difference if you work with a selection that you have made before. You have to deal with what you have. Or, you have these unlimited possibilities on your stick.' Phillip relates to us an anecdote about one of his DJ gigs in Japan when he simply forgot his USB stick. He only had with him a set of records and had to rely on them. Initially stressed, he ended up delivering a great set: 'I played such a beautiful set. I think it was one of the best in recent times because I had to work with what I had. It makes you so creative.' This highlights another pragmatic difference between formats: you can lose or forget your USB stick, but it is highly unlikely that you can go to a gig without your bag of vinyl.

Finally, there are micro features of the medium that may potentially contribute to its individual and imperfect character. It perhaps takes artists' idiosyncratic approach to recognize these details, and to revel within the subtle world of minute architecture of the groove. Lawrence English is adept at playing within such structures and observes the non-musical features of vinyl to be just as important as its musical content:

> The lead groove of vinyl is like a prelude of noise before music, there is an anticipation aspect to this mode of listening to music. It's like a plane taking off, gaining speed and then – the sonic boom.

Similarly, Mieko Suzuki points out that the uniqueness of the analogue medium can best be identified at the start and end of a vinyl record, or in between songs. This interstitial space is not a lack or an emptiness, she believes, but in fact allows the listener to identify the special features of the medium. It is, one might say, a 'positive lack', perceived as a distinctive feature of vinyl, in contrast to the digital nothingness between songs on CDs or digital files, or the capacity for 'gapless play' settings on some digital playback devices:

> *Mieko*: The CD is much clearer and vinyl sometimes has noise on it. And also, it sounds different. The way to listen to it is so different, you play ... Sometimes like in between the first track and the second track, you know. Shhhhhhh! It's not noise, but it's just ...
>
> *Ian*: Just the needle on vinyl.
>
> *Mieko*: Exactly! The grooves in between the tracks.
>
> *Dominik*: So the perfection and clean sound of the CD was something actually unattractive for you?
>
> *Mieko*: For me, yeah.

The observations couched within the above conversations allow us to identify vinyl as a special playback medium. It is not perfect or pristine, or of absolutely the highest sonic fidelity, but has unique affordances which, as Robert Henke points out, give vinyl a presence in its own right. Robert discusses this dimension in a remarkably lucid explanation of how we *hear* vinyl:

> I think the effect is indeed a medium, in the full sense of what medium means, it mediates and it has its ... It has its very own presence by itself, that you can't ignore. The whole promise of the CD was perfection, which it more or less delivers. It's a digital medium, you put in a sequence of numbers and you read out a sequence of numbers. So there's no room for interpretation here. In theory, the perfect CD player is invisible. With vinyl it was never the case, and the restrictions of vinyl go much further: after 20 minutes you have to turn it over, these restrictions of vinyl mean you have to store it, you have to pull it out of the sleeve and put it back in the sleeve, so you are exposed to this whole culture of packaging and all these things, it's very important. So you make a record and you

> have this amount of space you have to fill, or you leave it blank. But you know there is this space, and as a consumer, you buy the vinyl and you are exposed to this, so there's so much more to this medium than these little CDs ... With vinyl it's a different thing. People have a much more emotional relationship to the vinyl. Because it's bigger, it demands a different listening, a different way of listening, it's a process that just demands more attention.

A somewhat tangential story from Henke serves hilariously to further illustrate how there may be a clash of interpretations regarding the appeal of this multifaceted distinctiveness that analogue mastering offers when applied creatively. In short, the clash Henke describes below is one of commercial interests, which exploit the sign value of vinyl, with artistic interests wanting to exploit the full spectrum of what we might call *medium value*. During his time at *Dubplates & Mastering*, Henke was contracted to master a hip-hop record for a big-ticket customer. As Henke puts it to us, this is where 'the role of the engineer comes into the game. The thing is that not all distortions are good distortions, and at least to a certain extent it is a matter of taste – what kind of distortion you want to allow in this process and which kind you don't want to allow.' Henke decided to cut the vinyl master 'hot', according to a particular aesthetic sense and the style of the famous independent cutting house he worked for:

> [These] German hip-hop guys, I think signed to a major label already, decided it would be cool to try this out, and so I did the usual magic, and did the same aesthetic judgment that I had for a club 12-inch, which included cutting it 'hot', which means it's punchy, it's loud but it's also distorted, a bit edgy, and I was really pleased.

Upon hearing the test pressing on vinyl, the artist and the record company were not so pleased, and fired back to Henke very quickly about the sound on the test vinyl product. He recounts the sequence of events and his reaction to it:

> The first thing that happened the next morning was a phone call from the label saying 'What the fuck?!' I said, 'What the fuck, what the fuck?' They said, 'Well, the artist is completely unhappy with the sound.' I said, 'Hmmmm, alright.' So I tried to talk with them and understand. They said, 'Yeah, the vocals are not loud enough and the balance between the instruments is not right any more.' And I thought, actually it's all wrong: the balance between the instruments is perfect, the vocals are right there, but not piercingly loud. But this was a judgement coming from someone with a complete different aesthetic background. And afterwards, I redid the cut very, very conservatively. So, I made a boring cut. Something technically OK, no question there, but also nothing where anyone would say 'Pheeeww ... Wow'. More something like 'Yeah it's a good sound', but the specific aura when you put the vinyl record on and listen to it and go 'Oh man, what a sound' was completely absent. Well, I got a bottle of really expensive wine for that cut. They were really happy. And, of course, the second cut took me half an hour.

PLAYING THE VINYL: CORPOREAL AND RITUALISTIC AFFORDANCES OF THE VINYL

While the matters of hearing and sound may be hard to adjudicate as the degree of subjective preferences and sentimental attachments colours the way people talk about music they listen to, the corporeal aspect introduces a different, perhaps more graspable phenomenon to the story, especially through the work of the DJ. Playing with vinyl demands a wider range of movement and also encourages more tactile and expressive register of bodily protocols compared with computer interfaces. For Michael aka Puresque, this translates to an enhanced sense of flow while mixing with vinyl:

> Sometimes I play 12 hours for myself at home and I forget about time. And this would never happen with the digital medium, it would never happen. In the end these CD players got really, really good. But, the feeling of playing is just different with them. Maybe it's about the body language, you have another body language by holding the record, and maybe changing the needle, I don't know. People feel there is something else going on when you play vinyl. When you turn around, you pick up the next record and play it, you are always in motion. And it's like, this is what makes music, it's about dancing. Music is about dancing and vinyl makes me dance, I don't know, it just makes me dance.

Here we can discern another dimension of the difference between the analogue and the digital. A medium that allows your machines to do the mixing job for you impeccably removes the burden of certain musical skill from DJs' shoulders but with it all the claims to the beat matching craft are gone too. While these 'democratizing' and convenient effects of electronic technologies may amaze many, they also 'solve' an issue that is seen by some prominent professional DJs as secondary. Andreas Baumecker explains this situation in a following way:

> If you are a carpenter and you only just sit at a computer, but you haven't learned how to physically work with your hands on materials and stuff, then I think it's not really being a carpenter. It's the same with a DJ ... And it's not about the syncing, really. It's about how you work the tracks, it's not the syncing.

Apart from the physical aspect of playing experienced by the DJ, there is a visual dimension which exists for the spectators who observe the DJ at work. Phillip Sollmann aka Efdemin reflects on this in an interesting way:

> Sometimes the sound is not better any more because the system is more focused on playing with CDs. That's another problem these days. But in good places like Panorama Bar of course they take care. It's more *focused* on the vinyl. And, yeah, I think it looks better, the DJ looks much better.
>
> *Dominik*: This body aspect and the bodily connection ...?
> *Phillip Sollmann*: Totally.

Peter Runge notes another aspect of visual attractiveness of playing the vinyl. He thematizes the directness of eye contact with the process of picking up the sound from the medium. 'By seeing it, you know what you should do. You don't need a lot of explanation because you see what happens.' Seen in this light, DJing appears to be work in the traditional sense of the term. The DJ comes across as a more 'transparent' figure to the spectators and this fact can additionally lend a sense of honesty to the craft and art of playing for people. In turn, this translates to the discourse of authenticity and expertise surrounding vinyl DJs and grants a special aura to playing with vinyl. Because of this, analogue DJs tend to think of vinyl as medium *par excellence*, as Michael aka Puresque conveys:

> For me medium is vinyl. I feel more comfortable with it. If somebody is good at playing with CDs, it's totally fine with me as long as it's not like someone standing there with a controller, because I hate it when DJs don't move.

In fact, computer-based DJ software implies an obviating of the need for human DJs. Phillip Sollman makes this point when he notes that we might once reach a stage where 'we don't need a human DJ anymore because the selection could be easily done better by a software algorithm, which could make a "perfect" set. This is exactly the opposite of what I'm interested in. I want the DJ to surprise me somehow.' This is precisely another valence to the humanness of the analogue medium. The club parties are paradigmatic effervescent rituals of late-modern culture. Vinyl is a kind of totem within these ritualistic situations, as we show in Chapter 5.

Finally, analogue record affords a set of typical ritual practices in domestic spaces and amateur contexts. It demands attention and ritualizes listening to music. In terms of attention, it is like a guest in one's apartment, meaning that you can't ignore the vinyl – playing requires periodic and regular treatment. The convenience of digitalization is in the possibility of reducing music to the background. Vinyl is always physically present and you will sooner or later be reminded of that. It invites one to ritualize and celebrate the act of listening. One way this can occur is that it can effectively compel one to focus on the minutiae of composition and thus delve deeper into the carefully delimited structures of the LP. Indeed, the slogan used by Rhino Records in their series of classic album reissues is that vinyl affords listening to 'music the way it was meant to be heard, one side at a time'. Lawrence English calls this imposed pause an 'intermission'. Importantly, these aspects of the vinyl as an attention-riveting medium and artistic message are explicitly appreciated by the youngest groups of contemporary music consumers,[24] not just those who grew up with records as the main medium.

While digital listening favours lightness, mobility, portability and ease of transfer, and the CD is popularly held to erase the music's 'warmth' and undermine the notion of the two-sided LP, vinyl is the slow food equivalent of music listening practices. Precisely because vinyl does not lend itself to perfect portability, but invites special attention, it can function as a more demanding, ritualistic and thus reflective medium. Indeed, we observed urban venues that combined vinyl record store with rustic delicatessen with the Vienna-based shop, called *Tongues*. This ritualization is visible also at the level of maintenance that one might assume is purely mundane or even may become a chore. Just as a range of seemingly prosaic matters such as shopping and provisioning can be interpreted as token of love and devotion,[25] keeping vinyl 'healthy' carries with it similar meanings.

THE HIGH-SENSITIVITY MEDIUM

Vinyl used to be narrated as a high-fidelity medium. What has emerged out of the complex historical and technical accretion of meanings makes it more apt for us to describe it as a high-sensitivity medium. In this chapter we have shown that vinyl is a music medium that is replete with affordances conducive to it becoming an iconic good ritualized through certain practices of acquisition, collection, playing, handling and listening. Vinyl is a medium to play and play with. The vinyl enthusiasts we spoke to were unlikely to believe that vinyl is the most perfect medium. Most were more than aware of the limitations of vinyl. Nevertheless, many keep coming back to the special aural properties of vinyl. More than this, many believe that these idiosyncracies of vinyl are in fact special properties that can be aesthetically exploited. Vinyl is sensitive to human (mis)treatment and to effects of technical mediations, and it sensitizes us in turn to the qualities of these effects.

Vinyl's specific aural qualities matter for enthusiasts of vinyl who are able to discern the way vinyl sounds, in contrast to digital playback. Enthusiasts often laud vinyl for its 'warm' sound. In contrast to digital media, vinyl is often heard to be richer and more saturated, to fill out listening spaces better, to be at once smoother and less harsh, and to allow longer continuous listening without listening fatigue. Additionally, and again in contrast to digital media, an essence of vinyl's attraction is its durability coupled with its ultimate perishability. These facets of vinyl's condition lend it a certain human quality. It is a medium that requires care and attention.

Vinyl is a collectable medium and an artistic format, like books or graphic prints. This is of course directly the opposite of digital files, which can be gathered but with neither special glory nor effort of acquisition attached to their collection due to the relative ease of downloading mp3 files. It is hardly an accomplishment to choose, download and keep 20,000 digital albums, but it is something different to select, store and maintain 2,000 records. Acquiring the vinyl may be more expensive and time-consuming than other formats and it requires a more knowledgeable approach. You dig for vinyl, and while the virtual sites like Discogs aid the process and have somewhat transformed it, there is also a genuine joy, suspense and sense of quest attached to digging for a physical and relatively rare format. Going through crates and stacks of vinyl in second-hand shops may actually be necessary to acquire rare albums of obscure artists, promo singles, exclusive foreign high-quality pressings or special limited editions of live records. This is not the case with the virtual formats – if they do exist you simply get them, it's only a matter of several clicks and money. There is, therefore, a whole *archaeology* to vinyl culture. Broad knowledge and deep engagement are needed, or at least desirable, to inhabit this culture.

Vinyl's nature as an analogue medium makes the engagement with it so much unlike handling of digital musical files. Despite being a mechanically reproduced medium, it stands in opposition to digital files that, rather than copies, are absolutely reproducible virtual clones. Thus, nowadays the whole understanding of the analogue medium is different, symbolizing an 'organic', slow aesthetic engagement. It becomes special or even luxurious, and is therefore prone to domestic and club ritualization. In keeping with the basic definition of luxury, vinyl, as it is framed by digital contexts, may appear to be superfluous. While any given copy is perishable, the vinyl as a medium has a certain timelessness to it, too. As an audio principle, the analogue format is what it used to be; sonically perfect enough to withstand the pressures of progress and materially imperfect in the right measure, so that it feels *organic* and *authentic* without being awkwardly out of sync with its digital context. Thus, while vinyl is a medium, it is also a cultural message. Vinyl is also a vehicle of memorable experiences, something that marks personal biographies and histories of scenes. Because of this, vinyl makes emotional attachment to it possible. Of course, we acknowledge that it is possible to develop a similar attachment to digital objects, but as Phillip Sollman notes, while being very functional, 'the digital domain is somehow unromantic'.

While medium is a culturalized thing – a dense entwinement of technology and culture, functions and forms – we should not forget about what might be called the sub-level of thing: vinyl, like any other tool or instrument, is a particular physical object that possesses inherent properties and therefore exerts its own independent pressures on what people can possibly do with it. These material characteristics and place-specific 'environmental' entanglements tell us also a great deal about how a given artefact like vinyl comes into being in the first place. In other words, there are two irreducible elements to any cultural phenomenon that may be called socio-material etiology and aesthetic morphology. In the following chapter, we zoom in on these dimensions.

CHAPTER THREE

Thing

Qualities and Entanglements

CHASING THE THING ITSELF

While music and sound are to records what language and narrative are to books, there is special importance to the thing itself too. The actual matter *matters*. The 'no music, no records' approach alone can hardly suffice to understand why *this* format persists, *despite* a series of profit-driven, top-down efforts to irreversibly change our tastes and practices. No doubt the sonics is the food, but the haptics and pragmatics make it into a dish. Books are food for thought and – as the popular saying goes – ought to not be judged by their covers, and yet there is clearly more to books. The British singer and songwriter Morrissey defiantly observes: 'You should, after all, judge a book by its cover.'[1] One thing we may learn from vinyl's story is that music's not different. As we already observed, not only the *what* but also the *how* of music counts, making the vinyl's survival and revival worth delineating. This paradoxical comeback of a seemingly outdated thing in the age of electronic dematerialization shows that medium and materiality indeed does 'bite back'[2] and it reveals music to be more than meets the ear. All the senses are involved in consumption of music and at least some of us still consciously celebrate the multisensory character of music experience. If we are what we eat and what we eat is good to think with as much as offering nutrition, we also change as consumption forms change. Much of cultural consumption is subject to this phenomenon, including vinyl and other 'analogue' media. Just like the form of our narratives is already part of its content,[3] so the practical and haptic ways we engage with culture are part and parcel of its meaning.

So far we have discussed vinyl as a vehicle of musical experience and a particular listening mode. We focused on some of its key affordances, i.e. how practical object–human relations are focused by the analogue record which functions as a kind of historical 'material lens'. It is now clear that vinyl heritage is the archive of the canon of modern music and the format that makes analogue synonymous with 'warm' and 'human' sound. We looked at vinyl as a medium that is a message in a double sense – a durable music carrier and high-sensitivity audio object. Moreover, there are distinct stories behind this medium that coalesce into a kind of social drama and cultural style.

Vinyl as a medium has had its eventful social life, or cultural biography, and it took a form of a narrative arc that revealed it as a distinct mode of engagement with music. This chapter zooms in on vinyl's multiple qualities as a thing and its connectedness to other things without which it simply couldn't work the way it does. As these are the aspects easily taken for granted or altogether overlooked by many a cultural analyst, we try to bring it back to light. Indeed, we find the concrete, material qualities and entanglements of vinyl central to its resurgence in the digital age, a key to its status as *the other* of digital mainstream.

Drawing on our earlier description of vinyl as 'culturalized thing', we can say that it is as much a *thing* as it is *culturalized*. Such distinction is about striking a right balance when it comes to understanding the crux of the issue of the analogue record's presence in the digital age. Vinyl certainly could have made it to the catalogue of modern *myths* famously compiled by Barthes, who defined myth as 'a mode of signification, a form'. But just like it is a mistake to reduce vinyl to a mere instrument of art, it can hardly be adequate to approach it on mythological terms only and claim, as Barthes would, that 'myth is not defined by the object of its message but by the way in which it utters this message'. We believe that both aspects are significant – indeed constitutive – and that they remain in an intimate relation of reciprocity to one another. We surmise that it is precisely paying the attention to the object itself and its various entanglements that helps to explain why vinyl has not ended up as a *historic* myth forever confined to the archives but instead lives on as aesthetic artefact and technological totem.

As early as 1998, the German cultural theorist Wolfgang Welsch presciently reflected on the meaning of the material in the age of electronic 'immaterialization':

> Precisely those concrete experiences which are not accessible via electronic media have once again become important to us. In this way, we have learned to appreciate inertia in contrast to electronic hyper-speed, perseverance in contrast to global mobility, massiveness in contrast to indefinition, and instead of free transformation, constancy and reliability ... In addition to music, the style of youth culture requires material such as clothing for initial self-expression. Differences and status in the scene must be evident. They are evident in objects, which are, however, in a process of constant recoding and reassessment.[4]

To trace the cultural trajectory of vinyl as we did in the first chapter is to reconstruct this process of recoding and reassessment. But to understand fully how this process unfolded and why it assumed particular meanings, we need to comprehend what exactly vinyl means in terms of sensory experiences and how its physical properties contrast with the apparent dematerialization of the digital age. Yes, vinyl sounds different, but it also looks different, feels different and plays unlike digital files. Of course, the role of vinyl as an object that helped make differences in taste socially evident is amplified or rekindled rather than created by digitalization. Analogue records have always recorded not only music but also sense and sensibility of individuals, groups or even whole generations. They crystallized and continue to crystallize whole communities of taste, just like paradigms in science revolve around thought collectives. Things may have changed over half a century but, both back then and now, vinyl is a thing to identify with and celebrate.

To briefly indicate this striking continuity of concrete 'vinyl experience' over decades, consider two statements by two different boys spanning nearly half a century, the teenage Morrissey and Moritz Reisberger, a 19-year-old Swiss student and aspiring DJ:

Morrissey in his *Autobiography*:

> The small black discs are the first things that are truly mine; my choice, paid for with my own scraps of cash, reflecting my own stubbornness. These are the days when very few people collect records, so therefore whatever they might buy defines their secret heart ... The magical properties of recorded noise had trapped me from 1965 onwards ... I am spirited away watching and watching as these discs spin, calling up to me ... neat boxes of 7-inch discs explain me to any passing psychiatrist. I have no other identity and I wish for none. These were times when all were judged squarely and fairly on their musical tastes, and a personal music collection read as private medical records.[5]

Moritz:

> First I started to support the producers I fancy with buying their tracks (or the tracks I like) via iTunes. I'm still doing this. But some day I realized that this method only supports the Apple Company or Beatport, so I decided to buy vinyl, even though I had only a limited access to a record player ... It's just an other feeling of playing vinyl on a record player *vs* playing an mp3. Moreover, holding a 180g vinyl in your own hands, of which there exist only about 400 or 500 copies in the whole world, is such a good feeling. And especially for me as a student: 10 bucks for 2–4 tracks is a lot of money, so my decision to buy exactly THIS vinyl is (often) well-thought ... In the past sentences I often used the words *feeling* for my description and I think this is also a main aspect of my love to vinyl music. Vinyl music is connected with feelings! mp3s are the exact opposite! You like a track, you download it. Nothing special about it ... In this moment I am proud to be the owner of 24 vinyl records. Every vinyl is well selected. I can't spend 10 euro on it, if I do not like all the tracks, even if the producer is my biggest idol. I know almost every track by heart.

These passages invite us to consider the analogue record as a thing that records and projects a whole range of meanings and affords various experiences. They show how records inspire particular feelings, not just mirror our prior understandings of ourselves or of music. These statements are significant because – separated in time and space as they are – they tie together the music, the listener and the role of the character of the physical interface between them. Out of this nexus a specific affective and sensual space emerges. Importantly, these statements indicate continuity of vinyl's aura, present across temporal and spatial and genre contexts. They distinguish vinyl without traces of nostalgia or extensive prior exposure to the thing. In what follows, the impact of vinyl as such an auratic thing is unpacked. Well beyond its musical capacities, it is something to behold and touch, to display and to offer as a gift, a medium to play and play with. Before all those meanings and qualities are analysed, however, a kind of conceptual map needs to be outlined.

REPRESENTATION AND THING

Analogue records record in multiple senses of the term. They are things before they can be valuable artefacts or collective representations. To say this is to flip the notion typically held by cultural analysts who emphasize that cultural objects 'are not just "things", but rather reflections of the wider lives of communities and individuals'.[6] While sociologically useful in avoiding the traps of crude technological determinism, this statement may well be reversed. Professional critics and cultural analysts tend to think about artefacts in textual and abstract terms, and tend to treat things as only 'prerequisites' or mere 'containers' of and screens for 'deep meanings'. Cultural scholars excel at this approach. But realizing the profundity of the observation that the medium is the message is an important step towards approaching things seriously. We argue that rather than passive pieces of stuff or arbitrary signs and merely conventional media, things such as music carriers are rather complex agents replete with sensory qualities and entanglements that turn them into complex devices and equipments. They retain the objective not just subjectively attributed identity vis-à-vis human sensorium, and it is the case regardless of whether they are interpreted or not.[7] They work as icons and tools rather than purely replaceable semiotic conventions. They are indispensable physical interfaces of culture that co-constitute nearly all our meanings.

Once we understand this idea, we discern that there is more to things than mere reflection of ourselves, or passive screen for our projections. Things and persons are co-dependent. If our culture 'reflects' something it is that very fact. This vantage is as life-changing as the wonders of technology we so eagerly worship. It can lead us to appreciate how profoundly people merge with things in their actualization of self-expression. The 'thingness' of objects and their 'cultural meanings' are typically thoroughly spliced in social experience. While sociologists theoretically distinguish between such constitutive parts, it is precisely this indistinguishability between medium and message, thing and meaning, that is vital to the empirical experience of 'aura' or 'magic' of things. This observation corresponds well with Georges Bataille's remark cited in the preface that the poetic thrives on the mixed, on blending and fusing of separate entities.

Needless to say, cultural objects can fruitfully be treated as more or less faithful mirrors, or indeed records, that show us parts of our collective self. We have attempted in the previous chapter to indicate how such an 'archaeological' aspect of vinyl as medium can ethnographically be explored. It is certainly a valid and fertile metaphor for much of cultural research. But to stop just there, without asking what makes those material 'mirrors' work in the first place, means to run a risk of indulging in an idealistic anthropocentrism, especially when technology is under consideration. There is more to any such 'mirror' than meets the conventional eye. The trick is to account for very *materiality* of cultural mediation without resorting to an old-fashioned *materialism*. This means to start treating things as interconnected sensory contexts rather than separated and inert entities. We think that vinyl lends itself perfectly to the analysis of this kind.

The first move is to scrutinize qualities and affordances of a given thing in a phenomenological way. As Maurice Merleau-Ponty writes in the first lines of the chapter devoted to the thing included in his seminal *Phenomenology of Perception*, 'even if it cannot be defined as such, a thing has stable "characteristics" or "properties", and we will approach the phenomenon of reality by studying perceptual constants'.[8] The second move is to realize that just like artefacts are always suspended in the web of meanings, they are also caught in specific networks of production, dissemination and use, always a part of larger technological assemblages and spatial arrangements. The networks are not always – or even predominantly – purely relational or historically contingent structures as some, notably Bruno Latour, would argue. As Ian Hodder demonstrates, 'it is also the case that materials and objects have affordances that are continuous from context to context'; therefore 'rather than focusing on the web as a network we can see it as a sticky entrapment' or entanglement.[9]

These factors may seem mundane, or secondary to cultural development and seemingly sudden processes of resignification like the current revival of a medium. They are sometimes hidden from direct view, or on the contrary too obvious to be noticed, or else deemed by sociologists to be a concern of an aesthetician, engineer or archaeologist. We argue instead that these things matter critically for any student of contemporary culture and cannot be reduced to dead matter and excluded from the analysis with an excuse of the division of labour, especially when it comes to powerful cultural technologies.

When cultural analysts do notice the material surfaces of life, they are conditioned to construe them as canvass on which any meaning could possibly be projected, or as something simply, well, superficial. As material culture scholars have pointed out, however, the great irony is that dismissing material surfaces of things as 'superficial' is one of the more superficial acts that modern cultural analysts can commit now.[10] The present chapter shows that the story of vinyl – its qualities and entanglements as a thing – is a great case in point.

While quite a few socially salient things seem to exemplify the contingent, power-related or downright free-floating nature of meaning attribution, others resist such totalizing characterization. Vital parts of their significance appear to stem from their objective properties and how these figure in larger temporal and practical contexts. They are tools, the gear, the stuff our bodies use in direct and mostly non-random and non-redundant ways. While a tool can, of course, be put to different uses and be subject to various interpretations, being a humanly designed artefact with specific properties it can hardly be expected to serve all our purposes equally well and remain unrestrictedly open to any interpretation and every function. This significantly circumscribes the scope of plausible meanings or values likely to be associated with a given object in a given material context. For example, the vinyl record in an electronic age can hardly be expected to escape the binary of analogue/digital which is technological and material as much as discursive. Indeed, this discourse refracts the physical difference more than the other way around. Perhaps most importantly, such objects or tools are *experienced*, not only comprehended or decoded. They are *felt*, not just communicated. They are simultaneously heard and seen. They literally *work*, not just signify, and their movements in time and space matter. To quote Merleau-Ponty again, 'the thing is the correlate of my body ... and is constituted in the hold my body has upon it; it is not at first a signification for the understanding, but rather a structure available for inspection by the body'.[11]

This is a crucial aspect of existence and salience of concrete things. The signs or sign-objects that are also tools, and tools or things that become symbols are particularly interesting and complex class of social phenomena, irreducible to symbolism they may embody. They are *hybrid entities* of highly unique characteristics, but they can also tell us something more general about the way culture is variably formed and performed. In short, apart from being a socially and artistically framed medium, vinyl is this kind of hybrid thing. It is a tool and a toy. It is a distinct kind of thing with concrete qualities, inextricably connected to specific equipment with its own definitive characteristics and its own degrees of pragmatic freedom. These must be clearly laid out in any study of analogue records in order to further comprehend vinyl's iconic significance and that is what this chapter discloses in greater detail.

THING AND EQUIPMENT: BRINGING EXPERIENTIAL 'PRAGMATICS' BACK IN

In order to further conceptualize vinyl's modes of existence and how records are involved in pragmatic systems of turntables, needles, mixers, pressing machines and mastering devices, consider briefly the strikingly relevant insights coming from another philosopher deeply preoccupied with both phenomenology and ontology, and who advocated a congenial perspective way before any vital sign of the digital revolution and the advent of material culture studies. Evoking philosophical contexts here illuminates the subject matter as much as the other way around. To connect contemporary objects with earlier ideas about things means to open up a conduit of mutual contextualization between them. This way we learn more about both.

Already in his seminal early work *Being and Time*, first published in 1927, Martin Heidegger offered an understanding of the two concepts important for us here: *thing* and *equipment*. It sheds light on why we need to take seriously not only 'external' semantics of a given medium but also 'internal' pragmatics of what Heidegger calls 'things invested in value'. It also sheds some light on why a certain disregard for actual thingness of cultural objects has been conspicuous in Western thought.

> The Greeks had an appropriate term for 'Things' – *pragmata*. But the specifically 'pragmatic' character of the *pragmata* is just what the Greeks left in obscurity; they thought of these as 'mere Things' ... If we look at Things just 'theoretically', we can get along without understanding readiness-to-hand. But when we deal with them by using them and manipulating them, this activity is not a blind one; it has its own kind of sight, by which our manipulation is guided, and from which it acquires its specific Thingly character.[12]

Here Heidegger attempts to vindicate our bodily practices and to present things as capable of shaping people's practices. He reveals how deep the intellectual sources of neglecting things as 'mere' things run, trying – as Ian Hodder notes – to 'get away from a perspective in which things were seen as separate from humans'.[13] For this kind of cultural understanding, things and humans are united in embodied practices rather than separated. They're interdependent. That is why Heidegger is careful to point out that things that serve as equipment in our actions become meaningful only in connection to other such things:

> There is no such thing as *an* equipment. To the being of any equipment there always belongs a totality of equipment, in which it can be this equipment that it is ... Equipment always is *in terms of* its belonging to other equipment ... Out of this the 'arrangement' emerges, and it is in this that any 'individual' item of equipment shows itself. *Before* it does so, a totality of equipment has already been discovered. Equipment can genuinely show itself only in dealings cut to its own measure.[14]

There is a telling analogy here to conceptions of culture that emphasize that a sign gains salience only in relation to other signs. But this formal similarity stops there. While signs can be connected arbitrarily and get various meanings depending on conventional rearrangements, practical artefacts constitute or belong to a more restricted domain of meaning-making. It is a crucial point in new material culture studies. This is partly what Ian Hodder – explicitly acknowledging Heidegger's later works on the topic – means by entanglements being 'sticky entrapments' rather than purely relational or conventional networks.

Vinyl – and especially its current 'revival' – surely owes part of its meaningfulness to rampant digitalization and its own historically contingent narratives but these can hardly be disentangled from objective properties of the actual thing, as well as the equipment and material contexts to which it belongs. Put differently, the thing of human design becomes socially significant not only through semiotic and discursive contextualization but crucially through pragmatic contextualization, i.e. specific actions for which it was cut and particular experiences that it thus affords and effectively fosters.

The aptitude of this phrase for understanding vinyl goes beyond metaphorical use. As we shall discuss below, the analogue record is literally *cut* in the ways that entail specific pragmatic, sensual and economic consequences, and impose other actions and things as required rather than conventional. To paraphrase Heidegger, vinyl genuinely *reveals* itself for what it is under certain circumstances. Specific meanings of such a thing stem from this fact, and considerably so. Moreover, here we find a suggestion that we can become fully conscious of this fact – i.e. of the character of the equipment – when we experience and practically comprehend its entanglements as well as other similar things, and especially when practicality or functionality of the thing is called into question.

> When we concern ourselves with something, the entities which are most closely ready-to-hand may be met as something unusable, not properly adapted for the use we have decided upon. The tool turns out to be damaged, or the material unsuitable ... When equipment's unusability is thus discovered, equipment becomes conspicuous.[15]

Heidegger develops this last idea in a way that makes it highly relevant for the topic of vinyl's perceived renaissance. He shows that things can appear as 'unusable' not only in the sense of being broken or unsuitable, but in a broader sense of being displaced or 'standing in the way' of our concern, i.e. being something 'to which our concern refuses to turn, that for which it has "no time"'.[16] In the case of vinyl, the intertwined processes of introducing digital technologies and acceleration of capitalist economy had made it plausible for the music industry and its publics to initially frame analogue equipment as 'standing in the way', something for which there was apparently 'no time any more', or rather no patience within the profit- and speed-obsessed culture. By the same token, however, what appeared to be the efficiency-driven triumph of the new electronic and 'virtual' materialities in time made some people more aware of vinyl's 'realness', and thus revealed the wider scope of its meanings and value. This is a relational phenomenon, to be sure, but not guided solely by convention but by its own objective 'stickiness'.

This is exactly what Heideggerian thinking would expect: a problem, crisis or displacement can make us conscious of a thing's objective character around which the problem revolves. Displacement has a virtue of making something banal unobvious, or even 'magical' or miraculous. This perspective resonates with Durkheim's observation that 'collective feelings become fully conscious of themselves only by settling upon external objects'.[17] It should be clear then that what appeared to be vinyl's imminent demise at the hands of digitalism was a premature vision, and that dematerialization can neither be total nor lethal to hand-crafted objects. Once vinyl's stable properties could be reconnected and rediscovered in contrast to now routinized flows of new virtual materialities, they would stand on their own unique merit, ready to redefine and perhaps even re-enchant the new era as its complementary counterpoint rather than quaintly nostalgic residue.

To reiterate, the observed revival of an 'outdated' thing with such well-entrenched tradition like vinyl is not a purely arbitrary intellectual effect. Different embodied modes of knowledge and physical experiences are at stake. It is the material context and its phenomenological ramifications that push in this direction, making certain conventional attributions and metaphors more suitable than others. Cultural narratives may provide amplification or devaluation of this phenomenon, but they feed on objectual constellations of qualities and technological connections that can hardly be ignored. The original source remains there, just like the groove stays more or less the same and exerts its independent influence on what and how we can hear and say.

MULTISENSORY MORPHOLOGY OF VINYL

In a digitally altered world, the seemingly old-fashioned thingness and unique pragmatic qualities of analogue record could and did become somewhat conspicuous and unique. This reclaimed uniqueness made vinyl cutting-edge again. Importantly, its qualities as tactile artefacts and numbered pressings quite literally came to the spotlight with heightened force, some of which may well have been taken for granted when the analogue was the norm or the only commercial music medium. An important reason why we should look at the qualitatively unique 'thingness' of vinyl, its actual physical and sensory properties, and not only the narrative and musical references, is that it enables us to recognize its attraction as some-thing at once timeless, i.e. time-resistant, and time-responsive, bearing manifold traces of passing.

Our respondents often say that vinyl is 'alive', a living thing. This paradoxical allure of vinyl seems to resonate with our perennial needs and the basic character of our sensorium. It is also able to allegorize our own trajectories as humans – like us, it ages, wears off, gains individual character amenable to personalization and patina of elapsing time. This correspondence may not be terribly attractive or important to everyone, but it is not likely to dwindle without resistance or vanish unmourned either. Interestingly, there are quite a few very young people, like the above-quoted Moritz Reisberger, who recognize this condition as a value, despite having grown up with computers.

As the representative of an older generation, Peter Runge, reminded us, our ears still remain analogue. And they're rarely perfect, one may add. What seems to remain perfectly undisturbed, even if sometimes unconscious or half-articulated, is the need to touch, see, smell and experience media as pieces of art and tactile objects, not just convenience devices smoothly integrated into all-encompassing computer systems. Vinyl affords sensual, singular rituals and its actual properties are inherent part of the story. Talking about vinyl's qualities makes us more articulate about those needs, some of which may prove to be more like imperatives than whims. To quote Wolfgang Welsch again:

> Even if processors become constantly faster, our sensors, our motoric and psychic abilities do not do so. The processing capacities of calculators increase astronomically, but our lifetime, our reaction time and the time we require to comprehend do not. We are currently rediscovering this sovereignty and unwaveringness of bodies in contrast to the medial transformation of the world. To avoid possible misunderstandings: this tendency does not constitute a simple anti-programme, but is a complementary programme to electronic realms.

Let us therefore more systematically present these sovereign material characteristics of vinyl in relation to human sensorium and other objects. The goal is to get a better idea of where the vinyl comes from as a thing and what it is that makes it stick as a cultural performance. We first explore the main – sometimes seemingly obvious or banal – properties of vinyl's 'thingness' that comprise its everyday ontology, and then connect it with its embeddedness in technical and practical contexts.

DOUBLE-SIDED DISC

Unlike CD, vinyl record is a disc playable on both sides. The most popular diameters have become synonymous with the vinyl single as such: 12-inch and 7-inch (30 and 17.5 cm, respectively). For vinyl, not to be pressed on each side would be considered a waste, as the analogue pressing typically is much more time-, material- and energy-consuming than the production of a CD, let alone an electronic file. Judging by the experience of Optimal pressing plant in Germany, the production of a copy of a compact disc takes 3 seconds, as opposed to 25 seconds needed for an analogue record. The scrap rate is 3–5 per cent versus 15–20 per cent, respectively. If only for that reason, says the main production manager at Optimal, Peter Runge, you should value this thing.

The idea of a double-sided disc as we know it came first as a technological simplification originally conceived by German-American inventor Emil Berliner to improve on Thomas Edison's analogue cylinder record. Berliner's record was a flat disc, not a cylinder, and he called it a gramophone record, patented in 1887. This reduction of the medium from a three-dimensional bulky object to a flat nifty thing proved revolutionary. The development of the medium has gone through decades of experimentation and improvement which involved solving many practical problems, including finding suitable materials, proper cutting technology, or maintaining the required steady rotation speed of playback machines. Yet Berliner's basic idea has remained unaltered, making a ready-to-hand flat disc a medium of extraordinary longevity. Since the replacement of brittle shellac material with polyvinyl chloride in the late 1940s, the two main forms of analogue record have never changed and the material on which the sound industry settled became synonymous with the thing itself: *vinyl*. As we mentioned in Chapter 1, the 33⅓ rpm 12-inch LP was first developed and marketed by Columbia Records in 1948 and quickly became the golden standard of the industry. Responding to Columbia, RCA Victor introduced the 45 rpm 7-inch disc and released it in 1949 to commercial success.

It is telling that when we say '12-inch vinyl' today we refer to specific palpable characteristics of the record: its size and material. We distinguish it from the defunct *shellac* disc – which, importantly, never experienced any comparable 'revival' – using the same material criterion. 'Analogue' is another physical-auditory term employed, although – perhaps surprisingly for a musical medium – less frequent in vernacular conversations. Slang expressions such as 'wax' developed out of the same sensibility – the production of early records utilized this material. Even the most cursory examination of the names of contemporary independent record stores shows this reliance on the materiality and thingness of vinyl: Hardwax (Berlin-Kreuzberg), Wax Art (Berlin-Friedrichshain), Wax Museum (Melbourne), Tactile (Frankfurt), Substance (Vienna), Vinyl Pimp (London-Hackney Wick) or Side One (Warsaw).

Then and now, one side of a 12-inch record contains up to 20-odd minutes of complex musical material. Other limitations that we discuss below apply too, effectively forcing producers to break the musical material into halves or even more parts (double albums). Sooner or later the double-sided disc ends and must be flipped or segued into another record. The dualism of sides A and B is a kind of 'binary' logic of the analogue culture that the invisible electronic binarism of CD conveniently avoided. In some situations it may be seen as a definitive drawback but it nevertheless introduces a peculiar quality to our listening experience, even in rather extreme cases like splitting one song in halves. A relevant anecdote shared by Peter Hook of Joy Division makes this point clear:

> When I got back from holiday I bought the single ['Sebastian' by Cockney Rebel]. It was nine minutes long and you had to turn the record over halfway through,

FIGURE 3.1: Thing: A Wax vinyl, release 20002. (DB)

> which just added to the experience: it was part of the ritual of playing it, gave the song a dramatic pause and made me like the record even more.[18]

But the convenience of the continuous digital playback leads to relative disengagement with the medium. This detachment is compounded by the fact that CD typically disappears in a machine and the process of 'reading it' is removed from any sensual-bodily relation to the medium. The engagement with music is stripped down to its core – *hearing* the sonic information, compressed and delivered to your ears as a technically impeccable signal. The actual process of retrieving the music from the medium, *playing of* the music, is most of the time pushed beyond sensual experience or aesthetic contemplation. Transferring the digitalized music to computers and portable electronic devices ever deepened this process of mediated detachment. Music has become data, just like many other things.

However, as a flyer of German record fairs states, 'music is more than a piece of data'. While vinyl may be seen as an annoying thing due to its weight, size and double-sidedness that typically requires one to take care of the finished record, it rivets attention and invites contemplation precisely because of its materiality. It is liked not only for what it contains and emits. If it sticks around for so long it is literally due to its ability to remain in place and engage your senses and demand your attention. You must change sides. You have to take care of the needle, mechanically and directly dropping and picking it up each time the side changes, or when you wish to skip a part of the recorded material. The linearity of listening process is therefore inevitably interrupted and any intended interruption requires direct engagement with the format. It is easy to see why one would want to have access to a format capable of continuous playback and remotely controlled skipping. Digitalization solved the issue: it meant up to 70 minutes of music without a break on CD. Andreas Baumecker, who is a dedicated vinyl DJ and avid collector but not a purist, makes it clear:

> I especially bought albums on CD because there's this flipping of the vinyl which can be annoying if you have a lot of music to listen to or when you want to listen to an album from beginning to the end, to really dive into what the artist wants to express. With vinyl you have to flip the disc every 3 tracks. At that point I thought the CD would be nicer to run through and have the overall experience of the album, it may be better with the CD. Unfortunately, nowadays big record labels tend to master their albums to the max and all the dynamic of the music gets lost. It's a loudness war!

The invention of compressed computer files extends the potential playback time to infinity, permitting different kinds of easy sound manipulation. While this facilitates music consumption in a number of situations, it is hardly the ultimate goal of music listening. For one thing, our focused attention can hardly be sustained as a long uninterrupted flow. Without any segmented structure and breaks, our perception can rather quickly become fatigued. An unbroken chain of music may work well as a background sound or as a mixed DJ set, and even in those cases changes and breaks prove desirable. Andreas Baumecker notes how the long sets that comprise only digital files are tiring even if not compressed due to their digital sound character. It's that much worse when the file *does* happen to be compressed. As Andreas stresses: 'You should never play mp3 in the club, never ever. Full stop!' Importantly, uninterrupted kind of listening, for example in a bar or at home, may in fact resemble what Walter Benjamin called a distracted perception of architecture in everyday life rather than focused participation in a concert. It is more of a hearing than listening. This is a legitimate mode of music consumption, yet should hardly be the only, much less heralded as 'better'.

Last but not least, while many vinyl lovers would admit that the necessity to attend to vinyl runs sometimes against our laziness or a need to simply relax, some see it as an occasion to be surprised rather than a nuisance only. Andreas Lubich makes this kind of connection clear:

> As we all are a bit lazy you don't skip the needle from A1 to A3; you let it run and after several times you discover that track A2 you always wanted to skip is the best on the record. Things like that don't happen with playing digital files because you can easily skip them and then you find out that you never listen to certain tracks because you always skip them. That you are kind of forced to listen to a track, if you are too lazy to move, brings you new experiences ... Of course, it can happen to other digital media, but it's more common with analogue media like vinyl-records and tapes.

Working with the seemingly detrimental limitations or rigid structures like double-sidedness imposed by the physical thing may well inspire compositional creativity on the part of musicians. The geometry of the thing is one of the factors they simply need to deal with when they take the presentation of music seriously. One has to answer questions such as what musical parts will be separated by the pause of changing the sides and what tracks should be put 'together'. The pause itself may be used as an additional compositional act, one that introduces a dramatic suspension or simply a break.

Moreover, as the needle moves towards the centre of the vinyl disc, a slight but gradual loss of high frequencies becomes a fact. As Andreas Lubich explains, technically speaking the best sound area of a vinyl record is at the outer diameter of the disc and when played at the speed of 45 rpm. The louder the cut, the more space on the disc a given track will require. This is partly why 12-inch 45 rpm singles with only one track per side emerged in the dance cultures of the 1980s. For all others this condition meant that the most complex tracks would benefit from being put at the outer edge, i.e. as the first on a given side of the record. Tracks featuring less complex sound arrangements, or the ones intended by the artist to come across more mellow or less crisp, would be placed inside the diameter of a record. This is due to the fact that close to the inner diameter of the disc the needle has less time compared to the outer diameter of the disc to travel the same distance of the groove and accurately 'read' the cut inscription of sound in the vinyl record. This physical fact may strike one as a metaphor for some human acts of interpretation – the more hasty, the less precise it gets.

In the case of singles, the B-side had to somehow be utilized and the A/B division has traditionally suggested the importance or status of songs in the artist's catalogue. The other tracks, or remixes and other takes, accompany, so to speak, the 'main' piece. It is not uncommon, however, that these would in time emerge as valuable works in their own right. They may become 'hidden gems' or get 'rediscovered' long after the main hit has been overplayed and fallen out of fashion. They introduce a surprise factor into one's collection, not unlike the situation described above by Andreas Lubich, or give DJs a field of creative possibilities. In fact, in various dance scenes singles have always occupied the centre of attention and their 'additional' B-side material inspired new art forms, leading to the emergence of whole new genres and mixing practices. A story connected to reggae culture underlines this fact:

> The birth of dub is also due to the existence, as early as in the mid-sixties, of an instrumental side, called *version*, on the B-side of single recordings, which became both a tradition and a necessity for sound systems. Indeed, sound systems need versions to be 'talked over'.[19]

B-sides are also a place where we encounter 'previously unreleased' older tracks or the tracks that for some reason could not make it to the LP. There are also radio edits contrasted with extended versions, for the former usually meant a short track or truncated version popularly felt to be more suitable for radio airplay. There are alternate takes and instrumental mixes, etc. Thus, on the one hand, singles present a range of possible interpretations of what seems to be the 'final' and finite piece of music. On the other hand, they are succinct statements or even mini albums with significant original material which, when grouped together, can make for a great record, musically and as a trace of band's evolution. Reflecting on this aspect, the lead singer of Suede, Brett Anderson took the reissue of Suede's first album in a deluxe remastered form as an occasion to emphasize the attraction of B-sides:

> I think [the album] is quite an honest picture of what the band was like at the time: restless, angular, ambitious, drunk on the arrogance of youth. The sweet lunacy that convinced us that putting 'Animal Lover' and 'Moving' on the album rather than 'My Insatiable One' and 'To the Birds' was coursing thru our veins … but it was a different time I suppose and there were these things called B-sides which for some reason really mattered to us.

When in 2013 the collection of various B-side tracks spanning Suede's career, *Sci-Fi Lullabies* was released as triple LP for the first time, it came with a sticker: 'Brett Anderson's favourite Suede album.'

Singles can also be a kind of mini album whose double-sidedness is amenable to presenting different styles of artist's work. The 7-inch Miles Davis record 'Diane/ Well You Needn't' released with his album *Steamin'* contains the liner notes that explicitly state this kind of use of the vinyl single format: 'In this volume you'll find two contrasting sides of Miles Davis's personality and the flexible approach of the quintet as a unit.' The sides of the record render the 'sides' of artist's creativity legible. Even stronger statements have been made about Davis's iconic albums recorded around similar time, such as 1959 *Kind of Blue*, the best-selling jazz record of all time. In his essay 'The Last King of America: How Miles Davis Invented Modernity', Gerald Early celebrated the 50th anniversary of the album:

> *Kind of Blue* would not have been possible if the LP did not exist. It was jazz conceived for the record album, not only because of the playing times of the tunes but also because of how the album creates an overall mood. *Kind of Blue* is not simply a series of tracks, [it] had a sense of narrative, a cohesive inter-relation between the tunes. It was a work … The sense of the album as an organic whole added to its appeal.[20]

As the name of the format itself suggested, 12-inch vinyl Long Play indeed lent itself to a relatively extended yet restrained form that corresponded well with Davis's 'cool' approach to musical expression. This symbiosis of form and content turned *Kind of Blue* into 'a signifier of the hip and the cool, which made it timeless'.[21]

In sum, a mutually constitutive, partially objectively structured relation between musical expression and material form and geometry can be discerned. Both exert independent pressure on the process of playing and listening to music and it is this interstitial space in between that produces cultural situations, in this case musical ones. Double-sided discs may be seen as a *constraint* but one potentially conducive to creative *restraint*. Just like for generations of music lovers, from the above-cited Morrissey to Moritz Reisberger, the cost of records required a disciplined rather than voracious consumption and thus possibly more focus and self-awareness, so do the technical parameters of vinyl in relation to the production and listening processes. Thus, instead of being a setback, vinyl's double-sided thingness can constitute an inspiring material condition of action that corresponds with human needs for brevity, focus, structure, ritual, suspense, surprise, concreteness, each of which is embodied and technologically formed, not only thought of as a conventional concept.

CUTTING THE TEMPLATES, PRESSING THE COPIES

A series of carefully calibrated mechanical and chemical procedures must be undertaken for the thing called vinyl record to be created and to satisfy our senses. Typically, the impeccably smooth black surface of the lacquer master disc is first engraved by a special lathe equipped with a cutting stylus.

As Robert Haagsma evocatively describes, 'the audio material is being led to the magnets, which causes both horizontal and vertical vibrations to the stylus. The depth of the groove depends on the intensity of the audio material.'[22] A stylus etches a groove with a force of almost four tons per square inch. Horizontally encoded sonic information is the sum of the left and right channels (stereo effect), and the vertical modulation is the difference between the left and right channels. Today most of the cutting work in studios like *Dubplates & Mastering* or *Calyx* in Berlin relies on traditional old lathes, like the one once developed by Berlin-based company, Neumann. The fundamental principles of analogue recording remained basically unchanged after they had been refined in the middle decades of the twentieth century. Interestingly, according to Andreas Lubich's experience, the older types of cutting-lathes are more flexible than the last ones made when it comes to unusual cuts.

This kind of machine was chosen by the pioneers of Berlin techno who founded *Dubplates & Mastering* studio. Robert Henke, one of the master cutters there in the 1990s, describes the advantage of having your own machine, pointing to one of the crucial features of the analogue pressing:

> The process of cutting a record isn't a one-to-one translation from one digital medium into another one, it's a process which always changes the result, it's a little bit like – since I see the camera here – like developing a colour photo by yourself. It's a process which, if you do it five times, leads to five different results of brightness, colours, and so on. Cutting a record is a similar thing; there is no one single way to do it. So everything has to do with taste, and the taste is shaped by the music you do and therefore, you're just better off having your own cutting machine.

Cutting the first original lacquer disc is a complex topic in itself that could hardly be exhausted in a section of a chapter like this one. It has been extensively covered in specialist sources. Suffice it to say that the quality of what we eventually hear on vinyl depends not only on how a given track was produced by an artist or recorded in a studio, but how it is mastered, and how it is cut, i.e. how the cut is calibrated. At this stage it is not a vinyl but aluminum disc coated with acetate. If the special Direct Metal Mastering (DMM) production method is employed, copper discs are used and a different angle of special diamond stylus is applied. While nowadays computers are employed as control devices, the entire analogue procedure run by

FIGURE 3.2: A Neumann vinyl cutting lathe at Calyx Studios, Berlin. (DB)

actual engineers remains largely intact and involves the same skills and materials the industry used to require in the past. What is important and stays unaltered is the circular geometry of the medium and the way the sound signal is etched onto disc. As we mentioned, sound is transferred to the stylus of the lathe that moves continuously, so the resulting cut takes the form of spiral groove on the lacquer wherein the music is phonographically inscribed.[23] This procedure must control for several different parameters in order for the pressing to meet technical and aesthetic standards of recording. Interestingly, one part of the quality control process is visual and involves using a microscope attached to the lathe.

Dominik: What are the conditions that the master cutter takes into account?

Andreas Lubich: At first, the sound … and to preserve the integrity and authenticity of the music to be cut. Then there's the question regarding the lengths I'll get per side and what disc-size I'm cutting, which in turn effects what rotation speed and level I can expect to cut with. Knowing that, I know how to treat the material. If there is a lot of stereo content at very low frequencies, I have to narrow these a bit without compromising the audio or the musical idea of the track. I generally need to balance the tonal parts of the audio to be cut in order to the expected frequency-response I'll get at the playback-side for the outer and inner diameter of the record. This means also that I eventually have to decide which track comes to the outer

FIGURE 3.3: Vinyl production: the special microscope is an integral part of the Neumann cutting lathe. (DB)

or the inner diameter of the record. Then I have to decide if its better to tame the highs a bit for particular tracks because otherwise I would get too much distortion, or even to slightly emphasize the highs in a certain way.

Dominik: All this gives a certain effect.

Andreas Lubich: Yes, there is a lot of interaction between the media and the audio. Due to the fact that at the playback-side in the outer diameter of the record I get more harmonic distortion than in the inner diameter where I get a loss of highs, I eventually have to tame some highs for some tracks to be cut at the outer diameter to get a more equal sound over the whole side of a record. But for a dance record it also can be great to have that condition. Because while a track is playing at the inner diameter where the highs are less present, it's the moment when the track is typically being mixed into a track that starts at the outer diameter of a record. It aids the second track to come in, sort of … The early electronic dance music sounds were delicate to cut.

Dominik: What do you mean by that?

Andreas Lubich: You had to cut sounds at a level which is far away from what the machine and especially the cutterhead was made for.

Dominik: What is the physics of it?

Andreas Lubich: The difficulty was the amount of bass and type of excessive

> highs, beside the request for cuts at a maximum possible level in dance-music back in the days. So the higher the frequency, the shorter the wave-lengths and the more excursions the cutterhead has to cut within a given timeframe. Cutting high levels results in high amplitudes for the groove within the same timeframe. All this combined heats up the cutterhead drastically until about 200 degrees Celsius, then the security circuit disconnects the cutterhead to prevent it from being damaged. This is why these sorts of record cuts were called 'hot cuts'. The actual goal was to do this cut in a way that it can be played later without too many unwanted side-effects. For this amount of excursions for the high-frequencies and groove-amplitude a pickup has to be able to follow. It all is easier if it's possible to cut at 45 rpm as compared with 33 rpm as there is more space within the given time-frame and therefore it's easier for the pickup to follow and play back even extreme signals. But that works only for shorter side-lengths.

This longer exchange with Andreas makes it clear how – from a certain material point of view – vinyl was not necessarily an 'ideal' thing for electronic music DJs that often demanded louder cuts than usual. Nevertheless, it offered practical, tactile and visual qualities that rendered vinyl the medium of choice for dance scenes. For others, for examples collectors and many contemporary music lovers, these aesthetic considerations are important too, especially the fact that vinyl comes to you not as one of an infinite number of absolutely identical *files* but as a relatively limited and painstakingly crafted *pressing*, nowadays increasingly designed in various aesthetic ways to distinguish it even further from invisible electronic clones.

For this reason it makes sense for someone like Phillip Sollmann to have a project of collecting all the editions and pressings of the same record. Not only vinyl itself but also the sleeve differs from release to release, sometimes quite noticeably. Even if the spectrum of such differentiation may not always work to the absolute advantage of the record, the resulting diversity becomes a value in itself, something to know and explore, if not always marvel at. In Phillip's case it is Donald Fagen's *Nightfly* LP released in 1982 by Warner Bros Records. We describe this case in the next chapter as indicative of vinyl's ability to be a collectible commodity, one that can positively reinterpret our understanding of fetishism. But there is also another dimension to it worth mentioning. Interestingly, as Phillip explains, 'it was the first complete digital recording at that time. It was expensive and there was no CD to put it on. The whole process of recording was digital and well done. The sound is outstanding.' There is still more, however. The cover features a man in what appears to be a radio or studio room, seated next to a microphone and a turntable with a 10-inch analogue record on. The short sleeve note from Donald Fagen states: 'The songs on this album represent certain fantasies that might have been entertained by a young man growing up in remote suburbs of a northeastern [American] city during the late fifties and early sixties.' For Fagen, his youth memories overlap with a golden age of vinyl and their association with records finds its expression on the cover.

To ensure that the variability of quality between pressings does not diverge too much, a pressing plant that receives the lacquer master disc typically conducts its own quality control. After the lacquer disc reaches the pressing plant for the first time, three new special discs are produced by the process of electroplating that takes place in the galvanics room. These three plates are: the 'father' (the negative copy), the 'mother' (the positive copy, playable and thus testable template) and the 'son' or stamper that is mounted on actual pressing machines as the printing negative. The acetate disc is then discarded and thus causes an issue of recycling the aluminum core of the disc. The stamper maintains the same high quality for only about 2,000 copies and therefore bigger runs may require several 'sons' to keep the quality at the same level. Some of them last for 5,000 pressings. For a really large order of over 100,000 copies more than one mother is desirable. This is yet another material factor that makes a copy of analogue record more costly to produce and contributes to the aura of the 'first pressing' or first numbers of a given run. However, Peter Runge sees it as a myth and partially dispels it: 'There might be a slight difference, but you won't hear it ... If you are careful in mastering and electroplating in galvanics department, then you won't hear a difference.' What happens in galvanics department – that important stage of vinyl's gestation? What does it mean to be 'careful' there?

> *Peter Runge*: First we need something on a lacquer disc that leads the electric current, and therefore we need a silver layer on the lacquer. The silver's sprayed on, then this silver layered lacquer is put into a galvanic bath with nickel sulphurate and nickel pearls. This nickel grows on to this silver layer, when you put a current of 120mps forward, for two hours or something like that. Nickel is used because it's hard enough to withstand the flow of the mould and plastic, the mould and vinyl. To last for about 2,000 shots, to withstand opening and closing of the press, nickel is used for the stamper. Before that when wax cuts were used, and the records itself contained shellac, they also used copper or chromium to plate the copper. But these chemical processes are highly poisonous and therefore we are happy that we don't need to do that.

Except for picture discs, only virgin vinyl is used for the production of regular records. They owe their black colour to graphite that assures necessary sleekness. Friction between the playing stylus and the record's surface obviously cannot be eliminated in physical analogue media but it has to be attenuated. The vinyl mould used for records is therefore a pre-fabricated compound of polyvinyl chloride and graphite produced by plastics factories. So-produced records exhibit significantly lower background noise than the shellac discs used before the 1950s. Optimal has made a test with polycarbonate used for CDs, DVDs and Blu-ray discs. The result: it is also noticeably inferior to vinyl in terms of background noise. While vinyl is not absolutely perfect, it is good enough. Moreover, and crucially, it is precisely the slight degree of distortion introduced by its materiality that our ears hear as warm, saturated, rich sound. Symptomatically, even engineers describing the physical details of the analogue production process ultimately point to a certain added value that only vinyl can bring. In sum, the materiality of vinyl involves unavoidable risks and imperfections but these are exactly the conditions of its uniqueness. It is not necessarily better but when carefully designed it can certainly be uniquely outstanding. Despite all the theoretical technical limitations of the LP format, there's an ineffable magic in the sound of a good LP played back on a high-quality front-end that even high-resolution digital audio doesn't capture. Some have even suggested that the LP in many ways sounds better than the mastertape from which it was cut.

This last aspect points to vinyl's capacity to be not only an outstanding medium but also a surprising one. Several of our interviewees explicitly talked about the experiences of being astonished by how the analogue end product actually sounds compared to the previous stages of music production. Andreas Baumecker, who has the privilege of hearing the test pressings of *Ostgut Ton* music on the powerful Funktion One sound system inside Berghain club, noticed the difference that the analogue medium and analogue mastering process makes and told us: 'In a lot of cases I am actually surprised by how music sounds on vinyl, because actually vinyl production is a different process.' Michael aka Puresque related a similar experience as well, pointing to a degree of unpredictability associated with vinyl: 'You never know how a track turns out on vinyl. You have it at home, you listen to it, in the end you give it to your master guy and there is the cut and it comes out on vinyl and when you listen to it for the first time in a nightclub, it's like this special moment ... Sometimes, it's worse than it was before, but sometimes, it's like: *oh wow, it's even better than I wanted it* [laughs].'

Vinyl thus could emerge and indeed stay the winner of the analogue technological evolution. It is the 'fittest' physical medium even though it is physically more prone to warping than other tested materials and sensitive to scratches. This liability can be seen as a 'price' to pay for its being more flexible and much less brittle than shellac that could easily break when dropped. By the same token, it makes vinyl something to take care of, a resistant but also relatively fragile thing that – like the book – requires a minimum of proper maintenance and protection. If stored vertically in cool dry interiors, like books, they are, as Peter Runge says, a lifetime medium, one likely to outlive its owner: 'Vinyl is like black and white film, it lasts almost forever if you don't scratch it.'

While considerably more expensive to produce than CDs and with a footprint to reckon with, analogue records could have been even more costly if other materials were used for pressing the records. Peter concisely explains why vinyl is actually not only sonically very satisfying but also comparatively more sustainable than similar materials:

> A good thing about vinyl is that the melting point is pretty low, about 130 degrees Celsius, so we do not need to heat it up more than necessary. We have to heat it up to 130 degrees, cool it down to 40 degrees in every 25 seconds, one cycle. So it consumes a lot of energy to do that, and if you used different material with a higher melting point, this would be even worse.

According to Peter, the pay-off is nevertheless palpable: 'Vinyl should survive longer than a CD or DVD, and it will because it's only made of one material.' Not only is vinyl cut from one solid material compound, the production procedure is a tried-and-tested one, known inside out after decades of use. Peter confirms that pressing of the vinyl aged well:

> The actual process itself is quite the same, only the control technology of these machines changed, because it has had mechanical controls or electronic mechanical controls, and we changed it to computerised controls. But the machine body itself and the whole process of moulding a vinyl disc, is the same, like 60 years ago.

Moreover, the process of quality control is still based on human eye and ear. At Optimal over 30 people are employed just to make sure that the things they produce culminate in creation of satisfying vinyl: templates, stampers, actual vinyl discs, labels and covers – all is assessed by human senses. At every stage records are looked at, checked, inspected. A sample of a given run is played on standard turntables. Some special releases are hand-numbered before they are packed and shipped.

In sum, despite not being a one-off art object, vinyl record scores higher on the rarity scale than digital formats capable of infinite, perfectly identical copying. In fact, comparing the digital and analogue 'copy' makes it necessary to reflect on the totalizing meaning of the word 'copy' itself – the digital file is an electronic *clone*, the analogue copy is a mechanical *pressing*. In the case of the latter, the multiplicity of production stages and physical factors make vinyl more than a 'mere' copy. It is a carefully designed artefact whose production is supervised by many persons rather than a single machine. Production of vinyl remains a craft and resembles graphic artworks more closely than CDs. If a digital file exists on the market, it can be easily accessed at the same relatively low price from anywhere. Scarcity is not really an issue here. Because analogue records are more expensive and their number is finite, their production is serial in nature and usually limited, the problem of scarcity kicks in.

Nowadays more or less artificially induced scarcity becomes subject to criticism from vinyl aficionados rather than a cause to celebrate, as we discuss in the next chapter. Among others, Phillip Sollmann and Andreas Baumecker explicitly share their reservations about it in their interviews. But there's also another fact that contributes to making records relatively rare: the passage of time. They may get damaged if improperly stored or used, and they can sustain scratches. They wear out when we play them often and so do their covers. If sold out, even popular vinyl may not be released again and tends to be costly to obtain in second-hand markets. Phillip Sollmann and Peter Runge make illuminating comments about these aspects of vinyl as something more than replaceable copy and as something that concretizes the abstraction of time:

> *Peter*: Obviously vinyl is a copy, but it is still a touchable, tangible thing. I think people will have something to touch and to feel, and more and more people think this way I guess. This experience is not so easily exchanged for something else … it might be the case that people see that something I

can't touch, and which is not visible, can't be of real value. If I cannot really touch it, I cannot really give it to somebody else.

Phillip Sollmann: Sometimes if I have a record which is really old I even push the high frequencies to make the crackle more obvious, to make people hear that this has been played so many times. I love this one and it's old. Some people are really like, wow! Yeah, you can hear history, you can hear time. It's so great I think.

Despite being technically a copy hardly distinguishable from other pressings of the same item, vinyl is capable of absorbing time and getting its own kind of materially mediated identity. It is personalized through the etchings that master cutters usually place around the centre of the record. You know the disc was mastered by Andreas Lubich because he 'signed' it with a personal cut on the run-off grooves of the vinyl. He emphasizes the pleasure connected to this ritual practice. Many other messages or enigmatic symbols can be added. The matrix number enables one to distinguish between different pressings of the same title and thus identify particular runs. That's further individuation of vinyl. The cutting of the grooves can be exercised in different ways, making certain parts of the groove particularly visible.

Importantly, regardless of the technique employed, the structure of the song is visible to the eye. The record's technical information may not inform you about the playing time but you get to know the song's duration by playing it and you learn its progression and changes visually as the groove changes its look. In this sense vinyl is as much about sound as it is about look. Peter Runge emphasizes this aspect when he talks about understanding a given medium. With vinyl, 'you don't need a lot of explanation because you can see what happens'. Of course, we can't see everything, but we see something. We see an actual thing. That suffices to make a phenomenological difference.

'THE BLACK GOLD': COLOUR, TEXTURE, PATINA

The OYE record store in Berlin displays valuable, classic or signed records on its walls. Some of the records have beautiful covers; they look like pictures. Others are a kind of visualization of the store's social history: important works with handwritten dedications by artists and producers, often with thanks and greetings for OYE's successful mission. Among them is Gold Panda's DJ Kicks' album, signed and dedicated to the store with the following words: 'Keep sellin' the black gold.'

As mentioned before, the standard colour of vinyl is black due to the use of low-traction graphite material. As the value of old records grows and the new ones are the most expensive music format on the market, this likening of analogue records to gold somehow makes sense. But equally important is vinyl's status of a noble music format, the 'gold standard' of sorts when it comes to sound and long-standing tradition.

The sleekness and lustre of black new discs is a source of special visual pleasure. There is a glossy quality to them. Freshly pressed or well preserved, clean records are small circular gleaming mirrors. The centrepiece without groove dimly but accurately reflects everything and you invariably see your own gleeful eyes as you inspect a new purchase. This quality of vinyl discs has made them amenable to other, non-musical uses. For example, while wandering urban markets it is now common to see old and new records transformed as clocks or – when shaped or cut and moulded properly – bowls and plates.

Black vinyl is shining and gleaming as a material despite being the darkest in colour. But it is also the texture of the groove that adds special character to its visual effect. The texture makes the dark surface alive with a game of light. The light is always interestingly refracted and variety of patterns and stripes appear as we shift the angle and glance at the surface of the record. The reflected light – that unassumingly luminous and straight range of brightness running across the record – provides the iconic look by which we recognize vinyl record as such. It resembles the romantic reflection of moonlight on a lake's dark surface. It's this signature play of light on the grooved surface, this contrast between the bright reflection and the dark colour that may be credited with lending to vinyl at least a part of its visual magic. Vinyl's capacity to glint is important and very old dirty records that have lost their lustre look unhealthy and beg for special treatment. Finally, the same aesthetically pleasing contrasts of black vinyl makes it a functional medium for DJs as the track's structure is easily detectable even with low light.

Although to many music lovers the standard black vinyl sounds and looks the best, today records cover the entire rainbow spectrum of colours and more. There are clear and marbled records, some coloured ones are translucent at the same time. There are, of course, picture discs as well, but these are made of different materials and recycled, not virgin vinyl. As a result, their quality and durability is noticeably lower. Clear and transparent pressings, however, are as good as the regular ones. They are invariably used as a distinction strategy or celebratory feature. The 50th anniversary issue of *Kind of Blue* features indigo blue vinyl with the iconic 1950s Columbia Records label in the centre. Countless other new pressings and special reissues employ coloured vinyl, from hip-hop (for example, the orange vinyl of Viktor Vaughn's *Vaudeville Villain*) to experimental electronica (for example, Philip Glass's *Rework* album of mixes, whose two black and white marbled discs visually match the cover design). *Ostgut Ton* label tends to release 100 copies of each LP as a coloured special series available only inside the Berghain club in Berlin. The colours are carefully chosen, sometimes matching the colour of the font used on the cover, as is the case with the L. B. Dub Corp *Unknown Origin* LP. Some labels, for example American *Underground Quality*, press their music almost exclusively on coloured, marbled vinyl. Vakula's first release on his label *Leleka* is half-white, half-black. Visual design is limited mostly by a designer's imagination and at present a multiplicity of forms abound.

Joined by its cover, vinyl comes to our hands as an aesthetic package deal. The colour, texture, weight and overall design of the cover make it into a thing in its own right. The so-called gatefold sleeves open like a book and some of them do include booklets, posters or even whole books, as in the case of the aforementioned special edition of Miles Davis's *Kind of Blue*. As Wolfgang Voigt noted in the conversation with us, there are whole books about the cover art of records and awards for the most special or beautiful ones, from rock and soul to techno and minimal. The visual heritage of record covers and centre labels is a separate cultural phenomenon and exists as public aesthetic interest irrespective of musical content of the actual records. Quite a few releases have self-referential covers that present vinyl as an object worthy of visual admiration, and replete with variety of aesthetic meanings and iconic cultural references. We have already mentioned Donald Fagen's LP which showed how vinyl can literally wear its meanings on its sleeve.

Perhaps one of the most refined examples in this respect is the sleeve of Thievery Corporation's *Sounds from the Thievery Hi-Fi*. The main cover art features a close-up photograph of a tonearm and needle touching the vinyl's surface at the eye level as the record is about to be played. Initial crackling audible at the beginning of the record comes to mind. Blurred background and blueish light provide a perfect visual atmosphere to admire a traditional cartridge that picks up the sound. The back cover presents small pictures of a vintage gramophone and the duo themselves standing next to it with a Verve record on. Like Fagan's LP, the whole thing evokes a kind of cloud of impressions and establishes sensual connectedness with a particular technical and musical tradition. It exudes attachment to particular aesthetics and form. There are many less elaborate but similarly compelling covers featuring vinyl itself, or even the artist's own releases. A series of 2002 Jazzanova remixes were released with such covers, first featuring a picture of another Jazzanova record (*Soon*) and then a picture of this very record being taken out of its sleeve (*Days to Come*). An interesting more recent example includes a vinyl-only release by Vinalog on *Relative* label. Both sides of the sleeve present black and white photographs of a record's surface and one of the centre labels portrays a pressing machine. The groove of the vinyl comes to the fore and it is the play of contrasting light on the textured surface that creates a striking effect. The name of the photographer is written on the main cover rather than on the back or inside, thus underscoring the artwork's status as such. Apart from basic information, nothing else competes for our attention as we contemplate the pure visual form of the photographed vinyl.

Covers are self-referential also in a sense of harking back to another similar artwork. Tracing these connections reveals the wealth of artistic networks, influences, inspirations, connections and paying homage. Some such covers are direct visual citations, and here Thievery Corporation's early EP *Encounter in Bahia* provides a perfect example: the cover is a faithful iteration of Joao Gilberto's seminal self-titled album, the duo's great inspiration. Peter Kruder and Richard Dorfmeister made a similar statement with their early EP *G-Stoned* released in 1993. The cover is a black and white portrait of the duo staged to copy Simon and Garfunkel's *Bookends* cover (see photograph on p. ix). In short, a vinyl disc requires a cover, which in turn lends its physicality and qualities to further artistic uses.

Covers like the one on Vinalog's release make us additionally aware of the fact that the special visual effect of vinyl can hardly be disentangled from its grooved texture. Vinyl's surface has its micro topography despite being flat enough to be a mirror of sorts. If disc is the surface and music is the depth, then vinyl is a special medium because its depth is quite literally available to our sense of sight and touch as a series of dense circular valleys of the spiral groove. Moreover, the visible tactile groove – this micro depth within the surface – already *is* the music, as Andreas Lubich says. It is sufficient to *hear* it using any metal needle and a paper cone attached. It is the technical audio needle that makes the crucial sonic difference and raises the sound to the hi-fi level that vinyl lovers admire so much. In a sense, therefore, the surface can partially be spliced with the depth. This is one of the aspects that make the physical record compellingly iconic.

In principle, this textured surface is not to be touched, only the edge of the record. The surface is a kind of taboo. But as any forbidden and visually arresting thing, it poses a temptation, and when it comes to mixing, touching is at the core of the game. It is precisely the tactile part that retains sensual allure, absent whenever the principle of convenience makes DJs rely on the sync button and the mixing software. If vinyl is seductive, then the visual and tactile properties of its surface effectively join forces with the mythically warm sound. Among many others, Wolfgang Voigt emphasizes the fact that for all those sensual reasons vinyl is simply sexy. 'It has the most sexual credibility, if you like, it's touchy, it's warm.'

But the grooved texture is also a source of trouble. It collects dust, visually conspicuous because of the contrast with black vinyl, and we can only mitigate the adverse effects it brings, perennially unable to stop them or perfectly protect the records' surfaces. The more we touch and use vinyl, the more likely it is to attract dirt. This does not necessarily discourage people though. On the contrary, it lends a certain patina to records that invites associations of ageing and heritage that may be strangely attractive, up to a point at least.

Just like the harmonic distortion introduced by vinyl's materiality and the analogue mastering count as a technical imperfection but tend to please our senses, so can the impossibility of keeping vinyl perfectly clean and fresh count as an interesting or even strangely liberating condition. Phillip Sollmann voices this kind of reflection when, shortly before the release of his album *Decay*, we touch upon the topic of surprises and challenges that playing vinyl can pose.

> *Phillip Sollmann*: Perfection is the most annoying thing I can think of in these terms. This society is going in the direction of perfection on all levels, like with body …
>
> *Dominik*: Vinyl stands for resisting perfectionism in some sense?
>
> *Phillip Sollmann*: Maybe. Already the aesthetic aspect of it, having these problems with dust, it's collecting dust wherever you go. I dust it off and you can hear the dust. The dust destroys it. You can only play it maybe 100–200 times and it might not sound good enough any more and I like that. It's like your own body, it's decaying at one point.

As time elapses, records behave like silver or copper or gold, indeed. They get the patina of age and thereby afford another way of seeing time in the thing. Vinyl's aging can anchor our personal sense of time, it encapsulates memories by connecting us to circumstances when we bought it and may suggest another life in the care of others. It perhaps bears traces of parties and listening sessions and moving house. As labels change their logos, the 'original' ones become suddenly a visible mark of time's passage, an iconic reminder of the past. Reflecting on browsing through his own collection, Efdemin says that taking out some records is sometimes like 'a piece of your own history'.

SIZE MATTERS

When we ask Wolfgang Voigt about the remarkably persistent attractiveness of vinyl as an object, he concisely asserts: 'it's the scale'. Heidegger might equally succinctly quip: 'it's ready-to-hand' – or hands, to be precise, as it engages usually both hands. Vinyl is light enough to be effortlessly played but it is also big enough not to be overlooked. Observing the steady rotation of the 30-cm-wide disc on a turntable can be mesmerizing partly due to its very size. It is there to be spotted. Its hypnotic quality corresponds well with steady beats of house and techno music traditionally released on vinyl. Vinyl's surface is large enough to project humble and yet spectacular light reflections when played in a dark room with the solitary turntable's own light only.

Having a surface larger than the screens of most iPads and many contemporary laptops, the 12-inch record is itself a picture of remarkably detailed structure. While professional vinyl cutters need a microscope to control and inspect record production, to regular consumer's eye the finished object is already like an enlarged photograph, big enough to appear as a kind of blow-up full of discernable minutiae of visual design and texture. It is telling to recall in this context a cinematographic reference. In the USA a 1966 promotional poster for Michelangelo Antonioni's film *Blow-Up* which so evocatively portrayed London of the 'swinging sixties' actually used just an anonymous, iconically potent photograph of vinyl grooves and spaces between tracks. It was recently included in an exhibition devoted to the imagery of the film and its cultural context to illustrate 'blow-up as concept'.[24]

The visibility and visual attractiveness of playing with sizeable vinyl discs comes to the fore in DJ sets in bar and club contexts. Wolfgang Voigt again connects this aspect with perceived sexiness of analogue records:

> You can impress your friends if you play as a DJ with vinyl, it's more sporty, it's more sexy. Vinyl is sexy, that's the thing. It's something different [to] some guy sitting with a laptop and a mouse and playing like this, it looks like he's doing his homework at home, or whatever. And playing with records – you know what that is.

Playing actual vinyl records still remains synonymous with 'serious' DJing as well as DJing more generally, even if many DJs seem to have switched to electronic files now. The push-button performances may come across either as disembodied tinkering with machines or generic computer work. As Moritz Reisberger, quoted at the beginning of this chapter, says, it may strike one as opposite to what engaged playing with 'feeling' should be. Significantly older than Moritz, Phillip Sollmann could have become a purist more easily. While he has not, he nevertheless prefers to play vinyl and contrasts digital and analogue Djing, speaking about the overall look and focus it exudes:

> I'm not dogmatic. I play both. If I have something on CD only, or USB, I just play it because it's good, but I think most of the DJs that I really like are more vinyl DJs because somehow it's more serious, more precise. I think it looks better, the DJ looks much better.

Many clubs and their resident DJs attached to the ethos of authentic DJing stick to vinyl, or at least mix not only the tracks but also media themselves, with physical vinyl being often at the centre of attention to them. For those who frequently travel to play, vinyl might not be an attractive option any more. But some of them, like Phillip, still take literal pain to play at least some tracks from analogue records. It's a sign of commitment and style rather than sound quality, especially that – as he admits – the sound may not always be noticeably superior or could be downright worse. He also points out that an SD card with files can more easily be forgotten before the gig. Vinyl is too big to fail you.

That size matters becomes particularly evident with vinyl's sleeve. It matters because cover art matters. Again, Phillip Sollmann's words say it straight:

> The cover, which is very important, makes sense mostly with the size of the record. I think the most important aspect about having records is that you can browse through them, you can look at them, you can use them like a picture, you can read and open the cover.

He emphasizes this aspect when speaking about the aforementioned Donald Fagen *The Nightfly* LP:

> *Phillip Sollmann*: When I first saw it [the cover], I was so absorbed by it. It's so well done. If you look at this on a CD size, it doesn't work really.
> Dominik: The size matters?
> *Phillip Sollmann*: Totally.

This is hardly a biased statement of a vinyl-devoted house DJ. In fact, underground electronic dance culture for long time favoured so-called 'white labels' and generic covers. As Wolfgang Voigt notes, a certain air of anonymity surrounding the then underground house and techno scenes, prevalent especially in the early 1990s, corresponded well with this often conspicuously absent cover design. On the other hand, carefully curated minimalist use of large cover space distinguished many electronic music labels from very early on.

Without doubt, cover art has always been hugely important in other genres, especially in rock music. A piece of anecdotal evidence from Morrissey's *Autobiography* provides a vivid example of the seriousness of the cover issue in relation to format size.

> I pass away as *The World Won't Listen* compilation is released, and the artwork of which I am most proud is repulsively reduced for the CD format to an absurd fraction of the larger photograph ... a cheapened impression of the album sleeve ... In a state of homicidal seizure I demand to know why the CD image does not repeat the LP image. – *'But we couldn't fit the entire LP image on the CD because a CD is too small,'* says Richard Boon, unhelpfully. *'But they managed quite*

> *well with Sergeant Pepper's Lonely Hearts Club Band!*' As the years go by, and *The World Won't Listen* changes labels, the CD image remains heart-sinkingly abysmal compared to the majesty of the LP sleeve. These things count.[25]

Being five times bigger, vinyl cover can hardly fail to be the most suitable for albums' art. Even if fitted perfectly, CD covers cannot match the visual power conveyed by a thing that looks like an actual picture ready to hang on the wall. Indeed, when framed, record covers can be gorgeous pieces of art. Nowadays, record cover frames are commodities on the market. The furniture maker and global mass design distributor Ikea now sell in their stores frames designed specifically for showing off vinyl within domestic spaces. Their instore displays feature attractive and evocative album covers which suggest some affinity with their customers' tastes: classic rock and pop albums. Being displayed in such a way, the details of the artwork are obviously more visible and the whole thing more gripping. If the entire cover is a portrait of an artist we end up with a near-natural size head exchanging looks with us. Think about Miles Davis's albums again, like the striking *Tutu*, or *Decoy*, *Get Up With It* and *Greatest Hits*.

Although once keen on anonymity and minimal packaging, independent electronic music labels nowadays consciously curate their visual identity with distinct sleeve and centre label design. The cover is the important thing that supports the vinyl. To Phillip Sollmann, whose records under the moniker *Efdemin* often appear on the Hamburg-based Dial imprint, this is not surprising due to manifold social connections between the art world and music world. Dial's carefully curated and similarly designed minimal covers owe their style to the artistic background of the owner, Carsten Jost and artists associated with the label and the Smallville store in Hamburg, such as Stefan Marx, who has designed posters, t-shirts, stickers and skateboards as well as record covers. In an interview with *Resident Advisor*, Marx talks about his sleeve designs and how they are intimately relate to the material qualities of vinyl:

> I think of the covers more like an art edition, something you'd put on a print. I'm happy it turned out this way, I didn't want to design covers for some shitty CD I wasn't into. I really love 12-inches and hate CDs. It's just not big enough; you can't touch the paper with this plastic case around it.[26]

Last but not least, hundreds and thousands of records comprising one's collection neatly arrayed like books in library produce an effect matched only by, well, libraries or bookstores. The spatial and aesthetic impact of a vinyl collection simply cannot be replicated by the digital files stacked on your computer. In the digital world, the idea is the opposite – to make the thing invisible. The digital revolution is partly about an elimination of this impact and its downsides. CDs come closer to vinyl's allure, of course, yet this is exactly when we realize that size matters, for better and for worse. A proper space is certainly required for the effect to be awe-inspiring instead of overwhelming. But a multiplicity of thin spines also provides an unforgettable impression, one that vinyl producers found repeatedly worth picturing on the covers of their releases. Ninja Tune's 'DJ Food: Refried Food' series is just one of the many examples. A neatly displayed collection, even if comparatively small, carries more weight, both figuratively and literally. Individually and as a collection, analogue records feel more substantial than CDs. They are full-size things. They certainly feel like a legitimate 'collection' with multidimensional history and considerable cultural worth rather than a useful but invisible, virtual sound bank. Wolfgang Voigt emphasizes this point in an amusingly sarcastic way: 'Who would be impressed about it if you said: *These are my 5 million files*! Wonderful! Congratulations!' Efdemin offers a similarly concise punchline, just on a more romantic note: 'I think there are only some things that are as beautiful as record shelves, honestly.'

FORMATS: DIAMETER AND SPEED DIFFERENTIATION

Apart from bigness, there is one more important differentiation point between the analogue and the digital. Unlike the shapeless virtual file or completely uniform format of CDs' 12 cm, vinyl discs come in a variety of formats, each one capable of being played at different speeds and in special cases taking shapes other than circular. Even the smallest one, the 7-inch single format, is significantly bigger than a CD, resembling a small book. Today, when most singles are pressed on 12-inch discs, vinyl seems special not only due to its sheer physical nature but also the actual size: when in the cover, it is akin to a big art book or a painting. By the same token, releasing your album in a less widespread format of 10-inch or a single as 7-inch record distinguishes it.

An example of the former is Radiohead's *Kid A* album, all the subsequent re-presses of which were kept in the 10-inch format. There is an instant association for the fans of the band between the album and its vinyl format. Ten-inch records have been used by contemporary artists to showcase their iconic singles, for example 'El Capitalismo Foraneo' by Gotan Project, with a high-quality inner sleeve cut to the unusual size. Independent artists and labels utilize 10-inch as DJ promo copies, initially not intended for sale, for example United Future Organization's 'Loud Minority' that includes the B-side with Kruder and Dorfmeister remix of 'L.O.V.E.'. Sometimes the unusual appeal of a 10-inch vinyl is also combined with other special features, for example a strictly limited run of hand-numbered coloured discs distributed to a number of special stores. The so-designed object is eye-catching and rare, so even if put on the market without any cover it helps small independent labels to promote their artists. For example, London-based renowned independent store Kristina Records promoted such a release by *Minuendo Recordings*, the 250 copies, vinyl-only record by 2DeepSoul entitled 'Earth energy pt. 1'.

Examples of 7-inch singles are more ubiquitous. Typically playable at 45 rpm, they tend to have a large centre hole rather than the standard small one in the middle that requires the use of a special adapter put on the turntable's spindle. The large hole on the 7-inch vinyl once facilitated the handling of records by jukebox machines. The adapters used to play those records on regular turntables come, in turn, in a variety of material forms, in cheap plastic and more expensive metal. Seven-inch vinyl harks back to the exhilarating times of recording pop hits in the 1960s and 1970s when most singles were released in such format and when they were gradually becoming more accessible to the general public.

Be it British underground rock or American soul, the 7-inch record for a long time remained the format for releasing singles. American labels such as *Collectables* became known for their 'collector series 45s' that would publish all kinds of music, from Frank Sinatra to Cat Stevens. Covered by cheap paper sleeves only, they would often advertise 'nostalgic music makers' or 'all the great oldies' as well as some DJ equipment. When the more easily manipulable and thus more DJ-friendly 12-inch vinyl dominated the trade of dance singles in the 1990s, choosing to press on 7-inch became an additional special statement. Therefore it comes as no surprise that today it is even more of a speciality, particularly beloved among soul aficionados. Explicitly indebted to *Motown*, the contemporary beat maker and producer working under the moniker Tall Black Guy releases his singles as 7-inch vinyl. As is the case with 10-inch, the smallest 7-inch format also functions as a thing of material distinction, typically combined with other unusual aesthetic features. When *Music On Vinyl* re-pressed Kula Shaker's *K* LP, the 180-gram audiophile album was marketed as 'expanded vinyl edition' which included a purple 7-inch record of the hit single 'Hush'. The German duo Modeselektor put out their collaborative singles produced with Thom Yorke of Radiohead, 'Shipwreck' and 'This', as 7-inch records, the limited edition of 1,000 transparent orange and transparent yellow vinyl respectively.

Beyond sheer aesthetics conveyed by haptic and visual qualities, vinyl features barely audible but detectable differences depending on speed popularly measured in revolutions per minute (rpm). As noted before, higher speed means higher resolution at which sound of the groove is 'read' by the turntable's pickup system. Since the late 1940s two different values have been in standard use, 33⅓ and 45 rpm. The 78 rpm records yielded to the new competition permanently as the lower speeds proved considerably more practical. Combined with narrowing of the groove – for this reason called at the beginning 'microgroove' – labels were now able to pack more music on one side without losing the medium's high-fidelity sound reproduction. The old types of groove were several times wider and the friction between the employed materials made records deteriorate very quickly. Everything changed with the introduction of vinyl and microgroove. Now up to 30 minutes – if cut at a low volume – and typically 20 minutes of complex loud material could be fitted on one side of the disc at 33⅓ rpm. A still lower speed of 16 rpm had been used for some time but proved practically inferior to higher ones.

HOLISTIC ARTEFACT

Put all the aforementioned aspects together and vinyl reveals its nature of a uniquely holistic medium. Playing vinyl engages several senses at once. As you spin a record, you see the label and vinyl's glimmering surface. You can immerse yourself in the mesmerizing rotation, and you need to attend to the process of playing which is not really suitable to be just a background to other activities. In fact, vinyl's visuality and haptics make it prone to be a centre of meditation or ritual or both. Especially mixing the records can be experienced as a meditative and ritualistic practice that may consume most of player's attention, allowing a sense of flow and remarkable connection both to the medium and its sonic message. Many DJs attest to that and almost all those we talked with admitted it. Michael aka Puresque and Andreas Lubich explicitly refer to mixing records in terms of meditation.

> *Andreas Lubich*: 'When I am a DJ, I can't imagine playing with CDs or with Traktor from the laptop, but that's only because I'm very visual with that … Sometimes I don't even know what artist or track I'm actually playing. I just know that, for example, I play track B3 of that record with the red car on the cover … Listening to a vinyl record which spins at the turntable has also something relaxing. I don't know. It's just something meditative.

Andreas Baumecker, renowned for his long, exquisitely composed DJs sets, admits too that his attention is almost exclusively consumed by the act of playing:

> I have this certain work 'tradition' that I don't look up to the crowd a lot. It's not because I don't want to see them, it's because I really concentrate. I just like going right into the music and to just focus on music; I just play records together and I try to make them sound like one new track, and that takes a lot of … concentration. Because having records play at the same time, staying on the same speed, it's a kind of work.

Others emphasize not only visuality but also the peculiar tactile engagement that vinyl brings to the table. Phillip Sollmann:

> I think most of the people that are left in this scene playing vinyl they're addicts to this. Either they're collectors or they really love to play with their hands. It's a physical thing.

Vinyl is narrated as 'authentic' or 'real' in large measure because it is corporeal. It combines the seriousness of professional archive and geekiness with sheer sense of fun – it's an instrument to play and a toy to play with, it is a tool and an art object, all at once, or whatever you want it to be at a moment. It attracts people who are 'visual' or 'haptic' in their approach to music media and more generally. This seems to be particularly important to those into electronic music where traditional, haptically engaging instruments are typically not used. Mixing with vinyl makes you feel like actually playing something. Describing the difference between the analogue and digital, Mieko Suzuki – like Andreas Lubich – emphasizes it is a matter of taste and purpose but tends to prefer vinyl: 'I never got into CDs. For me, it's no value. Vinyl record, of course, is quite big … Also, the way you listen to it is so different, you play …'

Even if you're not a DJ, listening to music via vinyl means you *play* it in a more embodied sense of the term. Vinyl becomes an instrument of sorts. Digital Compact Disc delivered just what it was designed for: a clean *compact* presentation of music requiring no more than pushing a few buttons. But it hardly had a potential to be an engaging *instrument* in everyday use. It was more like a microwave rather than a gas cooker.

CD effectively achieved a technological reduction of sorts. Listening is even easier and more manipulable with a computer, although for a time this privilege came at a cost of significant compression of sound. Gone is the cumbersome physicality of the medium – it's mostly about the device and its capabilities. No sides, no sights and no flipping, just a remote control skipping instead. No dust or special care for the thing is there to consider. A machine deals with the tracks mostly on its own. In the case of CD players, the playing machine generally sucks the disc in, and with computers the tactile geometry disappears altogether, streamlined into screen visualization of digital files.

In short, as a holistic artefact vinyl is also a specialist thing. It combines its multisensory appeal with singularly calibrated technological identity. It is perfectly suitable to be a gift or a collector's item, even if it proved to be a less-than-perfect commodity on a mass global market and remains a mechanically reproduced copy. As collecting and gift-giving remain at the cultural core of many societies, vinyl is likely to survive further revolutions in the music industry. Moreover, it is likely to support or rejuvenate all that is necessarily connected with it. This leads us to consider the entanglements of vinyl.

ENTANGLEMENTS

As we have showed so far, vinyl is an intentionally produced artefact with definitive sensual qualities and physical properties stabilized over years of experimentation, testing and routine use at home and in clubs. Like any other medium, it works only because other things exist too, yet we tend to forget about it. We now wish to turn to them and examine their material connectedness.

In a heavily mediated world, records – like humans – are not only multiple, diverse and tied to conventionally ascribed roles or contingently attributed statuses. They critically depend on a whole range of other things and stable material prerequisites to actualize themselves. Not only the seemingly intangible content and visible material form, but also the physical – often elaborate – entanglements and networks make them what they are in our experience. No object is fully assimilable to the linguistic, aural and visual meanings it happens to carry.

To quote Daniel Miller again, if functional constraint on form of an object is generally a very loose one for everyday forms, it is obviously not the case for the machine parts and technical assemblages on which they depend.[27] And without all kinds of machines, like turntables, pickup systems, amplifiers and speakers, records could hardly attain their cultural eminence and exude specific types of aura with which music lovers credit them time and again around the world. If records move people – literally and metaphorically – it is because they too move when played, and it is the things called turntables that keep them moving. But even the best turntable will disappoint if its pickup system fails. It's a bit like with a camera, or an animal that depends on one of its senses to move and hunt, like a bat or an owl: even the best body won't fly without equally sensitive lenses, ears and eyes. Of course, the story of vinyl's entanglements does not stop here. You need an amplifier, and you may want to have an analogue tube amplifier if you are a sound freak or just on the purist side of things. You may want to have your maintenance utensils ready to hand to keep the business running smoothly. There's no DJing without mixers, those boxes that join turntables and make them work as couples rather than solitary TV-like creatures. Last but not least, speakers and their spatial arrangement constitute the crucial endpoint in any audio setup.

These entanglements of technical objects must be looked at more closely than is usually the case. They can't be taken for granted. Unlike conventional signs in language or art, the cultural tools and technical artefacts have more specific or rigidly defined usefulness which can subsequently be 'translated' into a sensual effect. Not anything goes here. There are rather definitive limits to bending tools for the sake of our needs that may not exist when it comes to manipulating signs to serve our wants. If there is no such thing as a perfect tool, then some are nevertheless more satisfying than others in a given situation. This is not to say that vinyl is merely a cog in a larger machine of technological and industrial works. If the whole of the music world tends to be bigger than the sum of its parts, then a part called vinyl is also more than a subtracted bit of this whole. This thing is certainly a special cog, the 'discog' of the larger phenomenon sometimes called by sociologists the *discomorphosis* of music.[28]

Here we try to complement the discomorphosis approach with perhaps more intuitive concepts of *equipment* and *sensory formation*. All the necessary entanglements of vinyl add up to the existence of specific equipment whose sensual qualities and uses give rise, in turn, to an entire sensory formation we simply call 'vinyl culture', or 'analogue culture'. As we indicated above, in our regular experience these things reach us all at once. It is telling that we use words like 'gear' and 'equipment' as singular nouns. But it is just a functional simplification of daily speech. As Heidegger underscored, there is no such thing as 'an equipment'. There's multiplicity of interconnected and intertwined elements and impressions that go together as tightly fused rather than loosely conventional experiential 'bundles'. We tend to approach such technological and sensory bundles quite unreflectively, even if we love them dearly. Andreas Lubich helps 'disentangle' the vinyl equipment and the necessary role of specific things from the point of view of the mastering engineer who anticipates not only customers' aesthetic musical preferences but also a kind of equipment they are likely to use:

> So often we forget about that when talking about vinyl. It's always just about the record, and that the record sounds nice, but it can only sound nice if it's well recorded, of course. This is given that it just needs to be played back on a proper setup turntable. To ensure a properly recorded vinyl record is what the mastering engineer has to care for. When I work on mastering and cutting a jazz record, or maybe a folk record, my target group in mind will maybe never use a Technics turntable [SL-1200MK2 standard DJ model], or these typical DJ pickups to play it. Therefore I don't need to check such a record with a DJ pickup. I need to check it with a decent pickup as used from the target group. On the other

hand it's important to check a dance record with a typical club system using a DJ pickup.

The technological duo of turntable/pickup system sits at the centre of vinyl experience. Certain knowledge and preparation is required from a listener to buy and then use it to optimal effect, commensurable with quality promised by the medium. It can be interpreted as something too time- and money-consuming. But if one makes time and money, the experience makes itself palpable. Mieko Suzuki says:

> Vinyl is not portable, it's all about the setup. You need a setup to listen to it. This is what I like, giving it time, making time, setup to listen to one record. It's different to an iPod. What is different is the setup. I love it! Sometimes I'm busy and can't make time. But if I do and I listen to a record, it's very luxury for me.

Turntables, like the Technics series mentioned by Andreas Lubich, are highly functional, iconic things in their own right. Such devices enabled the emergence of the entire practice and musical genre called *turntablism* whose masters, such as DJ Q-Bert, raised the vinyl playing machine to the status of a musical instrument.[29] There is a synergetic effect between 12-inch vinyl single and this particular device spread the world over and present in almost every club worth its name. Some are not regularly used any more due to the current spread of digital devices but they are not removed either. In domestic spaces, any turntable – but especially the audiophile ones – simply defines the listening room as much as the shelves with records. Andreas Lubich comes up with the most succinct and beautiful simile to capture this:

> Look at these high-end turntables, it's a sculpture. There is one more thing about listening to vinyl – it's having this sculpture, playing the music.

If the record's cover can be a picture and an entire collection evokes a tapestry, then turntables are indeed sculptures. In all those cases, the devil is in the detail. And one of the key details in sculpted presence of the turntable is its pickup system, or cartridge comprising the headshell and stylus, popularly called the needle. Predictably, there's a whole science to the needles themselves and audible differences are noticeable even to an untrained ear. Different pickups require different setups of the turntable's tonearm and anti-skating adjustment, a more arcane part of the 'pickup science'. While it quite commonly gets neglected, the needle in operation can make all the difference in the world, both for sound quality and record maintenance. DJ pickups, such as the iconic Ortofon Concorde series, have low compliance, i.e. better scratching and stability performance. Conversely, the audiophile systems feature very high compliance; as Andreas Lubich says, 'they kind of fly through the groove, and that's great for the record wear; all the small excursions of the groove can be played back, while a DJ pickup goes through the groove like a tank'.

In the end, the factor of time again comes into play as everything gets worse as we use it, and thus becomes potentially detrimental to things with which it is entangled. Peter Runge's competence of a doctor of maintenance sciences means he can't help but conclude wryly: 'There are different types of stylus, like spherical and elliptical, and some people say one is better, other people say the other is better. I think a new needle is better than a worn one.' In addition to the difference stemming from technical design there is a whole world of aesthetic design that applies to cartridges just like to any other piece of equipment. In this aspect the factor of time assumes different meanings: the old can be stylish or 'vintage' or just redolent of a particular era in design history. It's a matter of preference that can be creatively explored by the player.

When obtaining a new device becomes difficult or impossible, we realize how precious is the thing that we may have once taken for granted. As odd as it may seem, the production of the beloved SL-1200MK2 Technics turntable was discontinued around the time when the sales of vinyl went up again, signalling the now-celebrated analogue revival. They are now expensive to buy in second-hand markets, especially since they have always been renowned for remarkable longevity and sturdiness. The situation proved sufficiently painful for vinyl aficionados to organize a petition to Panasonic Company to reintroduce the legendary player. Moni Daniel from Israel gathered 5,000 signatures by early April 2014.[30] By the same token, however, the decision to stop production seems to have revealed a disappointing yet unsurprising inability of mainstream industries to act on cultural rather than strictly economic impulses. The success of the famous Technics model shows that things may be hard to replace, just like certain experiences they afford are not easily exchangeable or replicable.

FIGURE 3.4: Iconic Ortofon Concorde pickup. (DB)

In short, a given technological network like the one briefly described here is at once a phenomenological nexus and a carefully calibrated chain of devices which form a unique chain of interconnected entities. The complex of embodied knowledge, repeated practices and sheer fun associated with those things gives rise to a distinct sensory formation irreducible to the way we talk about it and independent from the musical content for which it is created. The virtual environment in which new miracles of technology like Ableton thrive is also such a sensory formation. When Marshall McLuhan spoke of the Gutenberg galaxy, he may have meant something like sensory formation too.

Crucially, failure of the playing machine, or its temporary absence or shortage, introduces a Heideggerian displacement that makes us more aware of the equipment's role and thus its value. However, it does not mean the destruction of the music medium itself. This may not be the case with files whose very existence and functionality depend on computers and integrity of hardware. As digital music consumption evolves away from object-ownership towards streaming and similar services, analogue record re-emerges as the principal *offline medium*. Some record stores self-consciously emphasize this; for example, Hardwax attaches special stickers 'offline–store only' to its exclusive merchandise. Various electronic music labels subscribe to this trend, releasing 'store-only series', for example Rotterdam-based *Clone Records*. The limited batch is then distributed to befriended physical shops whose owners sign the centre label of each item under the generic rubric: 'location'. Peter Runge once again mischievously observes that vinyl's offline character makes you invisible to any government or company as long as you don't pay for it with a credit card. An interesting paradox is that the most tactile and visual medium's use can most reliably be concealed. Since many independent record stores – as we shall note later – work outside electronic cash systems, they indeed become a paradigmatically offline and potentially subversive cultural institution. Vinyl resists easy homologation, once again. In short, vinyl's technological entanglements are integral to vinyl's sensory enjoyment, but their failure is not sufficient to deprive us of the medium itself. It is the very physicality of records as things that makes them special.

VINYL AS THING

Each way of accessing recorded music is a distinct mode of engagement with it that often gives as much as it takes away. The question is what it is that you want or need, rather than what constitutes 'progress'. There is genuine science and profound art to making and playing vinyl. It is a thing of immersive qualities despite its simplicity. We can certainly *say* that new digital technologies like Ableton are immersive but it does not *mean* the same and they are all but simple. The actual meaning of a thing comes from a constellation of experiences and the specific sensory formation to which it belongs and within which it performs its function. There is no absolute scale that would enable us to say: this is better. But that's hardly a problem. In the end, parallel media formations and hybrid arrangements serve multiplicity of our needs much more adequately than any homogenizing attempt at perfection. As

Andreas Lubich says, 'you're much more involved with the music when you listen to a vinyl record; on the other hand, the high-end audiophile scene is always in search of detailed, precise and authentic sound'.

This is, however, not how the dematerialization of virtual digitalism was presented to the public by the music industry in the first place. If anything, the thingness of vinyl was frowned upon and no general cultural mourning really ensued. Those who decided to keep vinyl at the dawn of the digital revolution were likely to be seen as luddites, not visionaries. A comprehensive narrative of progress and betterment dominated public discourses, first for CDs, later for files that for a long time were just severely compressed mp3 files. Like in matters of food, lightness rather than wholesomeness tended to be foregrounded. As CDs were gradually being displaced by ever-improved virtualization of the digital music, just like records once were by CDs, the thingness and tactility of music became conspicuously absent, and, if evoked at all, then as a burden successfully 'overcome' rather than anything remarkable or worth preserving. Huge private, institutional and radio collections were given to second-hand stores or sold out for peanuts at fairs and flea markets. In the US, thrift stores were full of one-dollar vinyl at the turn of the century, their basements filled to the brim, sometimes with literally millions of unwanted dusty records. They were sometimes not exactly beautiful or romantic places to hang out at. The success of digitalization seemed all the more convincing as those formerly attached to vinyl abandoned it and were ostensibly persuaded to buy the same music again and again in the name of cleaner sound and cleaner domestic spaces. It all looked and sounded like an excellent idea. And for many it genuinely was. A sense of moving forward seemed undeniable.

Yet this is what you see by looking exclusively at the headlines and slogans of the mass trade, or from a mainstream point of view. Peer beneath it, and a different, more differentiated landscape emerges, one full of lateral moves and deep details that by their very existence, even if relatively small or seemingly insignificant, attest to the existence of parallel rather than outdated musical worlds. There are groups of aficionados, audiophiles, collectors, DJs, underground subcultures and music lovers, for whom vinyl as the sensual thing and the beautiful tool has never gone away. There are those who discover it for themselves, having grown up with iPods and computers and thus treating them as the standard rather mundane technology. Electronic dance music DJs have been one of such strongly committed groups. Representing diverse genres, from dub to house to techno, they retained the special relation to vinyl as a thing during its lean years and endowed it with coolness and hipness not unlike Charlie Parker's and Miles Davis's recordings did over half a century ago.

Records are something to see, touch, choose and own, tangible property to get attached to, collectible objects to treasure, personal sources of seductive pleasure, made by identified others and shareable with others. Being less standardized and much more diverse than CD or files, vinyl is a thing well suited to markets that thrive on differentiation and distinction. While more cumbersome, its formal variability underscores certain aspects of internal differentiation of music styles and playing practices. Vinyl is also uniquely amenable to putting emphasis on a given title as special release.

As with everything, this capacity makes vinyl vulnerable to abuses of capitalist commodification, a condition that we touch upon in the following chapters. But there is a more innocuous side to this kind of fetishism. After all, genuinely progressive, innovative and highly creative communities emerged and continue to exist around it.

Generally much more affordable than graphics or paintings and more valuable than CD or cassette, a good vinyl makes for a good gift. It may be less universal in this capacity than the book, which requires no technology to read it, but having a turntable makes it that much more special. The necessity of a player is another surmountable limitation that makes this thing a curious object. In the end it may be hard to put the finger on what it is that makes vinyl special. There is no singularly overpowering 'cause' or condition of infatuation with vinyl. Rather, it's a more holistic emergent experience, uniting various senses around a piece of music. It is about entire sensory formation and its histories, not about any one narrative or sentiment, be it nostalgic retromania or hipsterish snobbery.

We have tried to show that a complex bundle of material qualities matter and different aesthetic aspects may play a special role for different people under specific circumstances. Yet it is certain that the tactile and visual constitution of vinyl is inseparable from its lasting appeal. In particular, concreteness of this artefact makes it stand out as a concrete medium at a time when immateriality of media becomes the norm and 'mediation' shifts its meaning toward increasingly abstract communicative processes. When space and time are turned into scarce resources, things start to 'clutter' our rooms and 'slow us down'.

But some things cannot and should not be compressed and their limitations may gently remind us of our own limitations and needs that can be neglected only at our peril. Wolfgang Voigt exercises his sharp and witty irony in this context: 'you don't want to download your meal!' Vinyl offers a perspective according to which limitations and peculiarities of the concrete world can inspire creativity and reflection rather than frustration if approached with patience and curiosity rather than greed. Things can subtly re-enchant our relation to materiality, space and time, especially when they are simple but aesthetically refined and carefully shaped objects. Tactile, visual artefacts are not only 'decorations' or meretricious additions, but also genuine phenomenological anchors for our rituals and memories.

For these combined reasons, to quite a few music lovers playing music is not just about sound and melody and beat, even if they tend to enjoy those things immensely. It is also about a visually constituted event and actual physical *things* themselves, often indispensable for the events to work their elusive magic. As the German art historian Hans Belting suggests, listening is seeing, just like seeing is complemented with spatially reverberating aural impressions. Sound cannot be touched, but it can be felt through the vibrations in our bodies.[31] What we certainly can touch is things that produce and emit sound, everything from vinyl to speakers. All this is connected, technologically and as a bodily feeling. The body in space unites the impressions and music on vinyl reminds us of this fact, even if it does so in a non-verbal way.

These conditions typically elude our conscious acknowledgement, and this realization can also become expressed within popular culture, as Lætitia Saidier of Stereolab[32] sings on the track 'Anonymous Collective': '*You and me are molded by things, Well beyond our acknowledgment. You and me are shaped by some things, Well beyond our acknowledgement.*' The love for records is a more or less deliberate cultivation of the synesthetic qualities of playing music with vinyl. The magical properties of vinyl mentioned by Morrissey in his *Autobiography* are not a subjective view or mere conventional description of idiosyncratic attachment to a thing. Instead, it is an intersubjectively established, shared sensibility inspired by the thing popularly dubbed vinyl. We find it in many other cultural testimonies, and our interviews feature it too. Jenus Baumecker-Kahmke makes this point particularly clear:

> There's just something that happens, when you have the finished music; even though it's been produced digitally, when it gets pressed on vinyl, there's just something that happens. I think it's something that even science can't really explain. I've talked to several mastering engineers and cutters and they always say it's like magic, like something happens and you get a certain kind of warmth and power that is on a good pressing of vinyl that adds the little kind of 'nobody knows what'...

As Phillip Sollmann struggles to put his finger on vinyl's allure, he eventually concludes: 'I don't know what it is but it looks good, it feels good.'

CHAPTER FOUR

Commodity

Value and Markets

BEYOND PRODUCTION: CONSUMING VINYL IN THE DIGITAL AGE

The traditional understanding of commodities is that they are things to be produced, bought and sold in markets. As things which are exchangeable, they are key units of economic action. Across many disciplines of the social sciences, the commodity and its forces and effects are theorized as fundamental building-blocks of social and economic life. Particularly the case in sociology, the commodity is absolutely fundamental for coordinating diverse factors such as labour, capital, technology and consumption. In Marx's colossal theory of capitalism, in the commodity rests the key to understanding the corrosive and alienating forces of modern capitalist production. Much more than this body of work, which has for a long time been the dominant perspective in sociology, suggests, commodities spark and coordinate cultural action, interpretation and imagination. In recent decades, much research has focused on the role of commodities and their consumption as constitutive of practices building identity, self and community. As David Howes demonstrates, by focusing on production and alienating aspects of industrial capitalism Marx 'neglected an equally salient development – namely, the *presentation* of commodities in stores and exhibitions. The birth of these "places of consumption" heralded a transformation in the nature of capitalism with far-reaching implications – the transformation from industrial capitalism to the consumer capitalism of today.'[1] As far as this salient universe of consumption practices and valuations is concerned, we now live in a very different world from that of Marx or even Benjamin, and thus a commensurate shift in focus and interpretation is required. Commodities, such as the vinyl record, may be seen as 'sticky things' onto which all sorts of cultural and social meanings are fixed, and through which systems of embodied practices and collective activities are formed. Undoubtedly, vinyl may be subject to speculation typical of art markets, or fall victim to profit-driven marketing. But that's only part of the story, just like the art world can hardly be reduced to its economic malfunctions and post-industrial excess. In fact, certain artistic commodities retain polysemy that enables different carrier groups to subvert the very logic of the master narratives that seem to govern the production and reception of culture. The story of the analogue record in the digital age we narrated in Chapter 1 is one such evocative situation. It galvanizes a world of new complexity which begs for fresh angles of cultural analysis and social criticism.

Commodities also extend the world of economic production and markets into the cultural, hermeneutic and emotional world of distinction and status, identity and collectivity. In short, people can use commodities as a bridge, or a boundary, linking or distancing themselves from others in their communities. People reside within a forest of commodity objects and we live through these material things. Commodity objects constitute much of what we know and do as social actors and are often also the means by which we come to know and experience it. Rich with symbolism, demanding our attention, sparking our imaginations and bodies, rife with possibilities for pleasure, devotion, distinction and play, we revel in and among this material forest of commodities. Connecting the worlds of production and consumption, commodities also unite the forces of economic production with the human dimensions of consumption and the psychically mediated, pragmatic aspects of purchase, handling, possession, care and disposal. Being the result of economic production processes, most of the objects we deal with on a daily basis (which are, or once have been, commodities) have not been directly made or produced by us. But, in a way, through visual, corporeal and imaginative engagements we actually do produce them, negotiating and constructing their meanings and using them to make ourselves and in turn a larger meaningful universe. As either a mass-produced medium for distributing canonical pop-rock recordings, or as boutique, cult object for representing the collective effort of local music scenes and music heritages, the vinyl record is one such commodity.

One of the fundamental arguments of this book is that the widespread digitalization of music listening and music consumption has radically transformed the meaning of vinyl as a commodity, negatively, but also positively for some music listeners. Whether we like it or not, the digital reframes the analogue. The digital age is synonymous with consumer-friendly omnipresence, offering instant accessibility and portability mediated by online electronic devices and the digitalization of material for cultural consumption, such as music. In this current era of music consumption, the possibility of downloading or streaming a song or album via a digital playing device means instant music listening. The experience of deferred gratification and investment of knowledge and time related to the search largely ceases to matter within the digital world. One might not even have to browse online for an artist's new album, for example, but prepay and have the songs instantly downloaded the moment they are released to the global market. In this model, there are typically some small differences in pricing depending on digital format, on national markets, and on whether one streams or buys the music files, but there is also a tendency towards uniform digital pricing, especially on major digital store platforms. In part, this is the result of the absolutely identical nature of major types of digital files and the globalization of consumption. The ease of duplicating, distributing and sharing, and the identical nature of the digital music file means there is little opportunity for dimensions of rarity or uniqueness to be introduced. This is, of course, completely the opposite of vinyl, where in markets for second-hand vinyl facets of rarity, uniqueness, seriality and other special qualities are determined not just by the absolute rarity of any vinyl but by the factors of context, location and condition.

Moreover, there are, in fact, multiple markets for new vinyl releases. On the one hand, they are driven by the forces of heritagization within music industries and reissues, and on the other by boutique and small-batch production. Either form of vinyl release has its own rules for how value is made, interpreted and exchanged. In this chapter, we explore how the value of vinyl as a commodity is created, determined and understood in an array of market contexts and how the value of vinyl as a commodity is relationally constructed relative to other mediums for music listening. Along the way we propose a revision of the concept of commodity fetishism inspired by our ethnography.

PATHWAYS TO VINYL'S VALUE: RARITY

Music itself is not a rare thing. Music is not only widely and relatively easily available to be accessed or purchased, but is indeed nearly impossible to escape in many everyday settings. From supermarkets to public transport and television, music is ubiquitous. It is true that many of our music listening experiences are made by way of compulsion rather than choice. This condition of omnipresence makes the apparent choice of playing vinyl all the more powerful. Moreover, for the large part, the music that is made available through commercial channels and media is merely a particular sample of the music available for listening, rather than encompassing all the possibilities and styles available for music and noise making. What is more, the digitalization of music sharing and music production fosters a relative democratization of distribution, and the possibility of small-scale or 'bedroom' production. Against all this, music consumption and production was of course up until relatively recently a mass, big business concern, with decades of globally diffused production of music media such as CDs, vinyl and cassettes, often in very large quantities. What this means is that there are various, but particular, structural and contextual possibilities for the production of rarity as the remnants of decades-old production are recirculated in second-hand markets at the same time that reissue markets for the stock of iconic older recordings emerge.

The rarity of particular music media, rather than necessarily the rarity of music *per se*, becomes a feature of these markets. Almost any recorded musical performance can be relatively easily downloaded; yet, in many cases, few vinyl pressings of such performances are available for sale, and those that are have been distributed around the world in ways which make finding them something of an effort, or at least something certain knowledges are required for. Often, in the case of vinyl, the markets where rarity is most visible are second-hand markets, though rarity is also capable of being produced in markets for new vinyl releases. Let's first consider some of the possibilities for rarity in second-hand markets, for it is there that unique features of vinyl as a material good are particularly visible.

The first feature is that vinyl can, and does, appreciate in value. Partly, of course, this facet of appreciating monetary value is something of a myth which fuels secondary vinyl markets. The reality, however, is often different, as the '50 cent' or 'dollar bins' at markets and stores demonstrate. In the vast majority of cases the opposite occurs: vinyl enters a state of decommodification, depreciates in value, becomes cultural marginalia and then – except for the most devoted diggers of the rare, curious or obscure – merely trash. Which vinyl records rise in value and which fall are tied inextricably to the biography of the artist or band, along with a range of other contributing factors related to the rise of specialist listening communities. The physical condition of the vinyl matters too, as well as the conditions of production on which the initial quality of a given record depends. There are vinyl records from artists that appreciate in value for reasons of genuine scarcity. Media stories appear every so often citing the 'most valuable vinyl records' which add fuel to these myths of the secondary market. Often the narrative of such accounts implies that either one might be a collector, or that one might have copies of these valuable vinyl records hidden away in boxes, or in the possession of an old aunt or uncle who doesn't play them any more, let alone realize their potential monetary value.

In the following section we explore some of the conditions for vinyl rarity through the example of the pricing of Sex Pistols' vinyl releases on the *Rare Record Price Guide*. This example, we acknowledge, is an extreme one. In fact, although very few people will ever handle these particular pressings pointing to the potential of vinyl to acquire the status previously reserved only for original works of art. It is a Warholian object in the sense that it is transformed from an element of pop culture to a super-valuable commodity comparable with 'high culture' items. The *Rare Record Price Guide*[2] lists various releases by the Sex Pistols, annotated by particular notes concerning its evaluation of monetary value of each release. The most expensive Sex Pistols' release, the 'God Save the Queen/No Feelings' 7-inch vinyl acetate release, is indicated to be worth £10,000. In 2012, the *New Musical Express* reported that one of only two known copies of this release sold on eBay for £12,860.[3] In assessing its value, the *Guide* notes that few copies were pressed, that the release was pressed in '77' (as opposed to 1977), that no catalogue number is printed on the release, and that the release was 'used by Malcolm McLaren to get gigs and a record deal'. The value of this release rests on a number of factors. First, it is released on acetate, rather than vinyl. Acetate releases, while not a rarity within some listening cultures, are not as widely distributed and were often used pre-vinyl release to promote an artist with club or radio DJs, and are a medium likely to wear more quickly than vinyl. The value of this object is therefore not in sound quality, in fidelity, or in the longevity of the pressing in everyday use. Like any rare object, be it a valuable vase, artwork or rare wine, the acetate release needs appropriate storage and minimal touching and disturbance if its value is to appreciate, or its potential for further play assured. The value is therefore not merely in sound quality, but in the value of the object as an important cultural artefact, a thing of heritage associated with a crucial current in contemporary pop and rock music. As Wolfgang Voigt communicated in an interview with us, reflecting on the power and symbolic attraction of vinyl and its association with the mythologies that surround popular music, 'vinyl was tracks and records to touch, it was like legend spinning around'.

The more important factor determining value in the case of 'God Save the Queen/No Feelings', therefore, is the story – indeed mythology – of the Sex Pistols in making this acetate release valuable. Without its global cultural meaning via its association with the Sex Pistols and also, in this case, the hands of their manager at the time, Malcolm McLaren, it might have become a degraded and forgotten object that punk historians and blogger aficionados of underground music scenes might occasionally refer to or even be aware of. Enriched by the fame of the Sex Pistols, the object becomes one of the most valuable 7-inch collectables around. Its value therefore resides not so much in the value of the material itself and in its natural properties – though being acetate, it introduces some extra dimension of scarcity – but, more importantly, in the fact of the material object of the 7-inch single being placed within the cultural narrative of such an iconic, infamous and widely known band in the British punk movement. As Emile Durkheim notes in *The Elementary Forms of Religious Life* (1995 [1912]: 228–9) regarding the magical qualities of certain objects:

> [t]he whole world seems populated with forces that in reality exist only in our minds. We know what the flag is for the soldier, but in itself it is only a bit of cloth ... A cancelled postage stamp may be worth a fortune, but obviously that value is in no way entailed by its natural properties. But collective representations often impute to the things to which they refer properties that do not exist in them.

A lightweight disc of acetate is in itself worth little and easily destroyed, but to do so would for some be a type of iconoclastic, sacrilegious act.

Crucially, it is not just the materiality of this object which is important, but also the fact that as a material thing it also embeds sound. Moreover, as we have illustrated in greater detail in the previous chapter, it is a sound of particular quality and formal properties. Hence it is the *kind* of materiality that counts, that is vinyl relative to magnetic tape or CD. All these things are material objects that are entangled with other objectual systems, but they afford different listening experiences and playing practices. This might seem obvious, but this multimedia dimension of vinyl is crucial to its popularity. As Wolfgang Voigt reiterated to us, 'vinyl is a picture and in this picture there is music'. Such a statement is a deceptively simple observation. Through the surface grooves of the material thing we access the music, but the object – like any icon – affords us an entrée to important histories of popular music, each of which has particular cultural and, ultimately, monetary value. In addition, therefore, one of its incredibly powerful features is that such sounds are historically and culturally located – that is, the fact that the medium has music 'printed' onto it and it is 'legends spinning around', as Voigt says; and that this music became a focus of widespread 'collective representations' among certain musical enthusiasts, as the classical sociologist Emile Durkheim alerts us to. This is why the aforementioned example of the Sex Pistols' acetate pressing can become exorbitantly expensive and why even a regular reprint of *Exile on Main Street* by the Rolling Stones costs twice as much as many other rock albums.

Clearly then, the music is not the only thing here – and this is a crucial point. Digital files also store or embed sounds, are portable and exchangeable, but (aside from the different types of digital format) no one digital file is different to another and in fact they are endlessly reproducible and circulatable. The provenance, seriality and historicity of the unique or rare material thing – the vinyl record itself as a material container or representative of this bundle of heritage features – creates an aura that is the product of its accumulated historicity and cultural meaning. This is what may turn such a thing into a valuable commodity.

Various releases of the same Sex Pistols tracks also occurred in 1977, this time on vinyl 7-inch and also released on A&M Records, which are valued between £7,000 and £8,000. The later Virgin release of the 'God Save the Queen' 7-inch vinyl single, backed with a different B-side and presumably released in large numbers to take advantage of the band's rising profile, are listed to be worth around only £10, though a copy printed with a plain blue sleeve without the iconic representation of the head of the Queen, of which the *Rare Record Price Guide* says only two copies are known to exist, is valued at £1,500. While rarity is therefore sometimes a product of serendipitous factors in the production process which cause random differences or even errors to occur in the end product, the general feature of rarity is the closer one gets to the original or first pressing in terms of seriality, the more valuable the item. To put this in a much wider context, a digital file of 'God Save the Queen' can be purchased for two US dollars; an original vinyl pressing can be worth up to 10,000 times more. The difference is accounted for in the 'magical' quality – the aura – of the material container that brings the person who possesses it into more direct contact with a legendary moment, famous group or iconic personality of pop musical history, or simply gives a feeling of owning something special. Reflecting on what this difference actually means in terms of rarity and the association of purchase with particular life events, the Berlin DJ and producer Andreas Baumecker takes us back to the crucial dimensions of possession and ownership deriving from owning vinyl versus digital files:

Andreas Baumecker: Yeah. I'm sure you can have that with digital files nowadays as well, but I think it's more disposable, it's more like a throwaway if you have a digital collection. You can't really call it a collection because it's just zeros and ones that you have. I don't call it a collection really.

Dominik: In this sense, vinyl is more like an artwork, as you said before, you can collect artworks, right?

Andreas Baumecker: Yeah, it's like an artwork. It can get as expensive as artworks too, if you look at prices. But some records are *just* artworks, we have to face it. It's just that you own something, it's the owning of music that is fascinating.

PATHWAYS TO VINYL'S VALUE: POSSESSING THE ARTEFACT

This dimension of ownership is of course a crucial dimension of possessions in general. However, because possession of vinyl records contrasts directly within the cultural field of music listening practices, the fact of possession takes on a special meaning. Ownership of things entitles a type of power to trade and exchange, but more often it extends the self and social identity spatially and also temporally. As Russell Belk has described, objects afford an 'extended self'. What this means is that aspects of identity, memory and feelings of security about one's past and future are materially anchored by objects. To *possess some particular thing* offers a type of social efficacy and power which undoubtedly references the resources enabled to make the purchase, but which also indicates belonging to particular cultural groups, eras and scenes. Exploration and communication of identity, belonging and cultural knowledge become embedded in object relationships. As Woodward has put it elsewhere, humans are 'object-seeking social actors'.[4] This drive to possess is obviously manifested in a near-endless variety of object transitioning practices in people's everyday lives, from the large and expensive to the mundane and inexpensive.

In terms of music consumption, material possession of music media adds an important dimension to materializing one's past and one's tastes in music. The material dimension afforded by vinyl is crucial and unique, and it has this potential affordance in common with other material carriers such as CD or cassette. Musical taste, the love of music, and cultural expertise are not adequately signified socially merely by storage of digital files and players, which are invisible to others because they are encased within digital playing machines like iPhones or iPods which also, because of their designed features, strongly communicate a range of non-music meanings. Once again, it is pertinent to recall Wolfgang Voigt's amusing comment about the futility of the digital collecting: 'Seriously, who would be impressed about this ... "These are my 5 million files". Wonderful! Congratulations!'

For individuals, possession of vinyl might invite opportunities to revisit and remember one's past. Here, there might be an element of nostalgia, but it by no means dominates and, importantly, such opportunities are also useful for understanding and defining self as having a biography of cultural consumption or tastes. Socially, the practice of material ownership affords the crystallization of a sense of self with a history stretching back in time. One can point to the cultural and taste dimensions of self, revealing to oneself and others a sense of continuity and change in the objects which contain musical sounds. In our interview with him, DJ and producer Andreas Baumecker talks about his formative interest in 1980s music, revealing the way his identity is formed partly in past musical experiences as one anchor of self-identity and cultural biography:

> *Andreas Baumecker*: The most expensive record that I bought on Discogs was just 49 euro. And I know lots of people buy stuff for 200 euro, but it's totally ridiculous. I would never do this. But, that was specifically a record that I really wanted for a long time, and it wasn't available for a long time. It's some new wave, kind of early 1980s thing and I wanted to have that beautiful track, and I needed to have it. These are specific records that I value way more than any house or techno that comes out. I value songs a lot. So there could be this one specific 12-inch from Depeche Mode, or let's say Pet Shop Boys, or even Lady Gaga, that I value, because the song or the

remix of it is so good that it will always be like one of my favourites, the one that I connect with a certain period of my life. This is what I value.

Dominik: Did you find some of these in stores? Or it's mostly online?

Andreas Baumecker: Not really, I think I found them all in the shops at the time, not necessarily afterwards, and only certain items that I had no clue that they existed. There are some records from the 1980s like ABC or Frankie Goes to Hollywood that I only wanted because they had a very special format to it, like a shaped 7-inch. Especially in the 1980s the record companies had money to do this. The 1980s were insane. Record companies spent so much money for just one song in various formats … Those shaped 7-inches look totally amazing, and the thought of having the money to do this in the 1980s is insane. It's really cheap now (on Discogs), but sometimes hard to find. You can say that I collect these things nowadays.

Dominik: So the 1980s would be a period of special attention for you?

Andreas Baumecker: I grew up then, I'm a total child of the 1980s. I think the best music came out at that time. The best pop music is from the 1980s. I'm totally inspired by it. That decade was inspiring, in itself. So much different music came out in the 1980s and I don't really know if there's another age, a decade, when it really happened that much. The 1980s, because of the new technology and instruments, were totally crazy.

PATHWAYS TO VINYL'S VALUE: FORMAT-BASED PRICE DIFFERENTIATION

A further exploration of the mechanisms of valuing vinyl which takes into account the different media an album is released on reveals the multidimensional character of the way music listening is economically valued. To do so, we head to Tokyo, to the jazz section of the famed vinyl collection at Disk Union, in the vibrant pop cultural hub of the Shinjuku district, Tokyo. Disk Union is in fact not just one store, but a conglomerate of many Disk Union stores spread through parts of Tokyo, with flagship and headquarter stores in the districts of Shibuya and Shinjuku. Even then, as is characteristic of many retail spaces in Tokyo, the stores are more like boutique, specialized retail spread vertically over a number of smaller floors within the same building, rather than expansively over one large space. The effect is that diggers are concentrated with other diggers searching for stock of a specific musical genre and the ambience and decorative style of each space contains the markers of the genres sold there. Disk Union Jazz spans three floors, with the third floor devoted to new and used classic jazz vinyl. The selection on offer is a treat for jazz aficionados, with a range of second-hand vinyl records in excellent condition.

The emphasis in Disk Union, as is apparent in the key record store sites of the Japanese second-hand vinyl market, is on quality and rare second-hand vinyl. The general condition of stock is carefully assessed, both in terms of the condition of the vinyl but also importantly the state of wear and tear to the sleeve. Both contribute to the overall value of any second-hand vinyl record. Disk Union Jazz focuses on classic European and American releases, with major jazz labels such as Blue Note,

Prestige and Riverside given heavy prominence in the store's stock. On the day of the authors' visit to Disk Union, in early 2013, a scan of the featured stock presented above the general vinyl bins reveals that the most expensive vinyl is a first pressing of Tommy Flanagan's 1957 album for Prestige records, *Overseas*, priced at 180,000 yen, or about US$1,800. Featuring a glorious green print cover in classic graphic Prestige style, the mono LP is listed as being in 'B' condition, meaning there is some wear to the sleeve and the vinyl but that the integrity of the vinyl is sound. The value of this version of the LP here is in the fact this is a *first pressing* of Prestige 7134, with this dimension of seriality being an important pointer to the LP object's auratic value. The fact that there have been many re-pressings of this same album on vinyl points to its status within the modern jazz canon as a classic of the jazz bop style and this fact also places the original pressing as the most valuable.

It is not merely a matter of age, but also proximity to the sacredness of the original LP pressing which enhances value. A search of the Discogs database shows seven re-presses of this album since its release, with reprints published in Japan, Sweden and the US over that time. In 2012 there was a vinyl reissue by the label Analogue Productions, a reissue label that owns a range of sub-labels, including the Prestige Mono Series. According to the label, 'true to its name, Analogue Productions – and APO Records – works exclusively with analog tape. All of the reissues from this label are mastered from the original analog tapes.'[5] In 2013, one could buy this release for up to around US$60 from Amazon, or on the Discogs marketplace for around US$60 sourced from various Discogs marketplace sellers around the world. At around the same time, a 1986 Japanese pressing of the vinyl could be purchased for around US$100. In terms of non-vinyl versions, a CD of the album could be purchased from Amazon for around US$12, or a 'SACD' enhanced compact disc format for around US$37. An iTunes download of the album costs around the same price as the CD version, at around US$10–15 depending on the version purchased. Rather ironically, one iTunes version of *Overseas* features on its cover an evocative close-up photo of a vinyl record being played, as if to directly associate this recording with the rituals and pleasures of vinyl listening cultures and the analogue era of music production. It suggests to the purchaser that the ideal way to listen to this classic LP is on vinyl, though at the same time it encourages a tap on the 'purchase' icon so clearly identified in iTunes.

PATHWAYS TO VINYL'S VALUE: SMALL-SCALE PRODUCTION

More recent and contemporary vinyl releases appreciate in value when there is a relatively small – sometimes limited to a few hundred – number of pressings, or when an artist has gone on to become more widely known or important. For example, Boards of Canada's second album, *Geogaddi*, was released on a variety of formats in 2002, including a triple vinyl LP release. In the intervening years, the band became more widely known, their albums critically acclaimed, and in 2013 they released their fourth LP, *Tomorrow's Harvest*, after a six-year hiatus. Pressings of the 2002 release of *Geogaddi* became immensely sought-after, and scarce, fuelled by a feeling among listeners and critics that this was the band's best release. Prices for the 2002 pressing in online second-hand markets are routinely in the US$100–200 range, and sometimes as high as 500, according to discussion boards. We asked Nikolaus, from Rotation Boutique in Berlin, how he goes about establishing the value of records he sells in his store and also online through the Discogs marketplace, and this is where the topic of Boards of Canada's *Geogaddi* came up:

Dominik: What about establishing the value of those more special records that you put on Discogs for example? You have a certain stock and you need to make a decision of how to price them, right? How does this process of deciding what's valuable and what's invaluable, how does it work?

Nikolaus: Well, sometimes it's just sheer hype. If the distribution puts something out with 300 units special limited, but it's not really special limited because nowadays most of them are 300 pressings. But, it creates some kind of hype. Just check on Discogs how many people have it, you text them like you would do with any other rare materials or objects. I do sell second-hand on consignment for people, so that just helps if someone is selling his collection they just hand it over to me for selling. I have a collection at the moment of DJ T because he quit and didn't want his collection, so he just gave it to me and I sell it through the store or Discogs.

Dominik: Yeah, what about the stuff from the 1990s? Do you see that there is interest in this stuff or that people value classic techno or electronic from the 1990s more than before maybe?

Nikolaus: It totally depends. For example, when the LFO album was re-pressed for the first time on double vinyl, which is for me, personally, one of the most prominent examples of Warp music, I bought twenty copies, which is a lot for me. And, I got stuck with maybe ten because the day it came in it was not half as interesting as it used to be before it was re-pressed. It's difficult, now they're re-pressing the whole catalogue of Boards of Canada, and I'm really excited and I'm gonna buy a lot. But sometimes, you just have to wait because it's so obvious now you have all the channels of distribution: you will get it at every mail order, you will get it everywhere so it's not really rare and if I ask the people at distribution to tell me how many they press of the vinyl – is it going to be two thousand or ten thousand? – they won't tell me. Maybe they don't even have the figures or they just don't know what Warp is going to release through Germany, Austria, Switzerland and the UK and US, but I guess it's gonna be an edition at least of five thousand, it's not really small, and five years from now it's gonna be a rarity.

Dominik: Yeah, I was thinking about the prices of the original *Geogaddi* album, for example, which is 150 euros right now.

Nikolaus: Yeah, it will drop.

Dominik: It will probably drop when the reissue comes, right? But then again, like you said, it can some time become a rarity.

Nikolaus: It just depends. Sometimes also you're missing the *Lego Feet*, that first Autechre project which is really weird compared to the early Autechre,

> like mushy and fucked-up beats. It didn't really sell as expected, so it's hit and miss sometimes with re-releases, but still I appreciate that they make it available again.

The strategy of limited releases fits with a production philosophy which is appropriately called 'small-batch', which we might also understand as boutique or niche production. This is what David Harvey[6] called 'post-Fordist' production, referring to a situation where conditions of production shift from an emphasis on mass and scale to one where production is oriented to short runs in relatively small numbers, which cater to increasingly fragmented, 'fast' consumer markets. In the terms proscribed by arch-postmodern French theorist Jean Baudrillard, the vinyl in these markets is situated clearly beyond the logic of being a utility, that is, merely a medium for music listening, as there now exist a range of media for distributing music in massive numbers via digital files. Instead, rather than having utility value, it must be seen in terms of its sign value. And this sign value relates partly to the relative rarity of its serial production, but also to its association with historical origins of this now-lauded indie electronic act. As Wolfgang Voigt communicated to us concerning the scale and economy of contemporary production in relation to his label, Kompakt:

> It's smaller, of course, but it's more exclusive and expensive. We've got structures that are able to earn money on a hundred, two hundred, three hundred records. If you got a real strained rate of production on one side, the maximum price and take the short connection to the customer, it's possible and people are thankful for that, you know? Because it's something that is only available on vinyl, and this is working. There are still records that sell a lot, some, but not like in '99.

For musicians and record companies releasing vinyl, production of the analogue record as a physical commodity involves certain risks and opportunities which have financial and material consequences. A substantial risk relates to overproduction of vinyl releases. The risks here are both symbolic and material. Materially, vinyl stock needs substantial storage space. Literally, vinyl takes up space and in large numbers its weight is substantial. For most vinyl shopfronts which exist, especially for specialist vinyl sellers, there is also a large storage room or basement that most customers never see. Access to it is restricted, though possibly the most trusted and special customers may occasionally access such a facility. Here, additional stock, stock kept for regular customers, or stock sold online is stored, though space is of course limited and ultimately costly. And the weight of vinyl means its physical presence needs to be dealt with. Even for collectors, possessing large stocks of vinyl means dealing with space and weight issues. Head of Brisbane's *Room 40* record label and multi-arts organization, Lawrence English, points out in our interview that not only his personal possession but also the stock of the *Room 40* label needs to be stored at his house and therefore any excess stock is a real burden in terms of storage and care: 'I have around 5,000 records at home. I still buy regularly. It's heavy stuff. Four thousand records equals more or less one ton of weight!' Lawrence goes on to point out that weight is especially an issue for an old property, where a ton of weight along one wall of an old house, for example, can possibly place a structural burden on it. Moreover, storage practices need to be carefully considered, especially in the sub-tropical climate of a city like Brisbane, Lawrence's place of residence, where moisture and mould could possibly infiltrate improperly stored vinyl releases. While storage of weighty and sizeable vinyl collections is certainly a problem to be dealt with, it has also become a means of aesthetic expression. The means of storing and displaying vinyl has become associated with design, style and decoration recently through the book *Dust and Grooves*, which aims to document collectors in their vinyl storage rooms, and also in features on websites such as *Resident Advisor*, where DJs and their vinyl collections are photographed. The ability of the vinyl commodity to communicate non-musical, lifestyle-related meanings is clear in these contexts.

Whether organized by the artists themselves or labels, boutique-scale production of vinyl is manufactured in numbers which are judged to be bought up relatively quickly within collector, fan and DJ markets. The symbolic importance of the 'sold out' banner for small-batch releases is real. Scarcity and selling quickly creates a situation and feeling of rarity among buyers and stores, thereby pushing prices up in online and physical second-hand markets and also enhancing the reputation of a record label. As Lawrence English pointed out to us, limited releases also help to create a mythology around a record label, which, we might add, has the consequence of suggesting to buyers and fans an urgency of purchase in relation to future releases. An opportunity to re-press for a second run of any vinyl release represents an economically rational decision which acknowledges the necessity of small-batch production in relatively small vinyl markets with niche audiences. This would apply, for example, to Lawrence's own label *Room 40* which releases experimental, sound art and ambient styles, and also in electronic and techno markets. The prestige of advertising the 'second pressing' is symbolically good for both label and artist. As well as allowing consumers who failed to purchase the first batch of a vinyl release to catch up with releases they have missed the first time around, the second pressing also hopefully distributes the re-pressed product to widening circles of buyers.

Andreas Baumecker puts this shift to small-batch vinyl production into the consumer's context, showing how this small-batch production mobilizes buyers and DJs to visit stores more frequently or consult weekly emails from record companies in order to stay up-to-date with new stock.

> *Andreas Baumecker*: This is very new actually, it's started three or four years ago, when the vinyl sales were so down, that the labels didn't have enough money any more to make thousands of copies that don't sell. So they started small, limited edition series, like 250 copies. This made me realize, 'Oh shit, I have to look out and go hunting again for this kind of music.' Because I really wanted to have this stuff on vinyl. Not all of it, of course, because not all of it is good. And also it's become some kind of a new thing, labels offering limited editions to make it a little bit more interesting, but the music is shit, so it doesn't make sense. A lot of this becomes a marketing strategy these days, too, which is a shame.

Dominik: So it's an artificial strategy?

Andreas Baumecker: How can I say this? There are a lot of vinyl records that are available only through 250, 300 copies, and are really, really good. Finding those records can be – if you are a little bit behind and didn't see it at first – it can be really tricky. And a bit more expensive to get those.

Dominik: It looks like there's these kind of strategies to make vinyl look expensive, it is not necessarily a reflection of an increased demand.

Andreas Baumecker: Yeah. But, at the same time, if you look at vinyl, if you buy a 12-inch at 9.95 or 8.95 euros, there's four tracks and they're all good, and you wanna buy it, let's say, on Beatport. You should not do it, you should not buy mp3s, you should buy a wav file for the 'better' sound … And if you buy this on wav file, it can happen that these four tracks are actually more expensive digitally than the vinyl, which makes totally no sense. If you wanna have an LP from an artist with five tracks, like mini album, you pay way more money on Beatport for the digital file if it's wav, than the actual vinyl. Why would I wanna buy digital if I can have something in my hand that that maybe sounds and looks better, for less? There's no selection to this.

Dominik: I'd like to return to this rarity thing. Not only in terms of vinyl, but also CDs. I actually didn't know it about the maxis released on CDs being so rare, so perhaps, it's that now LPs are rare, because albums released on CDs were ubiquitous, so maybe it's just about maxis.

Andreas Baumecker: Yeah, there are certain albums that are also expensive to get on CDs, and they're rare because they were not re-pressed (and still have dynamic range because there was no 'loudness war' happening at the time of their release). Probably because most of the stuff comes back as the gold series or something, or limited edition, or re-mastered or whatever, so all this old stuff comes back with new mastering, which maybe doesn't sound better, but there's a lot of stuff coming back. But there's also the maxi 12-inch, which contained remixes that sometimes are not even on the vinyl when it came out, which again makes those more interesting to have for collectors, and that makes the price go up, because if people find out that what they have is rare, they put the price up.

What this last observation by Andreas indicates is that as long as the musical format is physical rather than virtual the small-scale production effect is likely to exert its influence on value creation, regardless of the format. There are further examples of the creation of value of commodities through carefully curated and relatively restricted vinyl production. Consider the case of Berlin's inventive techno label, *Ostgut Ton*. In the first eight years since *Ostgut Ton* started, they have released 72 12-inches and EPs and 14 LPs, and many of them have gone on to be regarded as dance classics. Arguably, they constitute one of the most original blueprints for a new kind of electronic and techno aesthetics. Many of their releases are now priced relatively highly online or in second-hand stores. If you're lucky to see the early ones in second-hand markets, they're probably significantly more expensive than what they originally cost upon release. We asked label head Jenus Baumecker-Kahmke about *Ostgut Ton*'s approach to having a regular number of pressings and also whether the label had a re-pressing strategy:

> *Jenus*: In the beginning of the label, there was no strategy to keep pressings at a certain number, or something like that. And we don't have a problem in re-pressing records. I can't really say how many, but the only reason why some records would not be available anymore is because we always have complete artwork. So, for us, it doesn't really make any sense to do a re-pressing of just a couple of hundreds, because then the printing cost is too high. Unless you want to have a reasonable amount re-pressed, then financially it doesn't make any sense.
>
> *Dominik*: What would be reasonable these days? It's relative, but from the point of view of *Ostgut Ton*, what would you say is the reasonable number of vinyl pressings? A thousand or …
>
> *Jenus*: I don't know, it's difficult to answer that, but I think the re-pressing numbers are sometimes less than a thousand. It's OK. You really have to calculate quite carefully when you are in this business, because if you spend too much money on new vinyl productions, then at some point you're going to reach [a point] when your funds are gone. Maybe you'll have lots of records that are not sold. So, I don't know. We're always kind of very busy with the upcoming releases, planning new records and I think sometimes when records were not available, more expensive to buy second hand, it was almost like we just didn't have any time to think about it, so we still re-press older records sometimes. Our music is for clubs and for DJs to use it, so it doesn't really make any sense to keep it artificially low.
>
> *Ian*: There seems to be a strategy that some labels and artists use, it's to press relatively small quantities and batches, and hope that they all sell and that prices rise and this reflects on the artist or label, but that's not quite your approach, right?
>
> *Jenus*: I totally understand that and I also follow a lot of artists that press very small numbers and I think it does make sense in some cases, and I'm a big fan of it, really. We also started doing limited coloured rounds and stuff like that, which is just something, I think, nice for collectors. It makes it more enjoyable for them to obtain that special thing. It's a fun thing but it's not about limiting the music. I think the music should be available to everyone who wants to buy it on vinyl.

In this interview selection, we can identify that small-batch production of vinyl becomes a sign in its own right. It is not just that small-batch vinyl production could lead to scarcity and eventually higher prices, but that by itself small-batch vinyl production points to authenticity, commitment to artistic values of effort and vision ahead of profits, and to the distinction of being able to be consumed by small groups of consumers. The logic of small-batch production is economic, but is also supported by cultural meanings. The two clearly buttress one another. Here's another example from our interviews. Wolfgang Voigt appreciates the art side of vinyl manufacture and what he identifies as the techno philosophy that strikes a chord with the independent, hand-made and, perhaps, punk philosophy of DIY, anti-corporatist production:

Wolfgang: The diehard fan scene around the world who will always count on this kind of techno philosophy and they give a shit about people playing only with laptops or whatever, they do this thing. A very good Berlin example is the label *Pom Pom*, which is made by the guy from the *Spacehall* shop here in Berlin. He releases for ages. He used to be distributed by us. The records are always black, and just black. There's nothing on them. You never know who makes them. It's really dark, Berlin, stupid, wonderful stupid music, totally weird, 17 minutes bass line, he does this amazing break. They're called *Pom Pom* and he doesn't talk about it, or gives a shit – it's black and that's it.

Dominik: And it's on vinyl …

Wolfgang: 'It's on vinyl, vinyl only. Of course, only vinyl. One track on one side. But he's not sentimental. He's not nostalgic you know. We all come from this but we are not crying about past times, you know. People say 'OK, now, now … the horse wagons are gone because the cars are coming'. We're not sentimental on technologies of the past. Vinyl is still important, some people buy vinyl, some people don't.

For consumers, the scale of small-batch vinyl production can present some risks of consumption anxiety because it may lead to a questioning of the motives or artists, record companies or second-hand resellers. This represents a situation where the 'sacred' activity involved in the independent production and release of music can become 'polluted' by the visibility of profit-seeking and those who attempt to push up market prices. When profit-seeking behaviours are identified as being the prime motive behind vinyl production, the 'sacredness' of the vinyl object is brought under suspicion. For example, Record Store Day 2014 has been criticized in some online discussion boards and magazine articles as cultivating practices of profit-seeking, because some of those buyers lucky enough to secure its special limited vinyl releases then resell their purchase via online markets at inflated prices. Online debates continued in the wake of Record Store Day 2014 about the practices of these profit-oriented 'collectors'. Although he is obviously a huge supporter of independent music releases and the Record Store Day ritual, in his article for *LA Weekly*, titled 'The Column! Are You Collector Scum?', Henry Rollins has also hit out at what might be seen as the fetishization of the collector's impulse – that is, a strong desire for mere possession of collectible vinyl that is blind to authentic and real forms of cultural participation in musical communities. In characteristic style, Rollins tells it like it is in relation to what might be seen as the massification of small-batch production and the exposure of the limited edition product as a sign of profit-seeking, rather than independence:

> Limited-edition, colored vinyl, 7-inch single with a non-LP B-side? Wait, it gets better. The first of three singles all featuring the same A-side but different

> B-sides. Hold on – the 12-inch version comes with a live track and a demo version of the A-side, but not the non-LP B-side that's on the 7-inch. To hear it all, you have to get all six releases. If you are someone burdened by a real life, all of this is boring and yet another example of the cruel and unusual machinations of predatory capitalism.[7]

The uneven distribution of globally limited stock creates a situation where very few copies of vinyl stock might reach local stores, meaning demand can easily outstrip supply in local markets. This is turn can create hype about a release, potentially enhancing its economic value in secondary markets. Andreas Baumecker identifies this is in relation to limited edition releases of the noted electronic artist, Burial:

> *Andreas Baumecker*: Two years ago there was a Massive Attack/Burial release with 1,000 copies, which is nothing special [the number], but because I knew it was kind of rare and because I knew it was a rare Massive Attack/Burial collaboration and I would play it a lot at home, I bought two copies. It's this thing that they make you *think* it's very rare and they re-press it three months later that is really not cool. I mean, it's cool for people who don't have the record. But to make it sell at the beginning, they make it look like there's only 300 copies and then re-press it. That's not cool, that's totally ridiculous actually – as well as those Discogs sellers that have one of the first copies and then wanna sell them for 10 times as much ... Buying two copies of a rare record that I value very much and I know I would play the record very much is some sort of security; if it fucks up, I have a spare copy. It's not that I buy two copies of the record because it'll go up in price and then sell it again. I will consider it maybe, in a few years' time when there is no need to get the second copy out of the shelf, I will keep it to this day, but there's a lot of people who make a business out of that and that's not cool, I think. It doesn't value the record, it just takes the piss out of people who value it.

In our conversation in Kreuzberg, Berlin, with producers and DJs Domenico Cipriani and Alberto Marini who run their own Restoration Records in Berlin, and their friend Borut Cvajner, a DJ and vinyl fan from Croatia, this reselling of limited editions among vinyl communities in Berlin was described as a 'factory of speculation' by Borut. While admitting that, as true fans of dance and electronic genres, they would be willing to pay 50 euros or more for records they wanted to own, at the same time they disliked speculators and felt that while paying something like 100 euros for a classic record might occasionally be OK, paying that for a record just two years old challenged their values for buying music. Suddenly, in this case, we see that the motive of profit-seeking was made visible, polluting the authentic artistic values which give meaning to their interests as producers and music consumers. On the practice of limited releases of vinyl, Alberto comments: 'That's people just putting out just 100 copies, and then 200 copies of the same record, and they sell it', to which Borut adds: 'And they sell it for 30, 40 euros each. And that's not good. There's a big speculation about the records nowadays.' The dimension of rarity loses its auratic power when it is seen to be artificially created, stage-managed or a result of selfish speculative practices, but retains authentic power when it relates to small-batch production which objectively limits distribution to the relatively few motivated shoppers who are at the top of their digging game. This leads us to the question of commodities as fetish objects.

PATHWAYS TO VINYL'S VALUE: A SYMBOL OF EXPERTISE AND VEHICLE OF LEGITIMIZATION

Despite vinyl being a matter of taste and cultural preference for those who choose to listen to music on it, it remains the case that vinyl is an important symbol of expertise, distinction and skill within professional music, DJ and club communities and that this symbolization of expertise can trickle across to the non-professional segments of buyer markets. In conversation with Nikolaus Schafer, we suggest that the word which comes to mind to explain the power of vinyl in this context is *credibility*, to which he agrees:

> Credibility, exactly. Six years ago, someone told me that it's more like business cards you can have, it's visible: 'I'm standing out, I'm not in the mp3 business', and people regard it a bit higher, and that's why a few mp3 labels have started pressing vinyl … a lot of labels that are putting out vinyl because they think it's necessary but they lose money on it and they make good money on the mp3 sales.

We can see this as an example of how symbolic power may trump strictly economic calculation. Then and now, vinyl is a vehicle of symbolic legitimization in the music business. Consider Keith Richards's observation of this phenomenon from the time when he started his career: 'In those days, being able to get into the studio and get an acetate back sort of legitimized you … Playing live was the most important thing in the world, but making records stamped it. Signed, sealed and delivered.'[8]

Within professional circles this logic of legitimacy extends to the vinyl being a type of gift, a token often gifted from DJ to booker, musician to label, and peer to peer. Compared to the logic of digital file exchange, the gift of vinyl does not merely cement peer networks and relationships, it demonstrates one has seriousness, knowledge and the capacity of professional networks to 'make' a vinyl recording. Digital files are surely shared and distributed as promotional free downloads, but being material and artistic, anything on vinyl is bound to be worthy of at least a listen. Robert Henke explains:

> From an artist perspective, it has tremendous symbolic value to have a physical artefact. You know you write a blog, you have a website, it's one thing … But if you got your box with your personal copies of the book which has just been released on MIT Press, and it's lying right in front of the table, it's a very different thing, because it shows that someone was willing to put all this effort into your word. For the artist, having the vinyl in your hand implies 'I went through all of that and I succeeded' and even if I do it all by myself, or mostly

> by myself, the moment when I get the finished product and I get the vinyl in my hand, I really feel like I achieved something, there's a sense of achievement there. And also a sense of achievement which is a group effort. Someone made the graphic, there's a guy who dealt with the manufacturing coordination, there's the mastering of this, there's all these people involved, and it accumulates into having this artefact. And that's an important thing to have.
>
> *Dominik*: The artefact stands for the collective social effort. It's a materialization of the social enterprise.
>
> *Robert*: And it defines an end point, which is a different end point than the potentially soft end point of, let's say, an online spinning. Because you could always say '*oh I changed the order of tracks, oh I changed the cover*' and so on. The vinyl is the final thing and if you make the wrong decision concerning track number 5, you have to deal with it for the rest of your life.

Robert Henke continues, pointing out to us that this credibility of vinyl to symbolize expertise and competence within musical communities works for both consumers or buyers of music, as well as for its makers. The key uniting both sides of this one coin is the cultural stuff of authenticity – authenticity as a credible and warrantable performative sign which members of a cultural community perceive as integral to the values and beliefs of that community. In this sense, vinyl becomes a symbolic commodity, possession or production of which points to certain knowledges and expertise. In the digital age, music can be distributed more 'democratically', as most of our interviewees acknowledged, but this capacity to flow and seep into a greater number of spaces and corners is not necessarily associated with artistic quality. In fact, democratization of music production can lead to great innovation, but also possibly to questionable quality and loss of value. As Henke observes:

> Buying a record is also a commitment, it's much more a commitment than clicking on a link, and there's … it has a certain ritualistic reality. You buy something because you want to belong to a certain social group, or feel like you belong to a certain social group, or because it has meaning to you, and you feel like it has a different meaning if you have it in your hand. It also indicates from the buyer perspective that someone put a lot of effort in this, you buy a nicely designed record and feel OK. But you have a higher expectation about the quality, if you see a nice vinyl release, you expect that the music can't be complete rubbish. What do you expect if you click on a Soundcloud link? Someone hands me a vinyl promo, I know that these people went through a remarkable effort to get this done, and the chances are higher that I listen to it than if they just send me a link.

Jenus Baumecker sums the matter up this way, distinguishing between the 'machines' associated with compact disc production and the chains of human expertise involved in vinyl production. Clearly, vinyl is made by a machine every bit as much as vinyl, but its production is much more dependent on competence and human supervision, and forms of specialist and expert knowledge, as well as viable networked links to production and engineering networks: 'I think there's a lot of human work needed to make a vinyl, when for a CD it's basically a machine that makes it. If you don't have the right person at every stage of producing the mother and the pressing, [it's a problem]. Every step of the production process needs to have a professional who knows what they're doing.' Peter Runge notes that approximately 30 people are responsible for quality control of vinyl production during every shift at Optimal pressing plant.

We also heard from our interviewees an extension of this idea about expertise and vinyl production to an association of vinyl with quality – and the related association of digital with loss of quality control. For example, Domenico Cipriani notes that 'the quality has been going down for this thing, now everybody publishes the music on the internet, there's no quality control so everybody can put it out there ... Somebody downloads it, plays it, but it's all the same, so the quality goes very low. Vinyl keeps quality higher.' Michael Kunz observes, however, that there is another side to this story too:

> Sadly, for most people the value is not there any more. Why do they do vinyl? They do it because you have to do it. To get the full promotional thing, you have to do vinyl as well. They have to be in the record store. I mean, most people, they don't care about making music, they want to DJ. They want their two gigs a week. They want to be Ben Klock. Many people use vinyl as a promotional tool.

Andreas Baumecker notices the same circumstance:

> *Andreas Baumecker:* Those labels that have been on the forefront of producing vinyl, and also the owners of the labels, are still playing vinyl, they still do vinyl promos. What I find a bit ridiculous is that there are so many labels, and the owners of the labels, who don't even play vinyl any more, but they do vinyl records. That leaves me with a bitter taste because it doesn't make it feel real any more. There's something wrong. If I know that a label boss is giving me these vinyl records, but I know he's not playing vinyl at all but he's using Traktor [software] in the club, then I really don't know why this person is doing a vinyl label. It makes no sense for me.
>
> *Dominik:* Why do you think people would do that?
>
> *Andreas Baumecker:* I really don't know, I have no idea why they'd do this ... just maybe to please their vinyl fans, the audience that's still buying vinyl. But I'm feeling kind of fooled this way. There's a big part of the business, people doing vinyl for a long time, who haven't been playing vinyl for years, so I really can't take that seriously, I have to say.

PATHWAYS TO VINYL'S VALUE: ANALOGUE RECORD AS ART OBJECT

While vinyl points to artistic credibility, specialist knowledge, network cultural capital and the performance of authentic immersion in music scenes, it is also sensitive to time and space contexts where its meaning can be reversed or polluted. Vinyl fused with other symbols of authentic knowledge and practice represents fused performativity, where there is aesthetic fusion between the material and discursive, articulation and reception: 'a coming together of background meaning, actors, props, scripts, direction and audience' where performances are experienced as convincing or authentic by participants.[9] Vinyl thus achieves most symbolic purity when surrounded by other objects, people and other commodities of the same universe of meaning, and also in particular social contexts where its meaning is seamlessly understood by participants. For example, a white label 12-inch vinyl with nothing printed on it except a numeric code is virtually worthless to most people, but possibly of immense symbolic and economic value in certain listening communities. Thus, in contexts where particular symbols, scripts or actors fall out of alignment – for example, vinyl is sold in shopping malls and department stores, vinyl is sold alongside CDs, or vinyl is merely a front for extensive use of digital technologies of DJing – then its auratic power is likely diminished. As Jeffrey Alexander points out in relation to the pragmatics of social performance as a source of social power:

> [T]he challenge for social performance is to make its component parts invisible. If they are not invisible, action will *seem* to be performed. Not seeming to be contrived, making a performance seem real, is the *sine qua non* for successful performance. To create verisimilitude is to seamlessly string together performative parts. Everything must appear to be created for the here and now.[10]

Vinyl thus has autonomous iconic power, but the strength of its iconic performance also depends on the fusion of other performative elements.

The vinyl revival based on limited series releases represents a shift away from the industrial mass economy. It is yet one more example of what David Harvey famously called 'post-Fordist production' – small-batch production which was responsive to niche markets and which afforded the development of consumption communities based around real and perceived differences in the qualities and characteristics of commodities. In the case of vinyl production, this return to boutique, small-batch production is a response to the mass economy of the internet and the fact that music splinters into many hundreds of locally framed genres and styles. The arrival of vinyl as a boutique commodity expressive of aesthetic qualities and artistic choices comes at a time when digital has become the hegemonic for music listening. Lawrence English points out explicitly that the positive outcome of frenetic digitalization is that the dissemination of musical cultural history – and also musical innovation and creativity – is much more democratic these days. Yet, for all the appeal of digital distribution in terms of efficiency and cost, digital formats are for the most part unable to convey additional information with ease – metadata such as artistic packaging, photographic material, information about the recording – which complements and extends the meaning of the musical sounds embedded in the vinyl pressing. Lawrence English observed:

> The record for me is inviting. The CD case was unattractive and had no functional elegance, whereas the LP had a publishing tradition. There is a heritage. It allows an aesthetic language to be developed and fully articulated ... Today vinyl culture

becomes an art book experience. We buy because it is beautiful just like art books are beautiful.

It should be noted that Lawrence English's *Room 40* label also releases cassettes, and that this reflects a more widespread return to cassettes among independent artists. As handcrafted objects that also happen to encase sound, the cassette seems to be informed by a similar logic to that associated with the independent vinyl renaissance, which is characterized by an emphasis on redeeming just far enough out-of-date but enduring technologies which lend themselves to artistic reframing through crafted production. The common factor here is that the sound is reproduced through technological means whereby the methods of sound reproduction are analogue and visible, and crucially, the musical object is encased in concrete material packaging which lends itself to artistic intervention and interpretation under conditions of scale where production runs in the low hundreds.

Examples from around the world of artistic-musical projects released via small-scale vinyl runs abound. A couple of different instances help to illustrate the general principles at play. First we will turn to an artist who has released music on the *Room 40* label, Brisbane musician and artist Heinz Riegler. Riegler has released two cassette audio editions on *Room 40*. His works deal in part with the relationships of sound to landscape and place. In 2013, Riegler collaborated with visual artist Allyson Reynolds to release *Score for a Mineral Landscape*, resulting from an artist-in-residency period in the Blackall Ranges area of Australia. Released in an edition of 30 units, and priced at A$300, the box set contained photography, works-on-paper, an essay by Lawrence English, and a 180-gram black vinyl with the 19-minute musical score on one side and a silkscreen print by artist Matthew Deasy on the reverse. The release is hand-numbered and signed, and the materials presented in individual sleeves housed within an embossed, clam-shell solander box. The logic of vinyl as commodity with artistic affordance and meaning is also relevant to larger print runs. Seminal ambient and electronic artist Brian Eno released his first album for Warp Records in 2010, titled *Small Craft on a Milk Sea*. A limited edition vinyl offering of the release featured a double 180-gram vinyl release, accompanying CD release of the album with an additional CD of extra tracks, and a print of a lithographic artwork by Eno.[11] The release was carefully and artistically packaged in high-quality paper stock encased in a box set. The emphasis is on design and artistic quality, with descriptions focusing on the quality of the paper stock used, the limited nature of the production, being 250 copies worldwide. Currently, the box set can be purchased for approximately £75 on Amazon. The uses of vinyl as collectable, artistic package extend outside of the EDM and art world, with releases by local scene bands in both 12- and 7-inch formats. Brisbane band No Anchor, self-described as playing 'harsh out sludge by three otherwise well-adjusted men', released their album *Real Pain Supernova* in 2011, a blend of huge fuzzed-out bass riffs, noise and thudding drums, on double vinyl LP in two editions of 150 copies, now both sold out.[12] Characterized by music critic Everett True as Brisbane's 'beloved intellectuals and doom metal aficionados',[13] the band describe the vinyl release format in this way, which emphasizes the sonic and hi-fidelity quality of the release:

> Mastered by Mell Dettmer [who has worked with Sunn O)) and Boris] this is NOT a substandard vinyl pressing of our digital album. To the contrary, this has been mixed and mastered specifically for the vinyl format and sounds exactly how we'd like it to sound. Also: as the songs are spread across two LPs, none of the songs get too close to the centre of each side ensuring a high sound quality. (No Anchor, *Real Pain Supernova,* 2011)

In 2013, Brisbane independent band the Kramers launched a *Pozible* crowd-sourced campaign to fund the release of their debut single on 7-inch vinyl. Their statement on the *Pozible* campaign site, 'Help The Kramers release a 7-inch', went like this:

> Hey friends! For a real long time we have wanted to release a vinyl 7-inch but haven't been able to because we have been under-aged kids with no money.
>
> We decided rather than to go through stress with a record label we would do this release as DIY as possible, we just need your help!!
>
> As honest as I could possibly put it, we need a thousand dollars, this will get 200 of our records pressed, and our songs recorded and mixed. This will be a valuable piece of Brisbane garage history in years to come. The records will come in a hand-folded A3 sleeve printed with art work on both sides. Made with as much love and care we could possibly put into them. We seriously hope you can give us a hand, we are local kids who certainly need it!

With a target of A$1,000, the Kramers' *Pozible* campaign to release their single on vinyl was oversubscribed by $62! Their example shows how the vinyl medium has currency for young, independent-minded musicians, whose statement suggests they value vinyl for its iconic symbolization of an indie and DIY ethic in music production.

This logic of releasing music on a range of disc materials can be stretched quite a distance, with the analogue nature of the vinyl disc amenable to being cut in different media and through a variety of techniques which enhance the uniqueness of the vinyl commodity. New Zealander Peter King is famous for his 'lathe cut' records, and runs an operation which cuts polycarbonate records using a different technique to the traditional one. His approach favours small runs, and therefore independent and artistic releases, and he has pressed records for well-known international artists such as Beastie Boys, Pavement and Lee Ranaldo. His website states that:

> As of 2011 Peter remains the only person offering domestic record manufacturing in New Zealand (EMI famously dumped their vinyl press into the ocean in the 1980s so as to force the uptake of the CD format). The great advantage of lathe cuts, for international customers, lies in their cost-effectiveness for small runs (anything from 20 to 150 copies) when compared to pressed vinyl. In the 1980s Peter was the only person in the world offering such a service and after cutting records for NZ underground icons such as the Dead C and Alastair Galbraith his reputation went international. It wasn't long before the sheer volume of work he had piling up in his shed necessitated the building of another 2 machines. Peter built these new machines from scratch, recycling electric motors and machine parts from the likes of old washing machines.

PATHWAYS TO VINYL'S VALUE: PACKAGING

The wrapping of vinyl, in the form of the LP cover, is also a key to its success as a commodity. Although mass-produced vinyl is a serial copy, its material presence, capacity to develop marks of ageing either on itself or its cover packaging, and its visual scale which is large enough for public display but compact enough for ease of personal handling and possession, means that as a commodity it is amenable to the twin imperatives of personalization and aestheticization. Let's first consider vinyl as an aesthetic commodity principally, though not exclusively, through its external sleeve: the record cover. The format's material packaging is extremely relevant to its enduring popularity. The obvious attraction of vinyl in this context is the large size of the photo on the LP record cover, about 500 per cent larger than a CD cover, let alone the small accompanying images included in such applications as iTunes. The scaled-up visual and material dimensions of the vinyl package also lends itself to references to record covers as artworks in their own right. Many books on artistic popular culture have been devoted to reproducing 'the best album cover art', or indeed sometimes devoted to the worst, cheesiest or most tacky album covers. A notable example in the 'best' category are the celebrated vinyl record covers designed for *Factory Records* in the UK, reprinted in the book entitled *Factory Records: The Complete Graphic Album*, which highlight the artistic and design legacy of Factory's futuristic record covers and emphasize them as *designed artefacts* whose visual language affords an important function much greater than simply encasing the vinyl disc inside. Key designer for *Factory Records*, Peter Saville, developed a visual style which was entirely fresh, drawing upon modern shapes and colours and particular font styles to set apart his covers. Notably, in addition to record sleeves, Saville designed various posters advertising *Factory* releases and events which no doubt featured in record stores, clubs and on the streets of Manchester from 1978 through the 1980s. In fact, his first design – serially numbered as 'FAC-1', according to *Factory*'s catalogue system – was a poster advertising a *Factory Records* party event featuring a range of *Factory* artists such as Joy Division and Cabaret Voltaire and using the tagline 'Use Hearing Protection'. The poster was reprinted in 2003 in a limited edition run of 500, demonstrating generally the relevance of material heritage, be it vinyl records, posters, costumes or musical instruments, for sustaining the mythical nature of music scenes. Saville was awarded the London Design Medal in 2013. Speaking in conversation with Peter Morley at the Global Design Forum in London, 2013,[14] Saville aligns his record cover designs with any other designed everyday objects, from cigarette packets to cinema tickets. Reminding us that the record cover is frequently seen as working together with the music, Saville commented that 'you can do great work for a mediocre record and no one talks about it. You can do mediocre work for a great record and everyone calls it iconic. The iconic label that much of my work has is because the records were fundamental to many people's lives.'[15] Saville has produced some of the most memorable and stunning record covers in pop music history, but what distinguishes them is their stylistic integrity, their relative semiotic arbitrariness, and their design qualities. Saville, for example, designed the iconic covers for Joy Division's *Unknown*

Pleasures LP, and New Order's *Power, Corruption and Lies* LP, among many others.[16] Writing in a feature article about Saville in the magazine *Wallpaper*, Nick Compton commented that:

> Saville's covers were something entirely new. They were mysterious (the covers for *Power, Corruption and Lies* and *Technique* made no mention of New Order whatsoever) and challenging. They were cool, though for reasons you didn't quite understand. And, for many, they were signposts to somewhere else, somewhere better or, at least, way more interesting. They were a gateway drug.[17]

Continuing, Compton talks about how he would place Saville's New Order LP covers face-forward at the front of his shelf, showing them off and swapping them around depending on his mood and to freshen things up, and how he played the vinyl, flipping it from side to side 'in an act of Holy Communion'.

PATHWAYS TO VINYL'S VALUE: VINYL AS MATERIAL HERITAGE

Because of its figuring as the sonically perfected, technologically hegemonic format for music listening up to the period of around the late 1980s, there is a perception of the vinyl record as the 'classic', 'real' or 'authentic' format for certain, if not most, types of music listening experiences. This perception allows vinyl to take on an aura of authenticity – as something constructed and experienced within particular settings – as an iconic medium of musical heritage, which in turn allows for its further (re)commodification.[18] For example, listeners who value high-fidelity sound reproduction and engagements with music heritage may consider that the 'best' way to hear an early album of the Rolling Stones or Miles Davis is via the format for which it was prepared and on which it was originally released – the vinyl LP. These artists and their oeuvre are coded as essential parts of the modern music canon. Importantly, serious listeners commit to the vinyl format as the preferred way of hearing and understanding – rather than merely listening to – these heritage acts. Sound and style, not just melody, are at stake.

This association of vinyl with canonical musical performances is expressed in the current patterns of vinyl production, especially in the reissue of classic albums in rock, indie and jazz genres. Catalogues such as Universal Records' 'Back to Black' series, for example, reissue important and popular albums in the rock and pop canon on high-quality vinyl pressings, and the Blue Note jazz label reissues canonical albums by artists such as John Coltrane and Miles Davis on heavy 180-gram vinyl formats. The record label *4 Men With Beards*, self-described as 'one of the pre-eminent vinyl reissue labels in the world', is another example. A simple analysis of their online catalogue shows a variety of key vinyl reissues by artists who are either important in the canon of alternative rock, such as the Velvet Underground, Iggy Pop, Wire and Bauhaus, or essential soul and jazz artists like Nina Simone, Aretha Franklin, Miles Davis and Herbie Hancock. This is a finely curated catalogue of reissues. The case of *4 Men With Beards* is significant because, for the most part, its releases are not focused on the most celebrated albums by these artists, such as Davis's *Kind of Blue*, Serge Gainsbourg's *Histoire de Melodie Nelson*, or any of Dylan's celebrated first clutch of LP records. While major labels and the public retain an interest in these iconic, relatively high-selling vinyl reissues, *4 Men With Beards* offers the rare and lesser-known releases from these artists, for example the latest reissue of Miles Davis's 1970s concert performances *Pangaea* and *Dark Magus*. In this sense, they encourage the use of vinyl as a way to engage with the complete and hard-to-find canon of 'important' music by key artists of earlier, often culturally formative modern eras. Vinyl's recommodification in this context rests with the mobilization of discourses of heritage within the pop-rock canon, and the promotion of vinyl as a key way to experience this.

As the previous section suggests, vinyl releases also have an advantage of material scale which is able to present the cover art in a size amenable to domestic or public display and which reinforces the idea that the vinyl package is a tangible component of musical heritage. The LP format's material packaging is relevant for understanding its aura, because it is the scale of 12-inch vinyl releases which are best able to convey important contextual information about the recording, not least of which is the cover image, but also inclusive of liner notes about the playing and production on the release. This facet of the vinyl as commodity means that some of the images used as album covers enter the popular imagination and become iconic. In the case of the Beatles' album *Abbey Road*, for example, one of the highest-selling reissue vinyl in recent years, the cover image is extremely well-known. In fact, it might be considered one of the iconic images in popular culture, and is frequently recreated and referenced by tourists and other media alike. The obvious attraction of vinyl in this context is the large size of the photo on the LP record cover. The scaled-up visual and material dimensions of the vinyl package also lend themselves to references to record covers as artworks in their own right, as we discussed above. Of course, there are many books devoted to vinyl cover art across musical genres but often focusing on jazz and certain iconic labels or cover designers, such as the Factory example discussed above, but also 4AD, and a range of jazz labels including ECM, Blue Note and Prestige.

PATHWAYS TO VINYL'S VALUE: SPECIAL FEATURES AND AESTHETICIZATION

But the most recent vinyl renaissance seems to be going well beyond just the scale of the cover art as a way of giving sensual expression to the materiality of vinyl and to enhancing its value as a commodity. Recent new and re-releases incorporate a range of other special material features which encourage the attractions of buying vinyl, relative to CDs and digital downloads. First is the increasingly frequent use of the heavy vinyl pressing. Standard vinyl releases have been pressed on 140-gram vinyl. Heavier pressings – frequently 180-gram pressings, but sometimes 200 or even 220 grams – are more durable and resistant to warping and are often advertised to buyers as 'Audiophile vinyl', though for the non-audiophile buyer the heavier editions have a pleasing heavyweight feel suggesting the importance of the musical content and also increasing the longevity and collectability of one's purchase as an apparently legitimate item of heritage. Other ways of promoting the distinctiveness of vinyl as a listening format include the use of coloured vinyl (although this idea has been around for a long time, it seems more popular in recent times as a way of promoting the collectability and specialness of vinyl). Some releases, for example, may press just the first few hundred copies on specially coloured vinyl, with the remainder pressed on black vinyl, in order to tap the impulse of collectors and enthusiasts. To use again Miles Davis's iconic oeuvre as yet one example, the 50th Anniversary Edition of *Kind of Blue* released in 2009 contains a transparent blue 180-gram vinyl record, plus exquisitely printed pictures and a richly illustrated, hard cover book about the cultural significance and production of the album. The release obviously costs much more than a standard vinyl or digital copy, but it clearly builds upon the idea that the album is an important part of jazz music heritage, and modern pop culture heritage more generally.

While music buyers will generally pay at least 100 per cent more for a new release vinyl album compared to a download, many new vinyl releases come packaged with a download voucher for the complete album, and sometimes additional special features like a cover art poster (for example, as in the re-releases of the well-known and famed photographic record covers for the band Roxy Music). Although a buyer might pay a little over twice the price for a vinyl record than a digital download, with the vinyl they not only get a download voucher but also the pleasure of possessing a large, artistic cover art sleeve. The latter quality may play a particularly critical role for the consumers of remix EPs (Extended Play) that rarely, if ever, contain download vouchers but happen to come in beautifully crafted sleeves – think again about Roxy Music's *Remix # 01*, exquisitely packaged in a well-designed gatefold sleeve and produced by independent London-based company The Vinyl Factory. The Vinyl Factory is a notable example of the way reissues and new releases are blended in ultra-high quality, collectible artistic packaging, as they describe: 'The Vinyl Factory is an independent British company that collaborates with musicians and artists to create ultra-premium handmade limited editions and accompanying exhibitions.'[19]

So, the power of vinyl's materiality in affording certain aesthetic opportunities is clear, but let's just briefly consider two further examples from our interviews. The power of the vinyl record stored en masse and in the domestic context is something that strikes a number of our interviewees and is also an important visual design convention, more generally. Phillip Sollman tells us that 'there are only some things that are as beautiful as record shelves, honestly' and that in preparing his new album titled *Decay* (Dial, 2014), he paid close attention to the cover design and material used for the album:

> I think the most important aspect about having records is that you can browse through them, you can look at them, you can use them like a picture, you can read and open the cover. That's why I'm really looking forward to the release of this one with a full cover artwork which I think is going to be my most beautiful record so far because it will have a different paper than this. We wanted to have it a bit like Japanese silk paper which uses also this indigo blue and these mountains

> are from Kyoto, so this is a collage of the mountains that were surrounding me while I was doing the music.

This intention of making a designed artefact to encase vinyl is something consumers also feel as a point of attraction to the vinyl as commodity. Dominique Lebel, a university student from the Gold Coast in Australia, purchased a *Deutsche Grammophon* release of Joseph Haydn's Symphonies 15 and 18 in a sprawling second-hand book and vinyl store in Fremantle, Western Australia. *Deutsche Grammophon*'s covers could also be considered iconic – their stylistic identity signifies classical music and their yellow-framed brand symbol is prominently placed on all LP covers. This particular cover features a glorious early modern painting of a woman. Not being a particular fan of classical music, Dominique comments on her reasons for buying this particular LP. Her reflection brilliantly points to the way the aesthetic features of the vinyl packaging can function even without primary reference to the music contained within the pressing:

> I could have chosen any record but as I said it was a two-fold attraction and the main reason I purchased this vinyl was that I found it visually appealing. The illustration is of a woman, which I felt overwhelming seduced by as I love this style of femininity, beauty, and of a Marie-Antoinette-esque era of excess, decadence, opulence and frivolity that appeals to me on a grand scale. So as unrealistic as it may appear, by owning this particular illustration I felt closer to achieving that ideal in my own life. Also I have a sentimental relationship and fascination with owning things and engaging with elements of that 1700–1800s life and culture of Europe. I've used the vinyl initially on display in my room and have recently moved it into the lounge room with my other records so I can play it!

More than just decorative packaging, both 7- and 12-inch vinyl can be presented in covers which enhance certain aesthetic affordances. As Kompakt Records' Wolfgang Voigt told us, the market for vinyl has changed from mass to boutique. People are now increasingly willing to pay more in order to get an aesthetically enhanced musical commodity. In the post-industrial markets for vinyl, price can now be a symbol in its own right, as Voigt identifies. Taste and distinction come into play. In the language of economists, demand for small-run vinyl releases are relatively price-inelastic, increasingly because of this aesthetic dimension, as Voigt identifies in relation to Kompakt's vinyl releases:

> On the one side, the die-hard of vinyl fans, they didn't buy for a certain period, price was important. The cheaper you are, the more you sell. But this mentality is a bit gone now, for a lot of people. When you get an interesting record, you don't care about paying 10 or 12 euros. It's not about this cash thing anymore. Vinyl has seen its down point let's say like 6 years ago. Meanwhile, it's coming back, there's a certain revival. At the same time, it's a luxury, collector's item. It's designed by individual artists, it's limited stuff like that and people buy as collectors, they want to have it on the wall, or in their furniture and in their record furniture at home. It's cult. Me personally, I do not think it's ideological or political any more, it has to be ... I say it's just a question of taste.

For Kompakt, the visual design of their record covers, for both 12-inch and LP vinyl releases, is presented using a distinctive, minimal inspired line of coloured dots or bubbles. Voigt explains the artistic inspiration for his ideas in art terms:

> I was coming from pop art and I was always feeling like this kind of Warhol idea, serial things. I like serial designs, minimal like make something like yellow dot, red dot, green dot, to push the collectors' impulse: 'You have the red one, you have the blue one.'

In contrast to Kompakt's main line of minimal techno releases, the 'Kompakt Speicher' series is accompanied by a large and brightly coloured representation of the city of Cologne's coat of arms, and has become a larger symbol of the Kompakt label, which is centrally on display at Kompakt parties and events in the forms of the Kompakt flag. Voigt continues:

> This eagle, this Kompakt Speicher icon, which hangs around, which is massive, like this, you know? And when we made this, it was a huge success directly, people liked it and then techno was not anonymous anymore; we had the logo and this was Kompakt, you know. Because the anonymous thing on records was good and right for a certain time, then it was not alright anymore and then we needed names, because techno also needs glam, and colours and also pop stars, you know. It's okay to be just somebody who makes great music and nobody knows you but you also need guys like Sven Väth, someone who brings glam shit into it.

Jenus Baumecker-Kahmke also emphasizes the importance of the visual dimension of *Ostgut*'s releases. Jenus works with the label's artist, Yusuf Etiman, a visual artist, in designing the sleeves for *Ostgut*'s output. Working directly with the artist, there is a back-and-forth process of selecting covers, but the bottom line is that the release must look like it's an *Ostgut* product, with distinctive font scales and types, and a suitably gauzy photograph as background, vaguely reminiscent of the 4AD sleeves designed by Vaughan Oliver in the 1980s and 1990s, which Jenus cited to us as an important point of inspiration:

> I think for me, the visual aspect of the label is, it kind of got me into collecting music when I was like a teenager, because there were certain labels that I found so attractive from the visual packaging that I would become a fan of the label and I would buy the next record without even having heard it because I wanted to have all of them. And at *Ostgut Ton* we just created a very clear graphic identity; we always use same font and same size. And that's kind of a limitation in a way that we put upon ourselves, but it also leaves us free to be very expressive with the visual, with the imagery, the photography, because it always gets tied with the same font. And the art that we use is strongly linked to the visual identity of Berghain and Yusuf who does all the layouts; he also does the Berghain flyer every month. So he does those two things, and even though they have separate identities though they sort of belong together aesthetically. Visually we're very tied to the whole Berghain thing, I think ... A lot of the visual artists that we use

> for our artwork are people that we know who are friends with the house that we've worked with on other levels, you know?

For the independent and small-batch releases, it's often a matter of DIY artwork, but this is identified as positive by Domenico and Alberto of Berlin label *Restoration*: 'Having our independent label means having the control of all the things, so that's good.'

ONLINE AND VIRTUAL VINYL MARKETS

The growth of interest in digging and vinyl culture more generally is promoted by a number of online developments, including a proliferation of stories and blogs about digging, a range of mobile device applications ('apps') developed to assist and augment vinyl record shopping and crate digging, and a number of websites devoted to documenting record stores. Notable sites include 'The Vinyl Record Collector Blog', 'Melbourne Vinyl', 'Record Junkie', 'Crate Kings' and 'Crate Digging', with a range of associated Facebook sites, including 'Strictly Vinyl', 'Vinyl of the Day' and 'The Vinyl Factory'. Many of these sites and groups are run by amateur collectors and enthusiasts, documenting the spaces of record stores they have visited, and often the covers of notable vinyl records purchased. For example, 'The Vinyl Record Collector Blog' is run by an amateur vinyl collector, who states on the site that: 'I've been collecting Vinyl for many years. Mildly obsessed. I travel quite a bit and when I travel to a new place, the first thing I do is find all the second-hand Vinyl shops, flea markets, etc. and I go to as many as possible'; while the tagline of the site 'Melbourne Vinyl', again run by a local vinyl enthusiast, makes uses of a popular vinylist slogan in its tagline: 'Vinyl Kills MP3: My mission is to visit every record store in Melbourne, Australia, in 2013.'[20]

Much of the remarketization or reselling of vinyl depends on matters of context and quality. Part of the excitement around the second-hand vinyl market, and indeed the enchantment, is in the chase for collectibles, colloquially known as 'crate digging'. The digger never knows what they might find and at what prices it might be offered. As we have suggested, digging is a type of serendipitous urban archaeology, akin to shopping for second-hand clothes or old furniture. The cultural added value resides in rarity and serendipity factors, both hardly available in the experience of the internet surfers. Of course, today the second-hand markets for vinyl are supported by internet markets such as 'Discogs' and increasingly by mobile phone applications such as 'Vinyl District', 'Discollector', 'Cratedigger' and 'iCrates'. This merging of the two spheres illustrates the point of the internet creating not simply a virtual, but also an augmented reality. For example, the iCrates app lets diggers do a search for any vinyl or CD they might want to know about, which can be especially useful for checking comparative prices while digging. iCrates gives users all information about the release, including label and catalogue number information along with a 'rarity rating' for each particular edition based on the 5-point scale, and then links externally to the comprehensive Discogs site which in turn allows diggers to access online markets where they can see different price offers by a variety of registered sellers, and obtain information about the price, condition and location of any vinyl they may want to purchase. This represents the globalization and virtualization of digging. While it lacks the excitement associated with physically visiting stores, it does allow the rapid dissemination of market information to diggers and it also allows vinyl to move to interested listeners around the world. Additionally, many physical stores – such as Rotation Boutique or hhv Selected in Berlin – also hold Discogs marketplace accounts and can send backroom vinyl stock to customers globally. Finally, many of the boutique record labels which are run out of physical stores also operate extensive mail order operations. German labels which also have a physical location in the form of record stores such as Kompakt in Cologne or Smallville in Hamburg ship vinyl worldwide, similarly with UK-based techno electronic labels such as *Honest Jon's* or *Hyperdub*. For fans of these specialist or sometimes micro electronic genres it means they are guaranteed access to vinyl editions which are mostly limited to small batches and often only available in local stores which are linked to particular music scenes.

For example, for fans of the Smallville label's characteristic take on minimal techno, the most complete stockist will be the Smallville store in Hamburg. For those fans of this genre unable to make frequent visit to the store, mail order is possible. The cost of packaging and the risks associated with sending vinyl – a relatively fragile and cumbersome object – are substantial, and add significantly to the final cost of purchasing records online. In addition to the environmental issues some might see as associated with vinyl production – for example, Niko from Rotation Boutique raised this matter of 'selling PVC' in our interview with him, as it contradicts his personal values and also the other local and ethical goods he sells in his store – mailing costs can also add many flight miles to the wider costs of vinyl consumption. At the same time, of course, contemporary independent labels, such as Clone Records from Rotterdam, release store-only series of their vinyl. It is also the case that shops usually sell unique vinyl at lower prices than online markets based on such all-containing websites as Discogs. For example, one of the authors has recently bought two original and well-preserved copies of *The K&D Sessions* in London and Vienna, each copy way below 100 euros. Recently, Miles Davis's rare European concert performance LP *Double Image* was priced at 90 euros online, whereas an excellent copy of it could be purchased for 40 euros at the same time in one of the biggest second-hand vinyl stores in Frankfurt. Last but not least, store-based buying enables one to carefully inspect a vinyl's condition in person and play it, whereas virtual marketplaces like Discogs give seller-generated classifications of vinyl condition and any notes relevant to describing vinyl wear and visible damage.

Andreas Baumecker neatly sums up the dilemmas associated with digging in the digital age. It's not as if one doesn't dig, but that digging is now augmented, assisted by online samples, and in the case of high-profile professional DJs, promotional digital files provided free by record labels. For busy professional DJs, it's not as if the ritual of digging has lost its excitement, but that time and the overabundance of recorded music which is digitally available simply doesn't make digging an easy pastime to engage in. On the other hand, and as a countervailing force, changing production markets which have led to small-batch production means buyers might be forced to dig more efficiently for vinyl stock and react much quicker to what's going on in the market:

Dominik: Do you still dig? Or is it mostly about scanning the market online, checking only certain labels? How do you acquire records?

Andreas Baumecker: I definitely have less time to go to record shops and dig. I do it in a different way. I actually have the possibility of ordering online, in a shop where I don't have to buy the records afterwards. If they come to the shop, I can go through the records, listen to them, and then choose which ones I wanna take, so I order quite a lot of records that come to my mind, I'm checking if it's good or not, and from that amount of records that come to the shop I choose which ones I want to buy. So that's how I buy records now. I receive a lot of digital promos ... but it's so much, that I really don't know when to listen to that stuff, sometimes, I just do it because I'm interested in the artist who sent it, but if there's too many artists, I find it really hard to listen to digital promos, I'll probably delete them, which is maybe not nice, but I don't have the time to do it.

Dominik: I remember that in the *Fabric* interview you had mentioned that a part of the fascination that you have with vinyl is the hunting for records, and the rarity of some of the records ...

Andreas Baumecker: Yeah! This is very new actually, it's started three or four years ago when the vinyl sales were so down, that the labels didn't have enough money anymore to make thousands of copies that don't sell. So they started small, limited edition series, like 250 copies. This made me realize, oh shit, I have to look out and go hunting again for this kind of music, because I really want to have this stuff on vinyl. Not all of it, of course, because not all of it is good. It has become some kind of a new thing – labels offering limited editions to make it a little bit more interesting, but the music is shit, so it doesn't make sense.

IMAGINED COMMODITY

One principal point that should be obvious to the reader from our descriptions is that vinyl is a commodity that circulates through multiple markets and carrier groups. Here, the distinction between new and second-hand vinyl matters. Moreover, vinyl is a commodity whose value is established in relation to multiple features of the object itself, such as marks of wear and tear, through its seriality production and patterns of its release and distribution through global markets, and through processes related to the rise and fall of artists and bands. Vinyl records by the Beatles and the Rolling Stones are still highly sought after and collectible across all vinyl markets, with value rising depending on the date of pressing, etc. On the other hand, second-hand vinyl records by pop acts of the 1980s like the Thompson Twins, Haircut 100, and Adam and the Ants are generally very cheap to purchase and reasonably plentiful in second-hand stores we have visited. Leftover or 50 cent bins generally testify to the forgotten decades of artists whose vinyl releases are no longer wanted except by the occasional collector and the dedicated, vigilant digger.

As much as *Pelican West* was a very pleasant light pop listen, its charms are now not widely known or appreciated, and it simply cannot compare to an early pressing of *Exile on Main Street*, *Blood on the Tracks* or *The White Album*. Simply, early vinyl pressings of canonical pop-rock acts become more valuable, more quickly.

This general observation can be qualified, however, when we take into account the relevance of location. In the right store, the first pressing Stones LP becomes a glittering prize with prime location above the vinyl stacks. In other stores, it simply won't be stocked, or it would be constantly overlooked by customers. Similarly, we observe that in markets like Berlin's famous Sunday Mauerpark markets in the district of Prenzlauer Berg, the many second-hand vinyl sellers are more likely to prominently feature vinyl from the Krautrock canon, Can, early Kraftwerk and Neu!, as well as from artists who might once have been associated with the city: the many albums by David Bowie or Nick Cave and the Bad Seeds are not only more available in Berlin, but seem to demand higher prices in the city because of the bands' mythical association with Berlin scenes in the second half of the 1980s. It is also no accident that Berlin's Mauerpark markets are a key tourist attraction, and musically literate fans might be willing to pay a few euros over the odds to take home some vintage Bad Seeds vinyl. Scarcity and rarity are objective matters, but they are relationally established. The contexts of production and commodification of other formats play an important role. Scarcity can also be manufactured and fit nicely with the ideology of much current vinyl production where the philosophy of craft, boutique and small-batch finds close partnership with strategies of distinction, and ideologies of DIY and credibility in musical artistic communities.

The reinvigoration of vinyl as a commodity has been remarkably successful also due to its association with the pop-rock canon, and the recent phenomenon of reissuing classic rock and jazz albums on vinyl. Of course, as we have shown, vinyl is extraordinarily amenable to this pattern of re-release as its physical scale and obvious capacity to be handled makes it a candidate for directly experiencing the heritage of the pop-rock canon. From gatefold sleeves, to heavy vinyl, to coloured vinyl, to vinyl mastered using different techniques, to including posters with albums, to including original liner notes or to adding in digital download codes with vinyl purchases: all these things enhance the ability of vinyl to materialize the experience of musical heritage. Fans of the Smiths may recall Morrissey's lyrics for the song 'Paint a Vulgar Picture', which seems to be apt here: 'Re-Issue! Re-Package! Re-Package! Re-evaluate the songs, Double pack with a photograph, Extra track (and a tacky badge).'

Matters of rarity in the second-hand markets are also connected to sometimes hardly distinguishable dimensions of myth and reality. Mythical notions of digging (discussed in Chapters 2 and 5) and stories of finding rare gems in yard sales are the currency of such discourses. Of course, there is always a mutual co-existence between vinyl and digital markets, not only in terms of recent vinyl releases including download vouchers, but in terms of the digital redistribution and playing of vinyl tracks, for example by DJs. A rather fascinating example demonstrates this point. In April 2014, the project 'CAT023 Caustic Window – Own the Legendary Record by RDJ' was posted to the crowdfunding site Kickstarter.[21] Only four vinyl test pressings of the album were apparently ever owned, one by the artist himself, Richard D. James, aka *Aphex Twin*. This album had never been heard outside those circles and was never to find commercial release. That is, until one of the four people in possession of a test pressing decided to offer it for sale at a very high asking price, around US$9,000 – too much for any one person to afford. Instead, a deal was struck with the artist and his record company to buy the album, convert it to a lossless digital format, and distribute the digital file to those who contributed at least US$16 to crowdfunding the purchase of this rare vinyl, described as 'the holy grail' of electronic music releases on the Kickstarter site. This example nicely illustrates the auratic power of the rare vinyl, but shows how digital cultures of crowdsourcing and musical files allow the material to become digital. We wonder how long it would take for illegal digital copies of the album to surface.

Against all of these factors of markets, it remains only to show how vinyl's price value is essentially animated and established through human means. Simply, it has to be. As Robert Henke points out, 'the value comes from the perception, so if people are excited, if they talk about it and write about it, this is the value'. To understand it fully we propose to consider vinyl as a type of fetish commodity that enables and encourages creative, devoted practices of sacrifice, effort and love, instead of promoting one-dimensionality. Without these impassioned drives and desires to possess vinyl, and the accompanying discourses of heritage and value which are attached to it, vinyl would of course become a victim of technological progress rather than a survivor. But what we actually observe is that it evinces the power of something that could be called a positive fetish.

For the most part fetish is understood as an entirely negative phenomenon, associated with Marxist critique of capitalist economy, or the Freudian idea of displaced desires. Heavily influenced by the singular vision of Marxism, sociology and cultural studies largely missed unorthodox ramifications of fetishization. To make a long story short, 'wanting too much to demystify the fetishism of tools and equipment, we lose sight of their very reality'.[22] The case of vinyl allows us to distinguish different valences of fetishization. While commodity fetishism signifies obsessive, potentially exploitative and narrow-minded compulsion which appears to distort the relation between person and thing, fetish more broadly understood can also redeem this relation. Fetish mobilizes cultural effervescence, dedication and personal commitment. It enables and inspires sacrifice that would otherwise be representative of pain and unacceptable effort. This passion stems partly from deep-seated human need, or even carnal desire, to ground our sense of reality through attachment to actual, concrete objects made by other humans, for example manufactured commodities. Robert Henke describes it in a lucid way:

> There are things that probably don't change, we can think about the virtualization of this world in many ways, but one thing doesn't change, we have bodies and we are still talking about us, we're not talking about an abstract construction, we talk about human beings. We are tactile, we respond to temperature, we respond to smells, to taste, to physical textures and we would probably never choose an avatar towards our partner we love, and so the virtualization of the world has certain limits. We like good physical products.

Sometimes getting such good physical products requires all kinds of sacrifices which only increase their value. Such sacrifices often mean significant monetary and time investment. Moreover, a fetishistic attitude directed to such products is conducive to a heightened level of dedication without which the extraordinary efforts would be hard to justify or sustained in the long run. Participants sense their devotion is somewhat beyond rationality, but immerse themselves nevertheless as a way of exercising creativity and coming into contact with everyday Gods.[23] The fetishistic kind of dedication allows utter immersion within a meaningful universe of a given phenomenon. A collector's passion provides us with salient insights into this positive spirit of fetishism.

Consider the story narrated to us by Phillip Sollmann. He has been assembling the comprehensive collection of multiple vinyl pressings and releases of a single album by Donald Fagen entitled *The Nightfly*. Apart from it being an early example of digital recording released on vinyl (1982), there is nothing particularly special about it. However, as is typical of analogue format, each pressing has discernibly different properties. Every cover is of a marginally different hue of blue. The details of the particular pressings vary depending on the country of origin, pressing plant, distribution company, etc.

Philip: The sound's outstanding, it's so amazing. This cover is … I don't know. When I first saw it, I was so absorbed by it. It's so well done. If you look at this on a CD size it doesn't work really … I collect this one since some years and I even have much more in the studio because they're so … I don't know why but they are so nice because they have so many different releases from different countries, from different pressing plants … At the moment I have around a hundred. Look at this? Where is it from? Greece or something. Look, they didn't have the good quality printing. You see the difference between the blues? It's so crazy.

Dominik: That's again something about vinyl that every single release is slightly different, they are not the same even though it is the same thing.

Phillip: Totally!

Phillip's engagement with the album shows how fetish is a balancing act of harnessing the energizing and absorbing dimension of person–thing relations, while keeping in check the obsessive qualities of such devotion. Fetish effectively pulls you into the game of playing with boundaries between unbridled worship and productive inquisitiveness. Therefore it is not a coincidence that Phillip describes the process as 'crazy', referring to the capacity of fetish to make one 'understand without knowing, or at least without knowing that one knows. It is to understand by feeling, by contact, by the "evidence of the senses" rather than the mind.'[24] Here the positive meaning of 'crazy' is suggestively revealed. Crucially, it is precisely the fact that we do not *exactly know* why fetish absorbs us so intensely that we derive energy from it. This is partly what artists and cultural analysts mean when they talk about 'the ecstasy of things'. Symptomatically, in the book that bears this title and explores the shift of late modern objects' significance from functionality to fetish, vinyl is featured prominently on the back cover.[25]

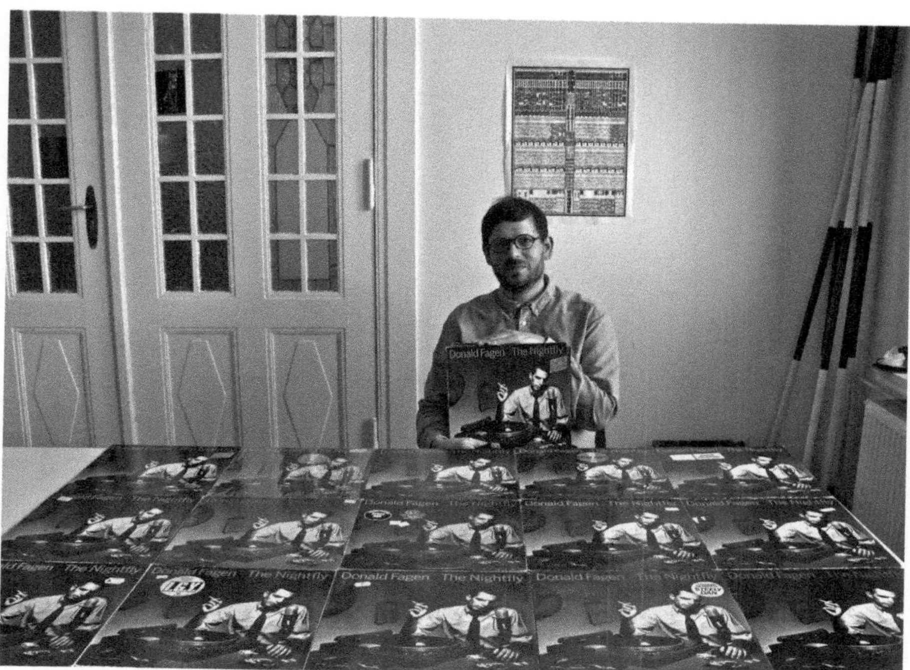

FIGURE 4.1: Collecting as positive fetishism: Phillip Sollmann, *aka* Efdemin, with multiple pressings of Donald Fagen's *The Nightfly* LP. (DB)

CHAPTER FIVE

Totem

Scene-making in Urban Spaces

VINYL EMPLACED

As a commodity that unexpectedly re-entered the mainstream market, the vinyl record is a *new old good*. It is now the most expensive but fastest-growing music format there is.[1] In the previous chapters we have shown that the historic legacy, material affordances and qualities, and market value jointly endowed vinyl with iconic characteristics that prevented it from being definitively categorized as outdated, obsolete and ultimately disposable. Instead, at the very least, vinyl may be described as a superfluous format that retains the possibility of signalling luxury or pecuniary value. At most, it is a hardly replaceable physical medium whose tactility and visual aesthetics uniquely complement its acoustic potentialities.

While it is clear that we are observing vinyl's rebirth inspired by its rediscovered characteristics, it is likewise clear that a resurgence of this magnitude and cultural significance needs to be connected to a spatio-social dimension, most notably to vinyl's situatedness in bohemian neighbourhoods, cosmopolitan urban spaces and music consumption venues. In particular, the following account emphasizes the way vinyl's salient meanings are created through its placement in and reciprocal relationship with urban scenes, especially big city music cultures of independent and underground kind. The key sites for such an exploration of vinyl's location in space and society are the institutions in which it is sold, traded and played. Crucially, it is *how* and *where* analogue records become subject to economic exchange and aesthetic placement that interests us here. As a physical and now relatively luxurious medium, vinyl tends to be ensconced within cityscapes, nested in specific ways in specific locations. It is never simply 'out there' waiting to be had, but framed by retailing institutions, social spaces and music venues.

This observation is consistent with the latest sociocultural findings that 'how people engage with the work of art shapes how they interpret it',[2] as well as with the argument that the city as 'experiential space' continues to have a major impact on the way society works despite the apparent dematerialization of social life.[3] Rather than mere landscapes or functional hubs, cities are dense socioscapes that frame and channel feedback between humans and things as well as host multitudes of artistic projects.[4] For these reasons, our focus on vinyl's urban presence employs material cultural approaches that augment studies of production and consumption of culture generally, and sound and popular music specifically. Showing how physical media and location interact to structure experience of seemingly 'immaterial' cultural values, we can push further our understanding of vinyl's successful persistence in the digital era. Ultimately, urban locations are places and playgrounds for communities and carrier groups that produce and consume culture, for example in the form of records. Such cultural objects are more than practical media or valuable commodities. They symbolize lifestyles, consolidate social groups, and help define places that host specific 'skeins of humans and things'.[5]

In other words, the central theme of this chapter is vinyl's life as *totem* in urban music scenes. In order for vinyl's affordances, qualities and commodity powers to be fully reappreciated, a series of spatio-social entanglements and connections must be accounted for. Just like vinyl needs a turntable and all other equipment to be played and heard, it is also inevitably introduced and used in specific physical settings and cultural contexts where performative combinations of people and things make its meanings effective. Moreover, we find that there is an observable affinity between vibrant vinyl culture and particular cosmopolitan urban settings. Broadly conceived spaces of independent culture merit attention in this context because they reflect an ethos of art over commerce, of deep cultural knowledge, and of 'do-it-yourself' cultural production. They exist literally and figuratively as off-centre neighbourhoods of big cities and as underground cultural scenes. The two are closely intertwined. Along with other potentially related signifiers of cosmopolitan scenes such as cafes and bars, ethnic restaurants and food stores, or galleries, artistic collectives and boutique fashion stores, they exhibit a distinctive cultural value.

While the analogue medium has always been important for the circles of serious audiophiles and collectors everywhere,[6] we need to look closer at much wider, and at the same time more localized, landscapes of cultural production and consumption – especially a variety of record stores and the club and bar scenes of cities – to comprehend the culturally transformative meanings now attributed to vinyl. Following cultural sociologists who pointed out that 'the influence of specialised cultural institutions like art on broader culture processes should be reconsidered',[7] we approach institutions such as record stores not as mundane or exclusively profit-oriented enterprises but sociocultural contexts in the full sense of the term. As we shall show, they do more than just sell music on vinyl. Moreover, in many cases their profit may actually be marginal, and it certainly was a decade ago when many vinyl stores found it difficult to break even, let alone make a reasonable profit. Stores are material interpretative contexts in which their social and artistic roles become palpable and shed light on how vinyl 'interacts' with people and spaces to produce exciting, new or transformative meanings.[8]

In short, it is not only the individual situatedness of a producer or a consumer,[9] but also the specific constellations of spatial emplacement and material entanglements that turn media into meaningful messages in their own right.[10] Theoretically speaking, cultural meaning works not only as symbolic-referential content but also as sociocultural event which is about 'reflexive indexicality'.[11] Practically speaking, things make sense only in conjunction with broader constellations of objects, i.e. in emplaced and embodied contexts of their use where groups of people can share the associated experiences and intersubjectively establish their value. As Ian Hodder argues, socially significant things are never isolated: 'Rather they are nodes for the flows of interlinked bundles of matter, energy and information.'[12] Cosmopolitan cities are such localized nodes, or systems of nodes.

Such a vantage point allows us to connect the production and consumption of culture as well as the professionals and the amateurs, whereby the key phenomena of cultural preference and taste are seen as 'collective cultural technique' rather than merely 'arbitrary election'.[13] In what follows we explore in greater detail what can be called the object-space-nexus, i.e. a series of concrete places where vinyl is bought, sold, exchanged and played. We focus on the stores and clubs nested in neighbourhoods developed and frequented by particular style communities. These communities can be credited not only with the commercial survival and current revival of vinyl, but also with broader processes of taste-making and increasingly significant acts of cultural selection and classification through their role of musical curators.

VINYLSCAPE: THE OBJECT-SPACE NEXUS

The role and meaning of social spaces are punctuated and energized by the co-presence and arrangement of sites and objects within them. In turn, objects exist within physically and materially structured interpretative fields where their affordances are clarified, made visible and shared. The sum of such objects, in conjunction and concert with practices and meanings associated with them, contributes to creating a particular cultural space imbued with local ambience or atmosphere,[14] traditionally but somewhat vaguely referred to as *genius loci*. Some of such objects may be strong cultural 'magnets' of sorts, auratic things around which specific social practices and meanings tend to coalesce. That is, the object itself – in this case, vinyl – becomes a quasi-totemic focal point around which social practices and collective feelings cluster, becoming 'fully conscious of themselves', to use Durkheim's apt phrase again. Our methodology here includes interrogating cultural meanings articulated discursively and established semiotically, but our investigation works from the object itself, its emplaced effects and its relation to other entities, human and non-human. Culture comprises sensibilities, values, ideas and feelings as well as 'external forms that such internalities take as they are made public, available to the senses and thus truly social'.[15] Vinyl culture epitomizes this definition.

Cultural objects and iconic media become important in helping to define the meaning and experience of certain urban zones and get energized by them in turn. Musical products and sound technologies are often implicated in this circular process. As noted by Will Straw in relation to the spacing of time within urban settings, 'the life cycle of cultural commodities may be considered in spatial and geographical terms as well. The paths and velocities through which cultural commodities move help to define the rhythms and the directionality of urban life.'[16] This directly applies to vinyl culture and independent cultural spaces. Here we may again draw on the world of coffee, for coffee roasteries and cafés tend to be signifiers or fully fledged totems of such spaces rather than simply useful gastronomic establishments.[17] Our argument is that vinyl is one such important object-symbol. In conjunction with other objects and physical sites, for example turntables, speakers, clubs, cafés, etc., it points to particular dimensions of urban experience associated with notions of alternative or critical attitude, decelerated consumption, 'cosmopolitan cool' and with practices of consumption which cross categories of new and old. In other words, such constellations of objects and places project and epitomize particular social 'messages'. Using the language of Arjun Appadurai's seminal work on constitutive global scapes,[18] we may apply his approach to talk about particular 'vinylscapes', referring to types of spaces where analogue records perform communicative and aesthetic roles in urban contexts.

Of course, the vinyl record is not exclusively an object associated with urban scenes and public spaces, and occupies a range of other, often mundane social spaces and contexts reflecting its status within phases and cycles of commodification and decommodification. Vinyl – like other objects within households and spaces of social exchange – is mundanely found in domestic storage spaces and devices like shelving, cardboard or plastic boxes, stacked behind sofas or atop cupboards, stored in back rooms, attics or basements underneath the house. For the most part, these represent non-market and non-public, domesticated contexts for vinyl. They are phases of vinyl's life cycle where it becomes part of the private lifeworld, incorporated into listening practices and patterns, or stored and packed away for later use, or for a phase of 'conscience time' related to the liminal phase of non-use, as the ultimate phase prior to disposal.

Aside from these mundane spaces, which are of course crucial and interesting in their own ways for patterning everyday lifeworlds, vinyl exists in marketized social spaces and professional entertainment settings, essentially physical stores and clubs, where its cultural properties are realized via display, archiving, categorizing, pricing, exchange or trade, playing and DJing. It is these public, marketized spaces that punctuate the energization and effervescence of vinyl that we deal with in this chapter. An illustrative example would be an underground club where vinyl is at the centre of the highly charged musical performance by charismatic taste-makers – DJs. Especially when it comes to what Bill Brewster calls electronic 'rhythmic music' and which is often at the centre of our attention in this book, club settings are crucial to understanding and describing the experiential meanings vinyl affords. He evocatively writes that 'rhythm requires a dance floor rather than a living room', and goes on to argue that 'Benga or Wolf + Lamb is not something that can be consumed at home, sat in front of the Bang & Olufsen, pen at the ready. It's elsewhere that those moments, those effects, the thud and thump are experienced ... It's no accident that many dance music journalists are also DJs, producers, participants.'[19]

The club is a studied example of youth entertainment and musical development. But it is also a 'liminal place',[20] an example of a site designed for ludic or transgressive leisure activities where daily routines are suspended. Some of the most special and iconic of them, like the Berlin-based club Berghain, are at once what Durkheimian sociologists would call 'sacred' places. In fact, it is not uncommon to hear people refer to Berghain as a 'temple', and to have charismatic DJs described as 'Godfather of house', 'Detroit wizard', 'Ibiza's magician', 'acid house evangelist', or even 'son of God'.[21] Record stores may not be commonly rising to such cultural stature, but some of them do assume a similar aura, sometimes referenced by the charismatic artists themselves. Think about the legendary vinyl shop *Hardwax* in Berlin and Shed's track entitled '44A (Hard Wax forever!)', which explicitly evokes the address and name of this iconic Kreuzberg-based venue.

Apart from these central commercial institutions, there are other settings for performatively reconstructing the power and qualities of vinyl, like bars and independent music labels, each of which has its own cultural strategies and rituals. As we shall show, some labels are closely intertwined with club venues, and bars remain in a symbiotic, spatially structured relation to the clubs and concert halls. Yet the record stores occupy the privileged position within vinylscapes because this is where people can come in touch with multiple records in the most intimate manner, including purchasing them. Considered in relation to such localized 'vinylscapes', stores can be grouped into heuristic categories with certain pathways of social connections and mutual support. They tend to have a unique approach – which is materially and visually coded – to housing, presenting and playing vinyl and this dimension has a bearing on how vinyl is to be understood in these settings and more generally too.

CURATED VINYL VENUES AND CULTURAL CLASSIFICATION

In contemporary markets where vinyl sales are still relatively low compared to digital formats, vinyl has primarily been encountered and acquired through independent store retailers. However, as sales continue to rise, vinyl is likely to be increasingly restocked in mainstream stores. Although quite a few independent stores have their own online service and/or sell their stock via Discogs, the independent physical stores continue to uphold the cultural life of vinylscapes as much as the other way around. In particular, the labels and shops that promote analogue versions of albums and singles act as crucial gatekeepers filtering the relentless flow of musical products. Before club and radio DJs begin to ponder their selections, labels and especially stores curate the musical output, suggesting what is worthwhile and valuable in the digital age of sensory overload and limited time. In a conversation with us, Robert Henke recalls this to be the enduring function of a record store such as *Hardwax* that caters to electronic underground scenes. But this seems to have always been the case in other scenes and more generally, too. As Peter Buck of R.E.M. noted, 'having someone curate a store made it easy to acquire records that you might never have heard about otherwise'.[22]

Within this framework, there is a continuum of independent retail institutions stretching from vinyl in archival and professional DJ settings to its location in spaces of lifestyle and fashion consumption. This continuum can be rendered more legible when looked at through the prism of a heuristic typology of stores. The idea is to distinguish – if only provisionally – various kinds of independent shops that are directly connected to local neighbourhoods and translocal scenes and thus intimately implicated in the cultural processes of keeping vinyl not only commercially alive but also culturally significant and eminently urban. Needless to say, few actual independent stores represent purely one type. Different kinds of hybridization can be observed, but the logic of recurrent combinations suggests the existence of relatively stable generic types of vinyl places with their own set of main characteristics. The recognizable patterns and symbolic boundaries are relatively clear. They reflect broader processes of cultural classification within music and the related acts of identity-construction. Moreover, while each store may have unique stock and represent the idiosyncratic taste of its owner and workers, what unites almost all of them is their being *curated* cultural venues committed to the specific values of the independent music scene as much as to the principles of economic viability. Record stores are like records themselves – they have their own individuality and character.

Of course, as a symptom of the broader revival of vinyl, the records are now also reintroduced to the stock of branded chain stores that only several years earlier had indefinitely discontinued this product or would have never considered stocking it. Because their role for the cosmopolitan dynamics described here is secondary, we largely leave them aside, arguing that such stores react to the trends rather than set them in motion. They tend to capitalize on, instead of contributing to, the narrative of coolness derived from the independent scenes. Moreover, as Peter Runge points out, in order to comprehend what is 'mainstream' one needs outliers: 'The "mainstream" is like the notion of "average" in statistics. Without the "independents" there won't be the mainstream … But the big players don't like these small numbers.' This is one of the reasons behind our decision to narrow the focus of this work to these carrier groups.

Thus, we will dwell here mainly on the 'outlying' but vibrant pockets of music market and distinguish three main independent spheres for marketization of vinyl, each supported by a discernible kind of shop, promoting particular labels and artists, and connected to specific clusters of entertainment venues, typically located within physically off-centre, 'outlying' urban neighbourhoods:

(1) Archival, multi-genre second-hand stores revolving around the pop-rock canon. Here the emphasis is on older and historically significant music, but a selection of new artists is often to be found as well; in addition to the pop-rock canon one often finds the streamlined selection of the 1970s and 1980s new wave and punk repertoire, as well as iconic jazz, funk and soul artists.
(2) DJ-oriented stores foregrounding brand new and/or reprinted records in electronic dance music (hereafter EDM) geared especially toward club scenes. Here the emphasis is on new vinyl, but second-hand records are sometimes included too, and there are professional DJ stores that in fact function as archives; in addition to the electronic canon of techno and house, other genres such as drum'n'bass, dubstep, electro, funk or soul can be found too.
(3) Lifestyle and boutique shops with strictly curated genres such as hip-hop and indie rock, both in their alternative and mainstream guises, with the emphasis almost exclusively on new vinyl, with select thematic cross-overs to pop music like r'n'b and rock'n'roll respectively.

Within each type, different affordances of vinyl become prominent and its meanings change. As far as stores themselves are concerned, the first two kinds tend to create and reproduce the 'sacred' and authentic meanings of vinyl, while lifestyle stores either attempt to capitalize on these totemic qualities or incorporate non-musical items to support their existence as independent record shops. In both scenarios they offer other cultural merchandise that creates and complements the taste of their clientele: CDs, books, posters, and designer clothing lines and footwear. All types of shops give material expression to the iconic qualities of vinyl and thereby recirculate them within expanded markets. This transference of iconic qualities within and across social spaces tells us a range of important things about vinyl culture in action, and about original, second-hand and special markets for analogue records.

This basic shop taxonomy serves as an orienting construct. Instead of being a definitive descriptive tool, it is rather an interpretative classificatory scheme informed by the actual practices of stylistic curating. One of its uses is to help concretize our claim that an elective affinity between cosmopolitan urban environments and the independent, vinyl-related music scenes evinces sociological stability across time and space contexts. It also reveals the capacity of vinyl to be a cult object for very different bohemian and mainstream publics, thus emphasizing its iconic potency. This typological approximation becomes especially important when we aim at demonstrating vinyl's *agentic* properties as an auratic thing, i.e. how it energizes and adds to a given urban setting, not just the other way around. Having said that, we aim to simultaneously account for the other directionality of influence. The meaningful impact of urban physical spaces themselves is undeniable, especially when considered in its sociological and aesthetic dimensions.

While we indicate the international scope of our findings by including first-hand observations from various countries and their major cities, we again pay special attention to Berlin and its vibrant districts. The conceptual rationale behind this focus is multiple, but it boils down to three observations worth clarifying. First, Berlin is a relative newcomer in the global game of metropolitan cool. It is a cosmopolitan centre in the making, thus laying bare how the scenes congeal into legible cultural forms. Second, Berlin's emerging status as a metropolitan hub, and even its reputation as 'a cultural myth of a city that defines its era',[23] has been recognized as strongly linked to its own effervescent club and underground music scenes which emerged out of the spatial and cultural conditions created by the division and reunification. German scholars underscore that Berlin's huge cultural 'boom' is related above all to music,[24] with techno being the city's signature sound, the post-Wall era soundtrack whose aesthetics and ethics is inseparable from vinyl culture.[25] Finally, there are at least 40 established independent record stores and many more bars and clubs just within the arc that stretches in an eastern and southerly direction from Prenzlauer Berg through Friedrichshain and Kreuzberg down south of the city to Neukölln. The main vinyl-related independent culture sites of those neighbourhoods have come to epitomize the independent cool and have promoted their districts well beyond Berlin, effectively demonstrating that 'neighbourhoods are the lifeblood of any city'.[26]

Of course, it is true that Berlin's urbanity and remarkable situatedness has to do with its modern history. However, a political economy that tends to credit lingering recent economic 'crisis' as a decisive explication of Berlin's uniqueness glosses over the relativity and one-sidedness of such categories. It reflects an attachment to political agendas more than the social complexity of Berlin's 'jigsaw puzzle'.[27] While cultural scholars broadly agree that Berlin evinces a pronounced *Eigenlogik*, i.e. its own urban logic and a 'uniquely politicized landscape',[28] they at the same time appreciate the role of more generalizable phenomena such as urban atmosphere and 'typical Western' issues of urban design, preservation and the meaning of material culture. As we have shown throughout this book, major political and economic issues, however important, do not fully account for cultural phenomena, certainly not for the ones that evince trajectories as unanticipated and erratic as the historical vagaries of vinyl and Berlin – arguably vinyl's European capital. Our study intends to develop a more balanced perspective, whereby both Berlin's sociocultural character and the city's new-found cosmopolitan meaningfulness get elucidated. In short, in Berlin's vinylscapes and associated independent culture spaces we see a vivid singular variation on a common but under-theorized theme of the interactions between cosmoscapes and independent scenes. Here vinyl is revealed to play a doubly totemic role. At once a global icon of musical cool and the symbolic 'currency' of hip underground local scenes, it feeds its cultural worth back to the cities that host it. The same appears to be true for other urban examples used below to elaborate each of the archetypal vinyl spaces.

STORES AS ARCHIVES

The last few decades have seen massive change in the way music is bought and sold. The behemoth chain stores of the 1990s and 2000s – Virgin, HMV, Tower – largely deserted the vinyl market during that period in favour of stocking CDs as the preferred medium of mass music consumption. Then, through the latter part of the 2000s, as consumers were encouraged to download, these stores came under pressure from the introduction and widespread adoption of virtual formats. The same principle of convenience that once promoted CD over vinyl now seriously threatened its right to exist. The arrival of digital virtual files rendered the physical digital format redundant. The future of the record store as an actual space was in question. The system of mass production and consumption of music had changed irrevocably, and with it the way people typically purchased their music. In the face of this massive transformation, many stores ceased business, or moved to a combination of online and store trading. One of the types of store which has been able to survive these changes is what we call the 'archival' vinyl store. By assembling a stock of analogue records that not only gathers and categorizes but also symbolically projects pivotal genres and artists in the pop-rock canon, these places have become emblematic heritage institutions of that canon, and are supported and celebrated as such. If in the 1990s record stores saw only those customers who grew up with vinyl as the standard format, the situation changed towards the end of the next decade. As the transition to digitalization was drawing to a successful conclusion, an understanding arose that if stores stocking physical formats are to make sense at all, they must go analogue, or risk irrelevance and bankruptcy. It is another aspect of digitalization's ironic effect that boils down to an observation that 'the technology that helped dismantle the mass record industry has helped us to circle back to an earlier, simpler, and more intimate time – a time when old record shops were independent little ventures run by music fans for music fans'.[29]

As much as they made available the musical outputs of the pop-rock canon, the stores themselves – as physical, social sites for accessing, visualizing, touching and purchasing the central musical objects of the pop-rock canon – could also become an integral part of the musical heritage and artistic feeling they promoted. As the name of one 'archival' store in Friedrichshain – *WaxArt* – indicates, vinyl is more than just a format. The defining feature of such stores is their coverage of the pop-rock canon across decades and sub-genre categories, or as stores which stock particular eras or styles in greater depth, sometimes giving access to tracks that have never been digitalized. It is especially true for jazz and soul music stores. Visits to specialized jazz stores like *O-Ton* in Berlin's Friedrichshain, *Mainly Jazz* in St Kilda in Melbourne, or *Academy LP* in New York's East Village are an opportunity not merely to purchase vinyl as a material-musical commodity, but to gain a sense of participation in a social scene and to come into contact with knowledge, 'sacred' forms and significant stocks of musical art in material form. Stores which house tens of thousands of records, like *Amoeba* venues in San Francisco and Los Angeles or *Spacehall* and *Galactic* in Berlin, have become key spaces for contacting and learning about the canon, for receiving what might be dubbed 'sacred aural texts' of the canon, and for visualizing and touching the artworks that gave artistic expression to them. Heritage stores communicate visually and through their very names this dimension. They make more legible the maze of musical forms by categorizing and thus mapping the universe of music. By the same token, such stores allow consumers to encounter the leftover, overlooked and currently unfashionable records which function as a type of cultural ballast of slow-velocity commodities currently 'exhausted'.

Importantly, then, major categories in the pop-rock field could be physically navigated and understood in the spatial layout of the heritage store. Musical styles and tastes were marked out, albeit according to sometimes idiosyncratic systems employed by store owners or managers, or particular taste communities, but these were also arranged in reference to genre classifications broadly accepted and understood in listening communities, which came to reflect locally understood meanings for particular genre categories and sub-categories.

The multi-level store *Disk Union* in the vibrant Shibuya district of Tokyo provides a legible context for observing these classificatory practices. Each floor specializes in particular genres, such as pop and indie, metal, jazz and rare groove, or techno and electronic. Consistent with density of building and office space in central Tokyo, each floor of *Disk Union* is small in size, around 30 square metres, connected by internal stairs or a small lift which opens directly onto the digging floor. The *Disk Union* chain assembles a very large bank of used and new vinyl. In doing so, it becomes an archive that houses a significant volume of vinyl stock that is carefully selected and curated, not just around genre but around the physical condition of the vinyl and the sleeve, and is therefore of high quality. While the store cannot hold every vinyl ever, the very scale of this enormous store gives one a bodily sense of getting in touch with the entire history of modern music. *Disk Union*'s collection, a commercial material archive of pop-rock history, materializes genre categories, pop music history and histories of music production. Its immediate social function, however, is to offer a space for enthusiasts and amateurs to 'dig' for this history.

The prototypical heritage store codes vinyl alphabetically within major styles. The heritage store is able to immediately mark its display of accepted components of the canon; the Rolling Stones, the Beatles or Lou Reed, for example, come to be marked out individually. The same types of marking-out are evident within other styles. In jazz, Miles Davis, John Coltrane or Stan Getz always have their own sections, while in independent or alternative stores we can often see heritage indie rock artists like the Smiths or Joy Division specially marked out within the broader canon. This is a material demonstration of a store's relevance or centrality to sub-genres within the vast universe of popular music.

There are also independent archival stores whose enormous volume combined with limitations of space precludes efficient classification. *Teuchtler* in Vienna features a huge collection within the rather narrow confines of its retail space. *Record Loft* in the heart of Berlin's Kreuzberg has significantly more space, but its huge collection is categorized only by rough genre-related principles, and diggers must find their own way through dozens of boxes and crates with techno and house records. Vinyl flows in and out, sold and bought, exchanged and traded, making fixed categorizations harder to maintain. One of the best examples of a big, open vinyl archive is an impressive shop in central Bogota, Colombia, reportedly housing over 85,000 records. Tucked in a hidden part of Los Angeles Mall at Calle 19, this one-room shop stocks all kinds of Latin American beats, largely uncategorized and densely packed in crates and shelves. The knowledgeable staff seem to be able to navigate their collection, but for most customers digging in the place means exposing yourself to excitements of chance and serendipity. Interestingly, in 2013, the entrance to the store featured a copy of an article from the Colombian weekly *Semana* entitled 'The Return of the Disc' – further evidence for the global scale of vinyl's revival.

Just as this type of store consolidates the canon, housing the canon marks the store as important for collectors and enthusiasts. Heritage stores work to trace historically constituted and locally contextualized global or specifically Western musical genres. These genres can span great and also relatively small time periods. In the case of paradigmatic heritage stores stocking the pop-rock canon, the period represented generally begins in the 1960s and ends in the 1980s; for jazz heritage stores the period covered is generally larger, including everything between the late 1940s and the 1980s. What defines the heritage store is its ability to collect into one place the most important and genre-defining outputs. Thus, while a store collecting the pop-rock canon could hardly be serious without records by the Rolling Stones and the Beatles, or Sonic Youth and New Order, a store with black music and jazz cannot contemplate not stocking Miles Davis, Keith Jarrett, James

FIGURE 5.1: Curating genres: 'Organic grooves' at HHV Selected record store, Friedrichshain, Berlin. (DB)

Brown and Marvin Gaye, and frequently has a separate section on important labels such as ECM, Verve, Blue Note and Motown, or particular styles and country-related music such as bossa nova, samba, fusion or funk. Stores like *Soultrade* in Kreuzberg additionally display all the iconic labels's logos and trademarks on the walls. *Musik Department* on Kastanienallee in Prenzlauer Berg likewise presents vintage record bags and sleeves on the walls, emphasizing this mundane and thus relatively neglected but conspicuous aspect of consumption culture. Likewise, those assembling the electronica and techno canon cannot avoid stocking Aphex Twin, Autechre, Carl Craig or Kraftwerk, and new work on now-canonical labels such as Warp, Ninja Tune, Good Looking Records, Kompakt or Planet E.

These types of stores also frequently offer evidence to shoppers to demonstrate their qualities as types of heritage sites, including – and spatially distinguishing – rare, exclusive valuable items such as first pressings, long out-of-print items, signed copies of LPs, special coloured or picture vinyl editions, as well as collectable and frequently not-for-sale items such as posters advertising gigs or albums. Their substantive focus on the pop-rock canon often overlaps with what we called in this book 'the golden age' of analogue records, especially the period from the late 1960s to early 1980s. The meanings that accrue to vinyl stores back then created cultural templates for the record business and survive to this day. This particular process

FIGURE 5.2: Vintage record bags at The Musik Department record store, Prenzlauer Berg, Berlin. (DB)

has been observed especially in the US and, by extension, in many other countries influenced by its pop culture, and it has been the case partly because 'record stores came of age in the late 1960s, a time when America was in a state of revolution. The underground record stores that sprung up in New York, San Francisco, and Los Angeles became models for stores in cities and towns across the country ... ultimately it was the passion for the music that kept people coming in.'[30] Finally, there are archival stores that function as up-scale antique stores, focusing exclusively on old and rare, well-preserved items, including some shellac era records and vintage equipment. A shop in the Parisian district of Montmartre emphasizes this role by its very name – *Phonogalerie*. Located in an old townhouse at Rue Lallier, it houses a large selection of old phonographs and music posters that iconize analogue culture.

UNDERGROUND AND INDEPENDENT ELECTRONIC MUSIC STORES

It is not accidental that when it came to the development of vinyl culture, major cities with robust bohemian classes like New York, San Francisco or London were leading by example, attracting the most passionate and in turn radiating the cultural energy internationally. The 'golden' standard of running stores 'by music fans for music fans' was adhered to by the next generation of vinyl lovers who found their niche in the inchoative underground scenes of electronic dance music (EDM) in the late 1980s and early 1990s. However, if the second-hand archival stores reveal the historical depth and stylistic breadth of the vinyl culture, the stores featuring EDM genres show the role of analogue record for the cutting-edge and underground club scenes for which the format has always had special pragmatic as well as self-reliant, anti-systemic and counter-cultural meanings. Although aesthetically very different, such scenes as early EDM or punk shared this DIY attitude. Cities like Berlin, London or Tokyo still support not several but dozens of such stores. The Australian metropolitan areas of Melbourne and Sydney have even their own special 'Diggin' Guides' with neighbourhood maps featuring 53 and 21 addresses respectively. The vast majority of those stores are independent venues, gathered in particular off-centre districts integrated into other cosmopolitan neighbourhood features, frequently connected to local labels, bars and clubs that could hardly flourish in downtown zones.

To be sure, some of the stores are very small and each of those cosmopolitan areas features a different mixture of genres and specific stylistic emphasis depending on local traditions (e.g. New York has strong hip-hop venues, London has been a home to drum'n'bass, Berlin is the current capital of techno, while Melbourne is comparatively weak regarding EDM, but famous for its soul, punk and indie rock culture). Yet, despite differences in emphasis, what connects these cosmopolitan centres is their ability to support nearly every notable independent scene, offering a variety of creative niches symbolized by the existence of specialized vinyl stores. Moreover, regardless of the specific national differences or time-trajectories, the variations of this type of vinyl store fulfil the similar role of musical taste-makers and stylistic curators.

In the particularly vinyl-strong independent electronic music scenes, analogue record has been first of all the 'DJ tool', i.e. mainly a club-oriented product. In some flagship institutions of this kind, for example *Phonica* in London, *Hardwax* in Kreuzberg or *OYE* in Prenzlauer Berg, many releases are explicitly described in these terms on the attached stickers. Nowadays the excess of musical information is such that DJs and producers would have to spend more time browsing and selecting than playing and creating in order to stay on top of their professional game as the informed selectors of tracks. In this context of cognitive overload and aesthetic pluralism, additionally exacerbated by the virtualization of music consumption, the relatively small physical store functions as a filter that makes many decisions not only easier but also more meaningful, offering educated shortcuts for busy professionals, especially those who, like Robert Henke, are far from being vinyl purist and whose strict time limitations make them often unable to regularly browse through stacks of newly arrived records. The store remains a place where records considered valuable are played, displayed and sometimes discussed. There is a definitive social aspect to it, both at the moment of selection by an ordering shop and when a consumer listens to and decides on particular records in store.

Forging of the close personal connections that more intimate, specialized record stores afford makes the curatorial and filtering role of such venues even more pronounced. Phillip Sollmann aka Efdemin describes it in a conversation we had about his connection to the owner of the Berlin-based store *Rotation*, Niko Schäfer and proprietors of stores in other cities that he visits regularly:

> *Phillip Sollmann*: Niko knows what I like and dislike, or what I could be interested in. There's always this little bundle of records that he keeps for me. Sometimes I even just take them home and listen to them here, and then give back what I don't like. This is so nice but that's basically all I can do at the moment when travelling every weekend and working in the studio. I don't have time to go to *Spacehall* or other record shops ... I also have 'my' record shops in the cities I sometimes travel to. For example, there is one very important record store in Stuttgart. It is simply called *Second Hand Records*. No electronic music but all the rest. One of our closest friends is one of the owners, so we can get very nice prices for amazing records. He's always like: 'Wow, you don't know this one? You need to listen to it!' We come back home with amazing records every time we go there.
>
> *Dominik*: So the record store is still an important institution?
>
> *Phillip Sollmann*: Yes, very important.
>
> *Dominik*: Because you have connection with the people?
>
> *Phillip Sollmann*: Yeah, it's a personal thing ... Through Nico I have discovered amazing music which I had no idea existed.
>
> *Dominik*: There is the expertise of a record store owner?
>
> *Phillip Sollmann*: Yeah. Plus his channels of getting all that stuff from DJs, old stuff, and then distributing it to the people who might want to play it. For example, he knows that I'm totally into the end of the 1990s techno. That's my sound.

Not unlike many other vinyl lovers we interviewed, whether professionals or amateurs, Phillip Sollmann underscores the financial and time limitations as being of great concern. For him, stores play an invaluable role of facilitating the demanding process of selection and bargain finding. They also open the doors that usually remain closed, or we do not even suspect exist. Becoming a regular of a given store channels and expands knowledge and it ultimately can yield a formidable expertise, evidenced by growing high-quality collection of a particular kind. Without a host of filtering mechanisms and evaluative experience provided by the knowledgeable staff of record stores, building such collections may prove virtually impossible. This is increasingly an issue nowadays. As the virtual social sites get cluttered with electronic noise and the digital space of the internet becomes not so much jammed but simply so wide that it ceases to be legible and manageable, a need for direct social experience of discrete physical objects in actual spaces and all things organic becomes palpable. In the process, the very boundary between the 'virtual' and the 'real' is being redefined along with the need to collectively share aesthetic experiences and knowledge. This emerging phenomenon, comparable with the increasing popularity of open-air organic food markets, suggests that the dematerialization and alleged deterritorialization of late-modern life is neither a linear nor inevitable tendency. Face-to-face evaluative interactions remain salient and efficient. Markus Lindner of *OYE* record store in Berlin emphasizes this point:

> There are no more filters in the digital business. It's like a total informational overflow. It's insane. But then we decide: we would like to offer this record in the store, so the customers encounter a selection.

Regular visits to the stores that cater to DJs and fans of independent electronic music make this phenomenon visible. This is the case not only due to the fact that professional producers and DJs vitally need assistance provided by record store staff's advice on the latest releases but also because some such stores function partially or sometimes even fully as archival institutions that decide what's worthy of people's attention and what is not. *OYE* in Prenzlauer Berg that stocks over 14,000 records, or *Spacehall* in Kreuzberg, which has one of the biggest stocks in Berlin with roughly 100,000 records, are particularly good examples. Typically, however, the electronic music/DJ store specializes in offering only what the owner views as key releases of particular styles of electronic music. Such shops can be seen as purveyors of distinct traditions, trying to distill the best of a kind and establish international links along the stylistic lines. As proprietors of the legendary Kreuzberg-based *Hardwax*, Michael Hain and Torsten Pröfrock say their store's motto is ***klein aber fein*** (small but fine). However, they are also careful to distance themselves from what they see as a rather artificial new tendency to force aura on vinyl through limited edition releases.[31] This tendency has been explicitly decried by most DJs we interviewed, especially Andreas Baumecker and also Phillip Sollmann,who admitted: 'it's getting on my nerves'. *Hardwax* is also an emblematic example of a store that stands for promoting specific cosmopolitan connections. It distinguishes itself by symbolizing the Berlin–Detroit connection in techno music. The store sells mostly new material and important, strictly curated reprints, foregrounding the back catalogue of the 'in-house' label *Basic Channel*. The classic records are displayed on the walls of the raw industrial interior, some of which include the sticker '*off line shop only*', suggesting that the format and the store-based selection, not the release's intentionally restricted quantity, is an acceptable form of exclusivity.

Peter Runge sees vinyl's revival as partially traceable to its very affordance of assuming the role of 'off-line' format and how it can fuse with an anti-systemic sensibility shared by the underground scenes: 'If you play vinyl, government people do not know that you do it … as long as you don't pay for records with a credit card.' As there are many independent record stores that are in fact cash-based businesses, from *A-1* in New York's East Village to *Audio-In* in Berlin's Friedrichshain, this feature of analogue culture indeed makes it opposite to the virtual world. However, as there are agencies wishing to control nowadays what is being played in clubs, vinyl's virtual invisibility may be restricted in the future to domestic use only. If that becomes the case, the meaning of 'underground', vinyl-centred parties may regain its former power associated with rave and early techno cultures. Vinyl's 'off line' character is perhaps the best example of interconnectedness of things as material nodes whose shifting networks entail shifts in meaning. It is also indicative of a degree of cultural open-endedness of aesthetic objects and how certain meanings of a given cultural commodity can become attributable in a new context.

Within the independent EDM scene, there are also second-hand stores for DJs and diggers interested in the scene more generally. One finds several such venues in Friedrichshain, for example the aforementioned *Audio-In* or *Power Park*, that stock thousands of recent and classical releases. Regardless of the specific stylistic profile of the store, this type of vinyl venue categorizes music according to genres and sub-genres, only rarely alphabetically by artist. The stores focusing more exclusively on new material either follow the same logic or organize their records by labels, like *Hardwax*. Since the independent labels of electronic music tend to epitomize, or at least adhere to, particular genres, this mode of classification effectively relies on stylistic differentiation, encouraging serendipitous discoveries based on taste rather than name-driven collecting. Many of those stores belong to bohemian or reinvigorated post-industrial and older residential districts. This spatial logic can be observed even in places with relatively weak EDM vinyl culture, for example Moscow, whose prime EDM store *Vinyl Gallery 33 1/3* is located in the post-industrial Vinzavod creative cluster, or Buenos Aires, where electronic music is promoted by *Exiles*, predictably found in the hip Palermo district. Some EDM stores add to their substantial collections also older genres, especially jazz, soul and funk – the ones that traditionally constitute a treasure trove of samples for electronic musicians. *Power Park* and *Audio-In* play this role in Berlin. *A-1* in New York's East Village or *Northside* in Melbourne's Fitzroy are such independent hubs within their respective environments. *Northside* is at the same time a label promoting local artists active at the intersection of soul and electronica.

The aformentioned Friedrichshain- and Kreuzberg-based stores are all within walking distance of legendary nightclubs like Berghain and Tresor, each of which runs its own label, with Berghain not only selling records in its mini-store but also displaying all covers (with first pressings inside) framed on the entry hall walls alongside Piotr Nathan's and Wolfgang Tillmans's famous artworks. Berghain's very name indicates its location roughly on the border of Kreuz*berg* and Friedrichs*hain*, and the club's staggering reputation feeds back to the aura of the small bohemian quarters that surround it, called *Kiez* in German. Its influential label, *Ostgut Ton*, evokes the 'magic of places' of East Berlin,[32] whose free and rough character made them attractive to hosting independent cultures. Some people go so far as to assert that this made the Berlin techno scene possible at all.[33] Importantly, there is nothing nostalgic in this constellation of meanings attached to ever-futuristic techno culture encapsulated by *Ostgut Ton* vinyl. But its leaders emphasize that the affordances of the reappropriated, enormous post-industrial space of Berghain make it 'the reference point' for sound creation.[34] In a conversation with us, *Ostgut Ton*'s manager Jenus Baumecker-Kahmke confirms that test pressings are often trialled inside the club on its voluminous sound system.

The off-centre position of stores and clubs within the city map and yet decidedly urban location of the scenes supported by them reflects the connection of EDM vinylscape with independent urban subcultures in contrast with the mainstream suburban culture. Other more outwardly gentrified neighbourhoods of Berlin that once had the rough precincts, still host EDM stores too. One can think of *Melting Pot* located right at picturesque Kastanienalle, or *Long Player* at cozy Graeferstrasse in Kreuzberg, each of which offers its own, carefully selected mix of electronica, soul and jazz. These stores tend to be remarkably self-conscious vehicles of independent cultural values and neighbourhood character. *Long Player* advertises itself as a 'Vinyl Living Room', whereas *OYE* proudly displays signed copies of renowned records, like the aforementioned Gold Panda's *DJ Kicks* album featuring the artist's writing: 'keep selling the black gold'. The very names of stores often evoke the independent and cosmopolitan values, for example *Other Music* in New York, *Submerge* in Detroit or *Melting Pot* in Berlin.

Despite the general emphasis on new records, even in small-scale professional shops one usually finds at least several crates with used or marked-down records potentially containing valuable releases. Almost every store visually promotes particularly coveted, newly acquired or new releases. Store proprietors sometimes contribute parts of their own collection to begin with, and the stock often reflects their aesthetic preferences. For this reason there are no two identical independent EDM stores, even if they cater to basically the same stratum of music lovers and DJs. What makes them similar is special attention paid to independent genres, and availability of professional turntables on which every record can be played before the purchase. These aspects have traditionally distinguished independent stores more generally, especially vis-à-vis branded chain stores where records remain sealed and are categorized alphabetically by artist. Even if opening a record were allowed, one would not be able to listen to it. This open *vs* closed record policy and the classification contrast symbolically underscore the difference between the corporate and independent approach to music, as well as a series of opposites between the generalist venue for the mass audience and specialized shops that not only sell the musical commodity but also support a distinctive set of practices and knowledge crucial for the thriving of specific musical scenes and their styles. Markus Lindner stresses this point when he says that 'music is taste, there is no bad music ... for me music is always in the context of socializing. Music itself is nothing.' He goes on to explain his motivation as 'not just to sell music'. He then refers to the importance of the scene: 'I always wanted to be part of the music culture and the club culture in Berlin. It is for me really important to be part of the scene.' These evocative statements reiterate our earlier point about the difficulty of conceiving of pure 'music' due to its inescapably mediated and socially constructed character. At the same time, we find Markus's approach typical of the EDM cultural circle, and find evidence of it among both those who supply the stores with new music – the record labels, and those who regularly buy them – the DJs. Wolfgang Voigt of Kompakt Records explicitly states that vinyl business 'is also about getting in touch with people. You wouldn't download your food from the internet; you have go to a restaurant, that's it. And people find out – after being alone and just exchanging music files anonymously, from iPod to iPod, etc. – that this has no sex appeal, it's no fun. And then they see that there's another culture to go to, a record shop, and this affects people.' Michael aka Puresque establishes an even stronger connection between records and scene-making:

> Vinyl to me is the most important thing in music because it created the scene. And the scene is not just about being in the nightclub, it's also this whole record shopping thing, you connect with other people, discuss music with other people, you support the whole art of the thing ... That's what makes it so special, you can never replace that with files at home, sitting in front of your computer listening to tracks.

Markus concurs. Although he deems new software facilities like SoundCloud or Twitter to be 'absolutely amazing tools', he has no doubt that 'the most important thing is still the face-to-face contact and whether you can trust someone'. It is clear therefore that record stores create social spaces conducive to emergence and perpetuation of communal values such as sheer fun, music scene and trust. It is precisely for this reason that selling and buying vinyl in physical locations remains viable and attractive. Nowadays when a record can be previewed online or is accessible in other digital ways, the physical accessibility of the vinyl may seem a somewhat redundant privilege. However, its social and pragmatic functions remain in place. Record stores are meeting-places. Moreover, they are friendship-makers. Attracting like-minded people interested in similar artists and notions of musical style, they channel social energy and make otherwise separated, disconnected or anonymous individuals mingle with each other. This old role of the record store finds its new incarnation in electronic music stores like *OYE* that organize in-store DJ sets and jam sessions, not unlike bars in the surrounding neighbourhoods. Markus Lindner promotes many such events at both locations of *OYE*, pointing to greater intimacy of such sets when compared with regular club gigs and possibilities to forge connections between people involved in music production. It creates opportunities to obtain signed copies of records during record release parties and to talk to the artists themselves. As the case of *OYE* shows, the store can become a fully fledged artistic enterprise that generates greater sales. Between 2012 and 2013 alone, OYE registered 60 per cent growth in vinyl sales. As a follow-up to these successful developments, the recently opened Neukölln outlet of *OYE* is now also the headquarters of *Hotflush Records* run by Scuba, who moved to Berlin from England. This is a good example of vertical integration, in this particular case how typically separated worlds of record companies and retailers are becoming increasingly enmeshed, at least as far as the independents are concerned.

In the case of the second-hand markets, the offering of the record to public inspection and hearing is quintessential of independent scenes. Analogue records have always been open to everybody who walked in, save the cases of rare and fragile old records, which remain valuable even when in less-than-perfect condition and therefore they get excluded from casual checking. The music on vinyl, especially when used, is to be tried just like any clothing item or shoes; it is to be touched, smelled and looked at like a book or an art album. The medium has a strong tactile component and is frequently treated as the ultimate palpable musical output for serious music aficionados and DJs. Again, this feature is self-consciously emphasized by the names of important stores such as *Tactile* in Frankfurt, *Hardwax* in Berlin, *Substance* in Vienna or *Fat Beats* in New York. This affordance of analogue records makes it possible for the independent stores to merge records with other style items, opening a possibility of transition toward the kind of fully fledged lifestyle shop we discuss above within the third type. This is also an affordance that, as several of our interviewees remarked, makes vinyl a perfect gift. Peter Runge suggests that giving someone files is not exactly a perfect present. He goes on to explain this in the following way: 'People want something that still is a tangible thing. This experience can't be easily exchanged for something else.'

A highly illustrative although now non-existent example of the hybrid assortments was the store *Breakbeat Science* on Lower East Side's Orchard Street in New York City. At its heyday in the early 2000s it promoted drum'n'bass and house music on vinyl, two underground genres that were then still popular. As tastes were changing, the store gradually evolved towards a sophisticated boutique/high-end haberdasher called *BBlessing*, described online by an online customer as 'throwback hybrid between hip and vintage'. By the time when only few records were being sold at the back of the store, the interior still featured references to music such as speakers and a door made of old vinyl covers. The well-known EDM DJ-oriented store *Freebase* in Frankfurt has also followed a similar path of change over the years, first by adding sneakers, t-shirts and sweatshirts to its line of products, and then by downscaling and relocating from the inner city to a more off-beat *Kiez* in Sachsenhausen district where three other independent stores were already located. While some shops may be forced to discontinue their operation or incorporate non-musical items to survive, others open in bohemian and 'up-and-coming' neighbourhoods, either using the mixed-item strategy right from the start or simply recognizing the growing demand in such urban zones. For example, in DJ-oriented *Bass Cadet* in Berlin's Neukölln the records with new and used releases from broadly conceived EDM share the space with what the owners call 'the finest selection of vintage clothes and accessories'. Even the stores on the more purist side of the spectrum, like *Hardwax*, feature a limited series of t-shirts and sweatshirts. As Neukölln district has gradually assumed a bohemian role previously played by Prenzlauer Berg where *OYE* headquarters is located, Markus Lindner has recently decided to open an outlet of his store to make his establishment part of what he sees as a vibrant and locally rooted independent scene, something increasingly rare in by now largely gentrified Prenzlauer Berg.

Finally, the stores that may broadly be described as alternative rock venues sell all kinds of music that can be considered extreme. In Berlin, *Stallplaat* (Neukölln) or *Core Tex* (Kreuzberg) that sell all kinds of underground hard rock, metal and noise music are good examples. These stores often feature other products such as books, posters, t-shirts and various scene-related gadgets. This is what makes them related to hip-hop and indie rock scenes that place significantly greater emphasis on the associated lifestyle, not only or predominantly on musical style. If the house and techno scene has always been relatively non-confrontational and open regarding the fashion aspect, such alternative scenes as punk or death metal lend themselves to easier typification. A careless or rugged and anti-system street aesthetic is rather strictly defined and its symbolic boundaries closely observed and maintained by the scene's main stores and their very names, like *Resist* in Sydney's Newtown district or *Radical Records* in Melbourne. Vinyl would generally be the preferred format here, even if CDs and cassettes can more and more often be found on display in such stores. Vinyl's status of 'the king's format of music' may be less self-consciously asserted in other scenes, but they offer their own spin on its cosmopolitan meanings.

LIFESTYLE AND BOUTIQUE VENUES

It is in stores devoted to assembling and presenting a range of iconic elements of popular culture which perhaps point to the contemporary cultural value of vinyl most strongly. The lifestyle or boutique store stocks vinyl as one important component of pop culture consumption among a smorgasbord of lifestyle possibilities. Such stores are cornucopias of alternative and revered movements in popular culture including, but not restricted to, its musical elements. As one media format and also as material symbol of the pop culture canon, vinyl is likely to sit among classic DVDs assembling movies by Kubrick, Tati or Truffaut, and books about important twentieth-century movements and moments in art, fashion and literature, such as Burroughs, Camus or Kerouac. These stores represent the capacity of vinyl to reach into expanded and reinvigorated markets, and the cultural affordances of vinyl to become productively entangled with other cultural consumption goods, though they are also spaces where boundary maintenance activities around matters of perceived authenticity and mainstreaming come to be exercised. In the following section, we explore in further detail the material, visual and symbolic qualities of vinyl within these lifestyle settings.

In the typical lifestyle store, vinyl has an overriding function as a sign object and its dance-floor oriented or archival meanings are marginalized. Vinyl generally accounts for a relatively small percentage of the floor space in such stores – around 10–30 per cent – though its presence performs an important role. Through its display on the store's walls, vinyl is a celebrated symbol of musical tradition, cultural survival and displayed as canonical musical or sophisticated popular art object. In the setting of the lifestyle store, it often comes to be representative of a collectable, essential pop-rock or jazz canon. An outstanding international example is the store *Tornamesa* in Bogota, Colombia. It combines bookstore, movies, music store and wine store. Interestingly, it stocks and displays its strictly curated vinyl collection in wooden wine boxes.

Another example of a lifestyle store is the chain of *Title* stores in Australia. The very name of the store cleverly indicates its mission: to stock the key *titles* of popular culture. The association of these stores' name with selections and titles – of books, LPs, movies – is worth examining. The stores stock not just a huge or comprehensive volume of titles like any archival book or record store, for example, but selected and strictly curated titles worthy of display on shelves and domestic furniture. These are titles that everyone who desires to consume and understand contemporary culture needs to own, and to have them on display *as titles* is essential. For those already familiar with the canonical performances and outputs of modern popular culture, *Title* also stocks a mix of new, fresh and avant-garde styles among its range. The emphasis on particular series of works, on key cultural

FIGURE 5.3: Vinyl as decorative ambience: the Dispensary Enoteca, Bendigo, Australia. (IW)

works by authors, producers or artists, and key labels is an important part of the mix of cultural goods in this type of lifestyle store. This combination of classical, canonical and cutting-edge gives the store a sense of being expertly curated. The store thus functions as a self-contained and coherent field of cultural goods, but one that is also cross-cutting in ways that are perceived as culturally surprising and exciting to consumers.

While the chain of *Title* stores in Australia perhaps best represents an ideal lifestyle store catering to vinyl's aspirations to be associated with canonical cultural outputs, many other lifestyle stores cater to different, explicitly independent or underground markets. In the section that follows we explicate some further international examples. Firstly, the store *Selected Store HHV.de*, located on gritty Revaler Street in the Friedrichshain district of Berlin, is also heavily curated and designed as a consumption space where vinyl is incorporated into a coherent materialization of lifestyle. However, rather than *Title*'s baby-boomer customer market which caters to fans of funk, soul, jazz and rock, *Selected* comprises a vinyl collection focused on hip-hop and electronica which is complemented by a range of lifestyle goods such as sneakers, t-shirts, skateboards, bags, or peak caps with slogans. *Selected* takes vinyl seriously, but it is the stock of clothing, accessories and sneakers which are most visible from the street-front and which are located in the central and front zones of the store. The back and side section of the store houses listening turntables (iconic black Technics DJ model) and a range of new vinyl stock comprising new electronic music releases, with a small selection of indie and classic reissues available.

Another prominent lifestyle store located where the Mitte district meets Prenzlauer Berg, near Berlin's Rosenthaler Platz, is *Rotation Boutique*, formerly known as *Rotation Records*. Since its inception in 2003, *Rotation* has been a well-known vinyl-only store in Berlin. It is frequently listed among the city's best record stores on blogs and guides to digging in Berlin, and is regularly frequented by professional DJs and tourists alike. With its location bordering the neighbourhood of Prenzlauer Berg, and adjacent to Rosenthaler Platz, a major Berlin intersection with many popular cafés, restaurants and fashion stores, *Rotation* is now situated at one of the epicentres of Berlin's completed gentrification. Significantly, in 2010, Rotation changed its name from *Rotation Records* to *Rotation Boutique*. As the owner Nikolaus Schäfer explains on the shop's website: 'In late June 2010, Rotation Records evolved into Rotation Boutique! After seven years, we felt it was time for something more than "strictly music". With our boutique, we want to become a platform for music, fashion, arts, culture and whatever we feel is good enough to share with the world.' *Rotation Boutique* principally stocks a range of club and street clothing to complement the array of new and second-hand house and techno records available. Three turntables are available to listeners and are visible from the street, and in a warning to amateurs that specialist knowledge and care are required to use them and that the store is not just about clothing but is a space for professional DJs, two turntables display a sign which says 'DJs only are allowed to use these turntables'. Nikolaus Schäfer responded to the vinyl downturn during the 2000s, when even some DJs were walking away from the format, by widening the range of goods he had on offer. Vinyl was still the heart of the store, even though it now occupied a much smaller area within it. Objects that were entangled within Berlin's independent art and popular culture scenes were now introduced, especially clothing and fashion that was ethically and locally made. Niko candidly explains the shift to a lifestyle boutique away from exclusively vinyl shop. Niko reached the crossroads with the first incarnation of Rotation. At the sage prompting of his girlfriend, he needed to reassess the store's direction:

> She said to me: 'Hey, you can go three ways with this. You can go small side street, you pay less rent and can do it for life. You're gonna end up grumpy as most of the self-exploiting guys at age of 50 end up. You can quit and do something else again. Or, you can build on the reputation that you have for seven years and just make it something else.' And yeah, that just seemed the most interesting and rewarding way to go to make that transition, that is, where it's more boutique and you offer stuff that fits together. It used to be that way in the mid-90s, where you had hardware stores selling vinyl. Also, it just made sense to offer something more that people could take away with them along with their vinyl. The significance of things for people as a souvenir is important; they've been to Berlin, they've been clubbing, they don't have a record player but they can take something home that they can remember now. It's gonna be a record cover, or it's gonna be a t-shirt, even if t-shirts or most of them are more expensive than

> vinyl, it's something they can use and relate to. Before we had record covers in the window, and a lot of people just walked past and they didn't recognize it was a store, and just didn't know what to do in there. And this is what I see in other stores when I go to a different neighbourhood. I find record stores can be just so specialized and kind of hidden away to most people. So, back to my store: it's still independent, we think that it is also very important to be independent rather than have brands that you can have in just every store. We also try to have sustainable clothing with people who have a focus on fair labour conditions. It is important that it's not imported from China where it's about exploitation in every way. And it fits very well, it's kind of unique. However, we also lost some hardcore vinyl fans. The audience widened up, you now have a bigger range of age, and also you attract both sexes and a few boys didn't like that too much.

Rotation Records' shift to *Rotation Boutique* of course drew upon its initial success as a vinyl record store that catered to professional musicians, composers and some high-profile Berlin-based DJs like Tama Sumo. By and large, these customers still frequent Rotation, as Phillip Sollmann attested to above. In fact, the store's reputation as a credible and well-curated space of independent electronic music culture allowed a relatively smooth transformation to a broader lifestyle boutique. It made sense in the context of Berlin's own transformation into a mecca of urban culture, art and music, which is generating tourism.[35] It also made sense in the context of the location of the store in an attractive hot zone of Berlin's gentrification. This kind of store may potentially offer a less intimidating atmosphere to the uninitiated. Participation in hardcore professional stores could be alienating. Specialist stores with their sometimes forbidding staff and mind-boggling genre sub-division may be hard to negotiate.

On the other hand, opening vinyl up to the general audience has its hazards, sometimes hilariously so. Niko recalls a repeated frustration with ignorant customers who mistake slipmats on turntables for records or inexpertly attempt to scratch on it. Some take photographs of themselves with headphones imitating the DJ. As Niko sees it, they have a general sense of this culture being cool and hip, and representing Berlin and the tourist perception of the city. He gives an example of one store in Berlin whose manager tends to refuse entry to bigger groups of young tourists because, according to his experience, they never buy, instead messing up and mishandling the stock.

This evocative power of vinyl as a DJ tool and totem of Berlin's vibrant club scenes makes it not only worth preserving as boutique merchandise, but also transferrable as a symbol of urban cool. An example of it is found in stores that have always been primarily clothing boutiques but established a connection to the vinyl scene by selling a carefully curated line of records from particular artists of labels. Located just up the street from *Rotation*, *Workaholic Fashion* is a paradigmatic example of such store. Here just a few record labels are supported, primarily ones considered to be typical of Berlin's sound, notably the B-Pitch Control label. Iconic Technics turntables can be accessed here by customers too, set in a minimalist side room of the store. The formula seems successful, as the firm now has a second venue, this time in more edgy Friedrichshain. This tendency to treat vinyl as a desirable semiotic component of fashion boutiques is now beginning to be registered in the mainstream clothing stores as well, not only through the ubiquitous inclusion of vinyl images in advertisements and store windows but through actual incorporation of new and vintage records in the store. *Urban Outfitters* in Berlin, for example, located in the part of the city close to *Rotation Boutique*, has a vinyl section – featuring both new and vintage records – right at the front of the store, categorized chronologically and mixed with a small collection of books and vinyl cover frames.

The evolution from pure record store to lifestyle store, as well as setting up mixed boutique stores, results from a series of challenges related to the long-term profitability of selling exclusively vinyl records and especially when only a small range of genres and sub-genres are sold. Clearly, a diversified portfolio of lifestyle goods, principally clothing, books and a small selection of personal items such as greeting and tourist cards, keeps the vinyl-centred lifestyle store economically sustainable. A similar example is found in the store *Outpost*, in Fortitude Valley in Brisbane, Australia. Located in a gritty laneway behind a famous live music venue in a district also famous for its clubs and music venues, *Outpost* displays a small selection of 12-inch LP vinyl and also cassettes, strictly from local artists. In contrast to *Rotation* where vinyl stocks number in the hundreds, *Outpost* stocks less than 50 vinyl and has no listening decks. Sometimes, however, the owner – also a soul, indie and ska DJ – displays a vintage portable turntable in store on which he spins second-hand records. Additionally, at live in-store events hosted by the store, live bands and turntablist DJs perform. While both *Rotation* and *Outpost* stock and present their vinyl in different ways, for both stores vinyl performs an important role of establishing the cultural, and specifically musical, contexts of the cities and neighbourhoods it resides in. The meanings of vinyl become entangled with the meanings of the store's clothing, each being mutually informative.

A final example comes from the store *City Country City* in Tokyo's district of Shimokitazawa. Located on the fourth floor of a building, it stocks a moderate-sized collection of second-hand vinyl across dance, soul, rock and jazz genres which is hand-picked by the owner during international buying excursions. The unique lifestyle dimension of *City Country City* is the fact that it also devotes much of its floor space to being a café. Serving coffee and a small array of pasta dishes, *City Country City* lets you browse vinyl while waiting for your meal. A similar concept of vinyl shop/café was Vienna's *Tongues* located in a quiet street in the city centre, or *Ukulele* shop/café in Moscow, likewise tucked away in a courtyard off a smaller street in the city centre, specializing in the jazz and indie rock canon with a range of classic and indie stock mostly sourced and sent over to Moscow by buyers in the US. Unusually, *Ukulele* was true to its name: as well as vinyl, it displayed and sold a large range of ukulele musical instruments.

In the ideal type of lifestyle store, vinyl is one of many types of companion objects which cluster in a highly stylized shopping space to provide a smooth landscape of cool cultural consumption. The role of vinyl in a typical lifestyle store may be emptied of meanings related to music scenes and listening subcultures.

The physical location, design and styling of the lifestyle cornucopia store is worth reiterating. Economics dictates that they aren't located at the centre of gentrifying areas or main avenues, but often on their edges. Nevertheless, such lifestyle stores as *Title* feature in newly renovated buildings, scrubbed and shiny in glass, steel and pale wood shelving. They have a heavy emphasis on street frontage and display, and often new vinyl releases or classic reissue covers are on display, alongside books on art and literature.

The larger context of the lifestyle associations of vinyl is frequently on display in the gentrifying streets and neighbourhoods in which lifestyle stores are typically nested. In this context, the vinyl fits nicely into the finely aestheticized material-cultural mix. Function and use of these accompanying objects is of course important, but sign value is just as crucial: vintage kitchen mixers become aestheticized and glamorized symbols of domestic labour, optometrists show off spectacles as modern works of industrial art, shoes and jewellery likewise are wearable art, coffee is drinkable art, the turntable is represented as an iconic modern symbol suitable for sophisticated lounge room display, the vinyl cover as a piece of folk or popular art. In this context, vinyl becomes one object among many in the larger picture of assembled lifestyle objects, but its frequent association with books and art albums makes it a special symbol of 'organic', cool or sophisticated culture. Adding a dose of cool sensibility, acknowledging history, giving material symbolization to educated listening practices and preferences that rest on rich cultures of popular music; it fits smoothly into new lifestyle zones of large cities.

In these lifestyle stores, certain shopping practices are typical. A browsing shopper – it is probably not right to call vinyl customers in these stores 'diggers', but rather dustless and dirtless 'gliders' – will typically not get his or her fingers dirty when perusing the stock in such a store. The records are all factory clean, probably wrapped in tight plastic, carefully displayed and presented rather than packed in category boxes, and the vinyl stock is organized by a small number of major genres such as jazz, rock and pop, or indie, and then also alphabetically by artist. A key feature is the display of especially interesting, iconic or attractive covers – the Jimi Hendrix Experience's *Electric Ladyland*, Aphex Twin's *Selected Ambient Works* and the Smiths' *The Queen is Dead* are all potential covers for display. Because vinyl makes up only a fraction of the space in such stores and because stock is frequently all new vinyl, one cannot expect to find records that are by definition rare or unique pressings. The suggestion of rarity and the connotation of heritage is achieved by stocking reissue, new records from the 1960s and 1970s, with a plethora of classic jazz LP covers by the likes of Miles Davis or John Coltrane, or indie rock LPs by Sonic Youth and Pavement. Here, vinyl is largely a sign object, whose aestheticization and entwinement with other cultural objects in the store point to heritage, authenticity and the staged emplacement of the analogue record as a means of distinguished curating and taste-making.

To critical consumers and diggers who invest vinyl with meanings of authenticity associated with organic scenes apparent in archival and scene-based stores, these highly stylized and managed types of lifestyle shops can be perceived as sterile and inauthentic, promoting vinyl as a lifestyle to be bought, rather than an object vested with critical and totemic powers of transcendence promised by the work of digging. For other vinyl enthusiasts, or just those fascinated by the iconic performances and outputs of twentieth-century popular culture, these new lifestyle stores are an exciting space for exploring canonical and cutting-edge popular culture. Whatever the case, vinyl remains a special object rather than a mundane product.

In the lifestyle stores more heavily immersed in local cultural, art and music scenes, such as the latter examples cited, vinyl as object is arguably just as selected and curated in terms of representative musical genres and styles, but these records are strongly integrated with companion objects in the store. Unlike archival and professional or underground stores where volume or stylistic consistency of vinyl is often a key indicator, in the lifestyle store curatorial authority, popular iconicity and homological coherence matter. In these cases, economics dictates that vinyl alone cannot sustain all the costs of running a physical store, though vinyl is a crucial part of the product mix in the stores due to its recontextualized status of an extraordinary medium. Outside of the cosmopolitan locations of big cities or art centres, the lifestyle vinyl store may sometimes be the only economically viable and culturally legible stockist. Wolfgang Voigt offers an insight into this condition: 'It depends on where you go. In some places, record stores have got more clothing, and people usually keep their music in their pocket, you know. They've never seen a record play: "What is this thing spinning around? It looks beautiful!"'

The power of authentic tropes connected to archival and specialist stores, as well as the importance of discourses of love and devotion to vinyl, can be gauged by seeing how they get incorporated or reinscribed within lifestyle venues. *HHV Selected* in Berlin organizes in-house events, just like *OYE* or *Spacehall* do, and promotes vinyl-only events. One of its flyers features a slogan that makes this aspect abundantly clear: 'Strictly Vinyl! No Bullshit! One love!'

VINYL AS TOTEM

We have explored the construction of meanings of vinyl within urban zones and physical settings through an analysis of store types. Working from the premise that things help to narrate urban space and, in turn, urban spaces are narrated by the co-presence of things, we have argued that vinyl as a meaningful thing is mediated by its location within particular urban sites. There is, we have argued, a medium-space nexus where particular objects have semiotic weight and iconic power within certain settings. Objects help to animate and define such settings, and the settings provide symbolic context and aesthetic reference points for the framing of such objects. Vinyl is one such object. Working with the idea of the vinylscape, we argue that vinyl has signifying capacity as a totem of independent, cosmopolitan music scenes, and is in fact inseparable from both imagination and practice of the associated urban lifestyles.

The reasons for this are worth briefly recapping. As a thing, vinyl signifies heritage, cutting-edge club scenes, high-fidelity format, and is tied up with narratives that position it as 'other' to digital mediums and the corporate technologies and networks through which they are managed and enabled. Further, contemporary vinyl production, especially within electronic music and indie scenes which characterize our major case of Berlin, is mostly produced in relatively small-batch or even boutique-scale pressings and tends to be equally an art concern as much as it is a business concern. This fact of economic production informs a discursive narrative centred on independence and authenticity crucial for the urban youth subcultures and alternative vibrant big city scenes. In addition, the huge stock of second-hand vinyl sold around culturally vibrant cities such as Tokyo, London, Berlin or Melbourne refers consumers to historically entrenched music scenes and makes them aware of the vast heritage of global flows and international sounds available on the vinyl format. Because of these factors, vinyl points to a particular mode of cultural consumption with critical possibilities, which draws on cultural heritage, expert knowledge, and which is energized by the existence of musicians, labels, clubs, bars and stores which release and promote contemporary and cutting-edge music on vinyl. Vinyl thus performs an important role in narrating the city in a way which points to possibilities of alternative consumption and cosmopolitan experiences. The articulated presence of analogue records adds to the cultural landscape of the city by diversifying not only its soundscapes and artistic traditions, but also its now increasingly digitalized mediascapes. The vinyl record can stand for a particular type of engagement with urban space and a related mode of acquiring vinyl which values local record shops as key institutions. For example, the vinyl release of the Third Side's LP *Unified Fields*, a collaboration between Domenico Cipriani and Alberto Marini with DJ and producer Steffi, includes the following text on its back cover: 'Third Side would like to thank all those who have been supporting us and all the people who buy vinyl, listen to vinyl, love vinyl. Support your local record shop!'

Focusing significantly but not exclusively on Berlin, we have woven these factors into our descriptions of store types. Berlin sustains dozens of vinyl-related institutions, some very successful, and still attracts thousands of people to settle in. It may be the economically poorest German metropolis, but it *is* a metropolis and – as Berlin mayor Klaus Wowereit famously said – it is sexy, perhaps the sexiest of them all. The saying is not: Berlin is sexy *because* it is poor. The sexiness factor derives its iconic power from elsewhere. Vinylscapes embody part of it, a viewpoint expressed by a number of our interviewees. We have distinguished its following dimensions: (1) vinyl's special pragmatics and ethics within independent cultures; (2) vinyl's aesthetic presence in stores and domestic spaces; (3) the commandable knowledge and effort, time- and money-wise, behind assembling a collection; (4) skills behind spinning it in clubs; (5) the intimate relationship with music and its cultural contexts; and – last but not least – (6) the city's spatial affordances that make production and consumption of music on vinyl a meaningful experience and an event. Vinylscapes we have presented here are neatly reinscribed within these dimensions.

In other words, the story of vinyl's cool and its counter-intuitive rebirth in the digital era is not reducible to the *aesthetics* of its immaterial content – the music and the values of its scenes. Neither materialist anthropologies, nor lay cultural discourses prone to claim that 'all that matters is music', could do justice to the elusive complexity of the topic at hand. Rather, we deal here with a phenomenological structure which is the 'synthesis of matter and idea'.[36] Importantly, this synthesis is performatively achieved through located rituals and strategies, whereby 'music lovers' continually redefine their taste using 'gestures, objects, mediums, devices and relations engaged in a form of playing or listening'.[37] Here we could broaden the analytic scope of Hennion's study from classical to contemporary independent music and argue that there is also *ethics* and potentially also *politics* to this phenomenological constellation which makes music performative in a deeper social sense. We might think about 'indie-ethics' and 'cosmopolitics' of vinyl as discernible variations on broader themes of urban counter-culture. Consider, for example, the popular slogan of vinyl culture that is reprinted on t-shirts and vinyl slipmats and visible in many stores around the world: 'Vinyl kills the mp3 industry.'

We also have to note, however, that the performative capacity of vinyl that we have explored – sometimes in superlative settings – is actually relatively precarious. Vinyl's meaning is constantly changing in relation to its users and contexts. There is not one single meaning of vinyl, not one hegemonic narrative, which is part of vinyl's appeal and cultural flexibility. Vinyl's polysemic qualities are in part informed by setting, context and the meaning-making activities of participants as well as by city and neighbourhood context, specific qualities of place and cultural practice, musical heritage of a given country or district, etc. In turn, these contexts directly shape and affect both the cultural and economic dimensions of vinyl's value. This means that while vinyl can point with potency and power to certain cultural ideals and values, this capacity is actually the result of complex performative fusions, materially mediated combinations of *mise-en-scène*, scripts and actors, allied with immaterial myths of place, urban legends and larger national and international contexts. The contemporary ascendancy of vinyl to the status of powerful symbol is thus also prone to performative failure when symbols, spaces, actors and practices fall out of alignment and vinyl becomes a mere thing. This range of possible cultural moves, corresponding to forms of cultural power, represents a continuum of possibilities from sacred symbol to mundane product.

The question of what happens when vinyl moves from carefully curated sites of lifestyle and spaces of independent critical power is interesting to consider. For example, if it moves back into the mainstream of chain stores and supermarkets, eco-supermarkets and bulk retail sellers – from gritty quarters of Friedrichshain, Fitzroy, Williamsburg and Kreuzberg, to Walmart, Urban Outfitters, Whole Foods and Amazon – will this shift indeed reverse, or at least halt the process of cultural elevation vinyl has been undergoing? If it did, it would only confirm our argument that the meanings of vinyl as an object are closely linked to the social spaces and cultural zones of its circulation. Following Steven Feld,[38] we may say that as these spaces and zones are sensed by people, their senses get placed. The urban emplacement of vinyl punctuates the sensual architecture of cities and it does produce social places, no less than built environments do, turning them into fully fledged cultural habitats.

CHAPTER SIX

Epilogue

Modern Icon

A NEW SPIN ON AN OLD THING

Digitalization seems to have altered everything in its path. It has destroyed some traditional ways of doing things too, in some respect to the point that what we have once learned is certainly no longer enough. The destruction has been creative, to be sure, but it has also been so swift and fixated on the perennial upgrade that for a time few of us paid attention to unintended consequences of the new revolution. One such ironic consequence is that convenience offered by the virtual mobilities of digitalization has made us sit more and meet less. Sociologists researching the icons of the new digital age observe that 'we are increasingly alone together'.[1] Another consequence is the phenomenon of 'data smog'[2] – a perfect accessibility to cultural data has a distinct flipside of creating informational noise or glut, as David Shenk put it. We feel confronted on a daily basis with too much too fast. Inflation of files, updates, apps and incessant flow of evanescent images may desensitize rather than inspire if left uncontrolled on our omnipresent screens.

But there is yet a series of other unanticipated cultural consequences in the form of persistence and resurgence of the old stuff that somehow withstood the pressure of the new, or in forms of hybrid arrangements between the new and the old. Some may see the revivals as micro resistance or everyday backlash against the new. Others simply rediscover an unknown pleasure. The technological hybridity may draw on both tendencies, but it also has its own dynamic of cross-fertilization and contrastive modes of action. Not everything old can accomplish this feat of cultural renewal and continuity though. A series of conditions must in fact be met for a rejuvenated or persistent thing to be more than a fleeting vintage craze or nostalgic prop of ageing generations. The phenomenon of vinyl's relatively modest but noticeably transformative resurgence owes its significance neither to a passing hype nor to nostalgic yearnings, although these narratives and associated sentiments may amplify some of its cultural cachet. We find that as far as music consumption is concerned vinyl has returned to stay; in other words, the digital may have to live with its other in the backyard. Moreover, the relation between the two formats can be one of creative symbiosis rather than indifference. By all accounts, ostensibly 'replaced' by the industry with a 'better' product, vinyl should have been dead by now, or at best confined to museums and antique stores as quaint *incunabulum*. But something else has happened instead. A series of new spins on the old analogue record have carried it to a new age through a path replete with inspiring ironies and paradoxes.

During the first phase of digitalization symbolized by CD, it was one carrier group in particular that can be held responsible for saving the vinyl – independent electronic dance music DJs who employed digital productions but stuck to vinyl as the medium for their artistic output. The standardized CD medium certainly revolutionized the music market by 'solving' all kinds of perceived imperfections of the previous format. However, revolving at their different speeds, records and turntables kept being freely used by DJs and producers to eventually spin a cultural revolution in its own right. Initially it was a sort of quiet revolution, even if done with unusually loud cuts. In the second phase of digitalization marked by ultimate preponderance of electronic files and virtual streams and iconically embodied by the Apple products, vinyl saw a socially broader renaissance exactly at the time when the digital revolution seemed complete. This is certainly about reappreciation of certain sounds, and asserting the depth and timelessness of the 'old school' hearing, listening and playing. Auditory warmth, richness and the much-vaunted high fidelity of the musical message account for vinyl's lasting and its air of 'holy script' for serious music aficionados. But these factors alone can hardly explain its rather explosive and quite widespread contemporary resurgence as well as its curious timing. We see it as a 'holistic' renaissance of the *concrete aesthetic object* at a time when screen-based digitalization of culture can be claimed to have reached certain critical mass and speed. This curiously timed resurgence speaks volumes about the continued relevance of tangible objectifications, communal experiences and personal rituals in our cultural life. In short, vinyl's appeal is about the meditative experience of sound but also about the ecstasy of dance, the beauty of expression and the sublime of collective effervescence. As we have showed in this book, vinyl proved to be perfectly suited for the task of enabling different experiences, a genuine cultural accomplishment with lasting effects. And then there is also this more private and introspective part of vinyl's aptitude for becoming the chosen medium for transmission and ritualized contemplation of musical experiences. We hear the echo of Ian Curtis's concise approach to vinyl in the words of his wife: 'Ian taught me that if you put a piece of music on, you sit down and listen to it. You don't get up and do the washing-up or anything. You listen to it.'[3]

If vinyl is a medium that is at once a message, then one of the key things it conveys today is: 'slow down and pay attention'. Among other things, its resurgence indicates a collective readiness to take such messages seriously. To collect and listen to music on vinyl now means to restructure our digitally regimented (in)attention, diversify shopping patterns and time use. It is about reintroducing elements of the 'sacred' moments and objects to one's mundane routines. In a time of fierce digital acceleration that worships fastness and growth, many of us have become not only omnivorous but also voracious consumers of culture. We have tried to show how vinyl's many affordances may make our engagement with music more focused and culturally 'sustainable', and thus more meaningful. This is a salient aspect of vinyl's emerging 'political ecology'.[4]

The more holistic approach to vinyl also pushes us to acknowledge that things are the most powerful signifiers as they engage not only our minds but our bodies and transform our engagement with space. Some of them are icons that epitomize whole cultural formations, whereby acts of cultural appreciation and social critique revolve around the role of specific objects. Therefore it makes sense to already talk about 'iPod culture' and claim that it enables as much as it closes off,[5] as well as to consider 'vinyl culture' to be a distinct attractive lifeworld with a unique and thus irreplaceable tradition.

The German art historian Hans Belting has provided us with a deeply informed set of concepts about media and icons.[6] Drawing on other congenial works of his discipline, he argues that understanding cultural phenomena requires a more inclusive, integrated and aesthetically variegated approach. In particular, the conceptual triangulation of sound, space and body promises a more adequate outlook as it joins together what often remains separate in academic research, despite being united in human daily existence. Citing Bernhard Leitner, Belting invites us to approach body as an integral sensorium of hearing which is not constituted only by the ear. Belting emphasizes that if we still happen to be 'enchanted' with things, it is because the visual, acoustic and haptic sensations of spaces and objects blend into one *experience*. He also states that when it comes to 'our innate ability of iconic symbolization, all the senses are employed'. We have found such a multidimensional perspective a necessary and fundamental addition to the standard cultural sociological accounts that, despite their thick descriptions of media discourses, remain glaringly 'thin' on all the phenomenological and objectual aspects of social life. It is by taking this new spin on vinyl's extended life that we wish to reveal its power not only to survive but shine, perhaps more than ever. Below we recapitulate how we have gone about it and what are the implications of this approach for our thinking about music and culture more generally.

ON METHODOLOGY: CULTURAL SPECIFICITIES OF THE STUDY

We do not claim that our research on the topic of the vinyl record is comprehensive. Indeed, it is not meant to be, and there are obvious strengths and weaknesses of our approach. A specific advantage is that we emphasize contemporary *vinyl culture* and focus on the vinyl as material object from a variety of perspectives rather than exploring just one aspect of it, such as vinyl consumption or collectorship, for example. We find that it is precisely the combination of different features that makes vinyl enduringly interesting for various publics. No single characteristic of analogue record could be credited with inspiring the vinyl revival in the digital age.

One of the biases in existing research on vinyl records is that it tends to focus somewhat obsessively on collectorship. The vinyl collector, who may be a crate digger of any age but is more often painted as a mature, intrepid or nerdy character, is often taken as the central figure in vinyl culture as if it is this user who somehow configures the entire vinyl economy and history. It is true that the cultural economies of second-hand vinyl and associated crate-digging practices are a distinct feature that derives from its historicity, relative rarity and seriality, and which directly informs important parts of its mythology. However, to favour this aspect tends to distort a contemporary general focus on the vinyl as material object. This emphasis on collectorship can trivialize the consumption of analogue records as the exemplary mode of vinyl use, thereby foregrounding a type of vinyl buyer who is in fact a special type, or even outlier. As Russell Belk's studies on collectorship suggest,[7] collectorship is a special, dedicated form of consumption. Looking at vinyl via explorations of collectorship can therefore reduce vinyl to a vehicle of special music consumption, as well as pigeonhole records as a class of collectable commodities with a distinct flavour of *negative fetishization*. However, we have tried to make evident that there is more to vinyl. Its revival is about rediscovery of engagement, sensuality, coolness, care, ritual, rarity and specific auditory experience. Importantly, its persistence throughout decades of mainstream neglect and re-emergence as a hip thing owes much to the passion of underground DJs and beat makers who revered the old records and kept producing new analogue discs when the very idea of physical carrier seemed to be called into question. Their story is not the one about transitions 'from vinyl to digital and back again'.[8] Their passion for the 'old school thing' sustained vinyl use regardless of changing technologies. This passion contains an element of what we have called in this book *positive fetishism*. Our method combines phenomenologically inclined observation and hermeneutic 'thick description' of both extant media texts and textual data generated through our own interviews to capture the multiplicity of vinyl's features and meanings. What emerges out of such an analysis is portrayal of a fully fledged artistic object and modern icon.

We are aware of the potential pitfalls of the main lines of inquiry adopted here. In his seminal work on cultural consumption, Pierre Bourdieu had claimed that sociology's 'aim is not to reintroduce any form of what is called "lived experience" but to move beyond the abstract relationship between consumers with interchangeable tastes and products with uniformly perceived and appreciated properties to the relationship between tastes'.[9] We see merit in advocating 'the necessity of including in the complete definition of the product the differential experiences which the consumers have of it', but we are not prepared to confirm that this is always a 'function of the dispositions they derive from their position in economic space'.[10] As we have traced a range of experiences people have had with vinyl and examined several modes of vinyl consumption in last decades, we feel more inclined to conclude that vinyl evinces a densely mediated and entangled power of agentic kind. Thus, it can be credited with at least partial 'autonomy' vis-à-vis socio-economic structures of mainstream societal makeup. Bourdieu was correct to observe that 'objects do not impose the self-evidence of a universal, unanimously approved meaning'. But we think he moves too fast – and probably too far – in asserting that 'even industrial products are not objective', while at the same time insisting that objective economic conditions of production 'necessarily determine' variability of taste and interpretation. To avoid a potentially economistic bias, we choose a more flexible and, in our view, more even-handed take on 'industrially' produced artworks of which vinyl is an iconic example. Objects are no less 'objective' than the socioeconomic relations that bring them to life. As they constitute our physical world, they 'objectively' inspire lasting 'subjective' attachment. And there is always a bundle of technological forces and cultural background representations about such things as 'progress' or 'authenticity' that come into play as well. What we heuristically call 'the digital age' is treated here as the key creative technological dislocation with both intended and unintended repercussions. It is a massive displacement of a kind that Heidegger would be inclined to see as revelatory even if it is somewhat myopically destructive too. But we wished to go further and ask how vinyl escaped the fate of 'outdated' medium in a culture worshipping incessant 'upgrade' and fast speed. This is why we have rephrased Regis Debray's key question turning it into one of our animating concerns: how does a traditional domain resist being dislodged by a novel technology?

In line with late-modern agendas in social theory and resultant methodological shifts, we treated vinyl as an example of 'vibrant matter'[11] that retains 'iconic power'.[12] It is a wonderfully paradoxical material signifier with singular aura and plural existence of a mechanically reproduced object that defied the 'objective', seemingly non-negotiable and linear logic of technological development. Vinyl is a signifier with specific qualities, affordances and meanings that require 'thick description', the method traditionally deemed necessary and most suitable for cultural analysis. That said, vinyl is at once a 'vivid entity not entirely reducible to the contexts in which (human) subjects set them, never entirely exhausted by their semiotics'.[13] In fact, semiotics can't be neatly separated from specific pragmatics and materiality. We have found vinyl a perfect ethnographic illustration and validation of Webb Keane's take on 'social analysis of material things', namely that it needs to 'recognize how materiality of signification is not just a factor for the sign interpreter but gives rise to and transforms modalities of action and subjectivity regardless of whether they are interpreted'. Furthermore, like other artefacts, vinyl remains a part of contingent spatial entanglements and rather 'sticky' entrapments of material kind that retain a degree of alterity from words, abstractions of human mind and intentionality of human will. We need to listen to sound, not just language. We need to rely on and share the life of the senses, not just the life of the mind. Put differently, we have to enhance our sociological 'thick description' with what Constance Classen calls 'sensuous description'.[14] Our research enabled us to learn from vinyl not only as a unique phenomenon but also as a type of iconic object that speaks volumes about layered character and variable agency of media. This is again in line with Jane Bennett's observation that the 'agentic capacity [of things] is now seen as differentially distributed across a wider range of ontological types'.[15]

Finally, we look at deeply felt personal and collective relations that people develop with such objects, seeing it as reciprocal. As Ian Woodward wrote elsewhere, 'in current studies of material culture the object-person relations is the direct focus of inquiry, and taken to be a matter of interest in its own right'.[16] The case of vinyl is certainly a case of distinction and taste games and problematic modes of commodification, but having zoomed in on its various aspects and features as engineered, designed and experienced by its different users convinced us to push certain important boundaries of these discourses. Here different other thinkers proved inspiring, from Hegel to Miller, Merleau-Ponty to Debray, and from Simmel to McLuhan.

In other words, a set of methods and concepts adopted here has been to explore the multidimensional cultural economy of vinyl production, consumption and mediation. This approach emphasizes the circulation of vinyl through multiple communities of consumers, artists, record labels, stores, vinyl technicians, and also its life in media discourses. Our wider framing means we are unable to fully account for each practice of vinyl consumption, for example. Clearly, there could be a whole book written on the types of vinyl consumers that exist. Noticeably, most of our interviewees are male, and while they couldn't easily be compartmentalized into particular social classes, they clearly share broad affinities of lifestyle, taste and cultural capital. Of course, there are diverse vinyl user groups we have largely ignored, even if we believe that much of what we have found will also be of relevance to these broader communities. It goes without saying that more work could be done on any of the topics we treat in this book. What we have achieved, however, addresses the contemporary economy of vinyl culture at a certain time through a number of constitutive aspects driven by a focus that prioritizes the material qualities and affordances of vinyl as a way of exploring its meaningful circulation within economies of music consumption and production. We found it indispensable to frame our study as one which aims to understand the survival and revival of vinyl.

Last but not least, our spatio-temporal focus locates vinyl where it has remained firmly entrenched throughout the turbulent time of the last 25 years and is being cultivated most intensely now – independent scenes in cosmopolitan settings. We have focused mostly on Berlin as a contemporary mecca of independent and underground music, especially in its electronic and club-oriented guises. It is at present one of the most saturated and still-expanding vinyl markets in the world, which is remarkable because Berlin has not always had this status. This central European metropolis is still a cosmopolitan and artistic centre in the making, and for this reason it is particularly revealing of people–object relations and processes of place-related value creation. As an urban form, it is less congealed, and therefore perhaps better corresponds with what some see as 'liquid' nature of our time. At the same time Berlin has had a remarkable track record of both the off-beat and independent bohemian cultures and cutting-edge technologies in the twentieth century, from the 'roaring twenties' to 'counter-cultural' atmosphere of West Berlin in the 1970s and 1980s, through to the exuberant 1990s brimming with techno. All were progressive in their own way, challenging the norm and developing a distinctly 'metropolitan culture' where the existential motto has always seemed to be: 'If it's so, then why can't it be otherwise?'.[17] The history of the legendary Berlin label *Basic Channel* is an iconic case in point; pushing the old Neumann cutting machine to its new limits inspired by the rising culture of techno and Berlin's unique spatial situation enabled a few local artists like Mauritz von Oswald or Robert Henke to realize a powerful aesthetic vision. The city is often cited as an important ingredient in this cultural brew that had vinyl as one of its key totems, a benchmark of quality and authentic simplicity at the time when the mainstream thought in opposite ways or did not think about it at all. In a recent conversation with Mauritz von Oswald, the legend of Detroit techno Juan Atkins gives an insight of a knowledgeable outsider to Berlin's importance for underground vinyl-loving dance culture: Berlin 'brought to the forefront the simplicity of music and simplicity of the beats'.[18]

In Berlin, vinyl is not just discussed and talked about as something extraordinary. Rather, it is lived, experienced, experimented with and enjoyed quite commonly. Among the young it is a part of a widespread hipster lifestyle, just like leisurely strolling and hanging in cafés belonged once to the lifestyle of the *flâneur*. Thus, 'going native' in Berlin's independent or underground music scenes partly means 'going analogue'. Likewise, the cool and the analogue seem intimately intertwined. Vinyl is easy to spot, even if far less ubiquitous than the glossy iPhone. At the same time, it is not trivial or banal the way new personal technologies have become, and thus less prone to become an obnoxious gadget, one anyway soon to be replaced by something still 'better'.

Vinyl's revival in Berlin made the analogue a cutting-edge experience again, almost as if it were a fresh invention. To many of the youngest music customers it may have appeared somewhat like this, and it is one of the more interesting paradoxes of our story. Vinyl's professional reappropriations and more general resurgence are genuinely contemporary, late-modern phenomena, in which experiences of media hybridity and renewed urban proclivity for sensual rituals of both commonality and individuality are crucial. These tendencies go hand-in-hand with an increasingly admired search for non-standard experiences which validate all kinds of improvisations, DIY practices, experiments and apparent throwbacks.

Therefore, it must be reiterated that our study captures a specific period in vinyl's long history and a specific cultural field defined by certain genres, scenes and user communities, even if it heuristically narrates a broader historical backdrop against which the aura of vinyl and its cultural 'depth' can be more fully comprehended. As the subtitle of our book indicates, we have considered vinyl during the most recent time, which profoundly accelerated cultural shifts and transferred an immense deal of cultural consumption to the virtual space of the internet. Vinyl's lasting and renaissance is a story of a certain *Zeitgeist* and its growing reflexivity. Again, this does not mean we believe vinyl to be an elusive vogue that somewhat contingently and passively 'reflects' fleeting desires of late-modern jaded publics. Rather, vinyl playing is among self-conscious aesthetic practices that drive contemporary redefinitions of a whole series of crucial boundaries between the concrete and abstract, real and virtual, authentic and fake, valuable and worthless, rare and common, organic and contrived, slow and fast, etc. These are not superficially symbolic boundaries but existential, embodied and deeply felt differentiations. More attention and care for vinyl overlaps with parallel contemporary processes of increasingly resonant passion for human craft, personal touch, rarity and individuality. To fully grasp it, one needs to live through those changes, not just read and talk about them. This is something to behold and to savour, slowly, to be sure.

For this reason much of our work has grown out of contemporary urban observations. As the key phenomena were becoming more graspable through direct participation in Berlin's spaces, not only through language, we were reminded time and again that lifeworlds are not completely explainable in systemic terms of any structuralism or system. Culture is inescapably corporeal, visually framed, spatially grounded and largely sensually mediated, even if it is also continually narrated, re-narrated and thought of. Human subjectivity and collective feelings get crystallized and reassured through contact and experience with material objectual manifestations, not merely by human discourses. It is within this hybridity where the 'messy'[19] sociological work of researching culture really poses challenges, but it is also here where we think it offers greatest rewards of cultural understanding. One of the challenges is, of course, to exercise a degree of critical distance while rendering our observations and feelings in words. While suspending intellectual disbelief often proves indispensable during the fieldwork that aspires to adequate understanding, it is our belief in a more intersubjective character of theoretically informed concepts that enable writing culture. We have tried to strike a productive balance between these spheres. The inevitable tensions may not be fully reconcilable, but they need not be. Just because the 'magic' of things seems 'inarticulable' within languages of societies that created them, as Michael Taussig, cited earlier, asserts, does not mean we are barred from understanding. In fact, the poignant realization of language's limitations – evident in Western culture throughout the twentieth century, from Hugo von Hofmannsthal and his famous 'Letter', to Ian Curtis's lyrics – paradoxically can strengthen it in relation to things, these things and pleasures one could never describe but nevertheless sees and feels their beauty. Similar reflexivity helps do and report on a research like ours.

In addition to the key sites of our study that shape various specificities of our findings, we must also consider the generational belonging, cultural location and roles of our interviewees and participants. The people we have interviewed and talked to are not vinyl tragics, unable to move beyond a familiar or nostalgia-infused medium. They represent different ages, from college students to mature masters of independent music business. All of them resolutely embrace new digital technologies, rarely if ever succumbing to purist or narrowly snobbish impulses. Many of them are experienced business owners, performers and consumers who have never given up on vinyl, to be sure, but this is for good reasons that mainly reside in its cultural relevance and material-*cum*-aesthetic specificity. Rafal Grobel, DJ and vinyl label manager, made it plain when he insisted that the either/or approach and comparisons of the good vs the bad are simplistic and counterproductive here. Analogue vs digital is not a matter of worse vs better. As he states, 'each solution has its pros and cons. I see no sense in fighting against one of them. The point is to use a given technology when it fits best.'

Primarily, we have interviewed independent artists and performers, the owners and managers of independent record stores, the managers and engineers of self-standing record pressing plants and mastering studios, as well as managers of independent record labels, all of whom – while crucial to the contemporary business of vinyl – nevertheless generally focus their vinyl production on small-run batches. Granted, few vinyl releases are very large these days relative to the number of digital releases purchased, which is in the millions for some popular single tracks. But, by comparison, there are vinyl releases by large media companies such as Universal or

Sony/Columbia where releases will often be in the thousands, and then there are independent companies such as *Ostgut Ton* and *Kompakt* where the scale of vinyl release is not only a fraction of this, but the independent tag matters for the nature and style of vinyl releases. For these smaller and independent companies, vinyl is a valuable sign in its own right, being a material symbol of authenticity, a carrier of a distinct and more carefully engineered sound, a reference to the longer history of the musical medium, and evidence of the company's commitment to releases with high levels of artistic and musical credibility vinyl releases afford.

VINYL: PHYSICAL AND CULTURAL MOBILITIES

The visible establishment of authenticity in these independent and underground cultural milieus facilitates the maintenance of vinyl's symbolic power within particular music cultures. Vinyl's unwillingness to disappear is based upon its continued relevance to contemporary independent scenes. Its capacity to work as a legitimate signifier of music heritage in turn energizes its wider circulation. Although challenged by the undeniable convenience of the digital medium, our study has shown that vinyl still retains symbolic and sonic currency as a signifier of highly credible and perhaps most authentic involvement in the music industry, on the sides of producers, music makers and listeners. The cultural energy vinyl acquires in underground and independent cultural spaces allows it to slowly and tentatively move back into certain mainstream settings. This trickle of vinyl back towards the cultural mainstream is not necessarily forever, and neither is it total. Now more than ever, the status of vinyl is both exciting and uncertain. It is, however, through meaning transformations that vinyl's cultural mobility is energized, involving a passage from spaces of independent and underground culture back into mainstream spaces. This journey also takes on a globally distributed, albeit decidedly urban and cosmopolitan character. We have shown the vinyl scenes in cities such as Berlin, and key metropolises of London, New York, Melbourne and Tokyo serve as centres of vinyl culture which attract records and labels to them as sales hot spots for rare and collectable editions and sites for scene-based cultural congregations, but also radiate the effervescent cultural energy of dance and indie rock scenes to other places. These places have strong bohemian communities that support vinyl, especially now when non-digital artefacts gain traction as distinctive and when off line practices are increasingly seen as off-beat and potentially even anti-systemic.

Again, this process of vinyl's cultural mobility should be seen as temporally established. In a music media environment radically transformed and continually upgradeable by electronic developments, this renewed edginess of vinyl is to some extent understandable as a type of cultural response to omnipresent digitalia and the way some listeners perceive digital media as tied up with the strictly profit-driven interests of global corporations. Vinyl, on the other hand, iconically undergirds and represents independent and artistic values, and its analogue nature means no company virtually owns or is able to track a person's musical tastes. It is no accident that along with club cultures and domestic settings, we have found vinyl to be associated with ethical, organic and small-scale producers of food and clothing, and to be played in neighbourhood and urban contexts where these cultures thrive. It is likewise telling that clubs that champion vinyl and authenticity of the party feeling of 'here and now' tend to forbid picture-taking, no doubt having the legendary Berghain club as the pattern to follow. Whether it is vintage or handmade fashion, organic foods, handmade jewellery or independent clothing boutiques, or other manifestations of slow and ethical consumption cultures,[20] vinyl seems to be a logical counterpart even though its ecological footprint as a product might be relatively big. It is, however, precisely the *kind* of engagement – both on producers' and consumers' side – that makes vinyl gel rather than jar with these new tendencies of conscious deceleration, high quality and DIY attitude. This may seem somewhat ironic given the survival of vinyl through its lean period was associated in some part with frenetic and hedonistic club cultures. This is yet another creative paradox of the vinyl-dedicated electronic scenes. While vinyl took from these settings authenticity, credibility, ritual power and sexiness, at the same time it also retained authority as a token of music and cultural heritage, and was associated with the discovery of forgotten and marginalized music cultures through the second-hand trade and the circulation of global vinyl.

COMMODIFICATION AND DE-COMMODIFICATION

The continued relevance of vinyl relates also to its capacities as a commodity. In the first instance, the longevity of vinyl as a material object, combined with its status as the dominant medium for music listening during the formative years and heyday of the pop-rock industry from roughly the late 1940s right through to near the end of the 1980s, means that second-hand markets for vinyl offer opportunities for music listeners to engage directly with musical heritage. The fact that this engagement is not always carried out under conditions of perfect knowledge in terms of markets, conditions and storage has rendered the myths of digging for vinyl even stronger. The current swathe of online markets and apps aid serious collectors and completists, but they cannot substitute for immersion in real social spaces where musical heritage can be explored, rediscovered and ultimately personally possessed. This discourse of vinyl as heritage object and archival medium also infuses markets for new vinyl. Top selling vinyl albums tend to divide into markets for contemporary indie and alternative music acts and markets for heritage acts and iconic LPs released through the 1960s and 1970s. In these markets, vinyl benefits from being a heritage medium, meaning it was the format on which these iconic LPs were originally released and for which they were technically calibrated. Vinyl retains cultural currency in this regard: authentic listening to this heritage canon doesn't demand or require vinyl, but it can be assisted and extended by it. In addition, new vinyl releases can benefit by parading their material, sensual advantages: full-colour gatefold sleeves; faithfully reproduced liner notes; free posters reproducing LP covers included; glorious, cool or perhaps tacky coloured vinyl; specially mastered and engineered pressings. All of these features aid the recirculation of the medium in mainstream markets. In independent markets, discourses of handmade and artistic production and the logic of the limited release afford the establishment of markets for new, reissue vinyl.

UNDERSTANDING THE MODERN ICON

There is probably no single concept or formula that could perfectly encapsulate the phenomenon as complex as vinyl. As Regis Debray succinctly states, 'a monocausal explanation is no explanation at all'.[21] It is precisely why a wider scope and more expansive rhythm of a book are needed to even begin to fathom the depth of vinyl culture. Vinyl effectively condenses and crystallizes so many different meanings that change across time and space contexts that it is perhaps easier to unpack them than to do vinyl justice with one name which could capture a kind of cultural condensation that it is. One heuristically useful way of recapitulating our unpacking of the analogue record in the digital age is to recognize it as a modern cultural icon. This qualification sheds light not only on vinyl itself but potentially also on how we can recast our thinking about cultural modernity.

In their introduction to the book *Iconic Power*, Dominik Bartmanski and Jeffrey Alexander offer a series of propositions regarding the nature of cultural icon and conditions of its social efficacy today.[22] They state that icons are aesthetic/material representations which, however, by dint of their very concreteness exist not only in the *re*-mode, i.e. as something reflecting or refracting other 'forces' the way discourses do, but may be described as independently causal and active on their own account. Most importantly, icons are potent objects whose surfaces do not simply represent hidden data and communicate information but constitute and transmit sensuous experience without which no culture can exist. As such they often are believer-friendly epiphanies or customer-friendly images. They are also exceptional cultural constructions in a double sense. First, they are instantly recognizable powerful symbols that travel through space and time. Second, they establish a strong relation between a particular riveting surface and a moving depth, one capable of blurring the structuralist line between sign and referent. To recognize and research icons means to delve into these two aspects and account for an intriguing mutuality between them. All this was noticed by the masters of cultural analysis like Roland Barthes and Claude Lévi-Strauss but left undeveloped, perhaps due to the fact that, as the German theorist of iconicity Gottfried Boehm writes, it 'irritates our common expectation which assumes a difference between the reality of the piece and its subject'.[23]

And yet, in concrete instances of cultural life we do see how this principle gets actualized. This is one of the reasons why icons exhibit a kind of power over us. The present book has attempted to tell a story of such resilient icon, powerful enough to have symbolized the entire technological watershed and then to withstand the seemingly lethal consequences of the next shift. Apart from all the valences of vinyl's attractiveness and its power, it is noteworthy that its surface comes perhaps as close at it gets to not just 'representing' but *embodying* its referent or 'subject'. In a certain palpable sense, the analogue groove *is* music. It is sonic abstraction sculpted and musical vibration congealed. Here we come closer to one of the key differences between the analogue and the digital that this book thematized and revealed to be of special importance in reconstructing vinyl's revival. Vinyl responds to our haptic and visual cravings that can't be fully satiated within the now hegemonic 'register of screens'.[24]

The hard discs with digital data make music invisible as they make it perfectly transferable. The hard 'wax' with analogue data brings music to the tangible visible surface. The former conceals the electronically encrypted signal that, as Robert Henke reminded us, leaves no room for interpretation and little error tolerance. The latter lays bare and even aestheticizes the electro-mechanically coded signal. It also leaves a degree of sonic interpretation and error tolerance, so that a scratched vinyl will still play and it will play noticeably different on different systems. As our interviewees told us time and again, no 'file' does or will ever have a history as humans have tended to define it until now. But every vinyl has history. It is an artefact that connects us to cultural heritage and – perhaps most importantly – to our own past. It is redolent of past moods, brings back memories, concretizes loose associations, punctuates our biography. It is a time machine of sorts. Some sociologists might consider it a 'mnemonic bridge', a potential link to the distant events from our lives, just like photographs or elements of urban design.[25] By the same token, vinyl can be a kind of investment in the future. What makes tangible objects like vinyl important to humans is that, being relatively unchanged, they give perceptually stable form to our feelings that often get dimmed by the passage of time and changes within ourselves. They lend that feeling of reassuring concreteness to the dreamy quality of our memories.

Thus, physical records record more than sounds. As their obdurate condition allows them to last and outlast their owners, they can record history, personal and collective. Unlike electronic discs hidden inside our machines, analogue discs are there to marvel at and exhibit 'hardness' that yields to reality in just a right measure to be compatible with a human sense of time and its passage that demands aesthetic concretization to feel 'real' and 'romantic'. All in all, Phillip Sollman, Peter Runge, Robert Henke and Wolfgang Voigt reflect concisely and almost identically on important social implications of the analogue/digital dichotomy. 'Nobody shows off their hard disc.' 'Perfection is a most annoying and unromantic thing.' 'We are still "analogue" beings.' These sensibilities translate in turn into a whole sphere of social distinction but, as we have suggested, not necessarily according to the rules laid out by Bourdieu. To the extent that vinyl may now be perceived as a luxury music medium, the socioeconomic problematic kicks back in. But if vinyl relativizes the notions of rarity, uniqueness and aura, it also does so to 'luxury', 'distinction' and 'necessity', and thus reshapes plausible evaluations of these terms. We find it instructive that our German respondents representing independent spheres would jokingly rather than critically say that vinyl is a bit like a Porsche car – you don't really need it, but it still looks and sounds good.

With a rich history, and its haptic, visual and sonic properties on display, vinyl is aural and auratic medium. Despite being mechanically reproduced, vinyl not only retained some aura but actually could be and did become a reinvented good within a fiercely competitive virtualized economy. To the extent that Bartmanski and Alexander are right to see iconicity as a vehicle of (re)enchantment that is an enduring feature rather than anachronistic leftover of civilizational change, vinyl's persistence and revival provide a convincing case in point. And as far as it is an 'imagined commodity' rather than a mere profit-generating product, vinyl helps concretize whole communities. Seeing vinyl as a multifaceted icon helps complementing the standard Marxist social critique of modern production and consumption and, when needed, to move beyond it toward more supple understandings. This book's approach yielded a story according to which the cultural potency of consumerist object is no less real than the potential danger of 'false consciousness' and negative fetishism. Despite a number of lingering effects of the latter, we have seen ample evidence of vinyl being a vehicle of cultural competence rather than misguided consumerism, a 'cultural performance' that fuses the assets of heart and reason as it inspires expertise and enchantment. This may be a relatively rare thing, just like the analogue record itself. But it does occur, and this is why in writing this book we have adhered to an interpretative perspective close to what Bruno Latour calls the 'variable geometry' of sociological analysis.[26] The vinyl story as we have narrated it here suggests that in addition to 'uniqueness without aura'[27] that putatively gnaws at our lives, a reverse dynamic takes place too – iconic aura continues to inhabit certain non-unique objects and ritual practices. To be sure, it can be used and abused probably in equal measure. If vinyl has proved relatively resistant to both neglect and corporate co-optation, it has been possible because it is much more than a music format. It is a resilient medium. It iconizes a sensory formation, a whole lifeworld – the situation cultivated by the independent figures we interviewed and listened to and which we set out to couch in a parlance of sociology. Behind vinyl there is a kind of love. On its surface, we find beats and signs of culture as it affords and shapes one of the most beautiful things there is – musical experience.

NOTES

PREFACE

1 Oscar Wilde, 2008, *The Picture of Dorian Gray*. London: Penguin Classics, p. 3.

2 Michael Bull and Les Back (eds), 2005, *The Auditory Culture Reader*. Oxford and New York: Berg, p. 13.

3 Dominik Bartmanski and Ian Woodward, 2013, 'The vinyl: the analogue medium in the age of digital reproduction', *Journal of Consumer Culture*. Online access: http://joc.sagepub.com/content/early/2013/05/30/1469540513488403.abstract

4 Bill Brewster and Frank Broughton, 2010, *The Record Players: DJ Revolutionaries*. London: DJhistory.

5 Regis Debray, 2000, *Transmitting Culture*. New York: Columbia University Press.

6 Ann Swidler, 2001, *Talk of Love. How Culture Matters*. Chicago, IL and London: University of Chicago Press, pp. 222–3.

7 Mitchell Duneier, 1999, *Sidewalk*. New York: Farrar, Strauss and Giroux, pp. 343–4.

8 Michael Taussig, 1993, *Mimesis and Alterity: A Particular History of the Senses*. New York and London: Routledge, pp. 207–8.

9 Bull and Back, *ibidem*, p. 12.

10 Bill Brewster, 2012, 'We Breathe Rhythm', in Ata Macias and Christoph Keller (eds) *Come on in My Kitchen. The Robert Johnson Book*. Frankfurt am Main: Ata Macias/Christoph Keller Editions, p. 206.

11 David Howes (ed.), 2005, *The Empire of the Senses. The Sensual Culture Reader*. Oxford: Berg, p. 4.

12 *Ibidem*, p. 4.

13 See Michael Emmison and Philip Smith, 2000, *Researching the Visual. Images, Objects, Contexts and Interactions in Social and Cultural Inquiry*. London: Sage, pp. 110–11.

14 Duneier, *ibidem*, pp. 341–2.

15 Dominik Bartmanski, 2014, 'The word/image dualism revisited: towards an iconic conception of visual culture', *Journal of Sociology*, vol. 50, no. 2, pp. 164–81.

16 See Robert Henke's excellent and informative interview with Rashad Becker, an engineer at *Dubplates & Mastering*, Berlin, available on the Monolake webpage: http://www.monolake.de/interviews/mastering.html

17 Regis Debray, *ibidem*, p. 99.

18 Georges Bataille, 2012, *Eroticism*. London: Penguin, p. 25.

VINYL AS RECORD: SEVERAL LIVES OF THE 'KING FORMAT'

1 Jonathan Sterne, 2003, *The Audible Past: Cultural Origins of Sound Reproduction*. Durham, NH and London: Duke University Press, p. 11.

2 Cited in: Hartwig Fischer, 2005, *Covering the Real: Art and the Press Picture from Warhol to Tillmans*. Köln: DuMont Literatur und Kunst Verlag & Kunstmuseum Basel, p. 12.

3 Paul du Gay, Stuart Hall, Linda Janes, Hugh Mackay and Keith Negus, 1997, *Doing Cultural Studies: The Story of the Sony Walkman*. London: Sage.

4 Michael Bull, 2007, *Sound Moves: iPod Culture and Urban Experience*. London and New York: Routledge.

5 George Lakoff and Mark Johnson, 2003, *Metaphors We Live By*. Chicago, IL: University of Chicago Press.

6 David Byrne, 2012, *How Music Works*, San Francisco: McSweeney's, p. 15.

7 Blaise Pascal, 1995, *Pensees*, London: Penguin, p. 28.

8 Constance Classen, 2012, *The Deepest Sense: A Cultural History of Touch*. Urbana, Chicago and Springfield, IL: University of Illinois Press, p. xiv.

9 Steven Levy in conversation with Rick Holland, *Electronic Beats Magazine*, no. 29, Spring 2012, p. 72.

10 *Ibidem*.

11 Michael Taussig, 1993, *Mimesis and Alterity: A Particular History of the Senses*. New York and London: Routledge, p. 208.

12 Regis Debray, 2000, *Transmitting Culture*. New York: Columbia University Press, p. 2.

13 Keith Richards, 2010, *Life*, with James Fox. London: Phoenix, pp. 78–9.

14 Michael Bull, *ibidem*.

15 Roger Moorhouse, 2010, *Berlin at War*. New York: Basic Books, p. xvi.

16 Consulted on 9 June 2014 at: http://www.library.yale.edu/cataloging/music/historyof78rpms.htm

17 Davis, Clive, with Anthony DeCurtis, 2013, *The Soundtrack of My Life*. New York: Simon and Schuster.

18 *Ibidem*.

19 Marc Hertzman, 2013, *Making Samba: A New History of Race and Music in Brazil*. Durham, NH and London: Duke University Press, pp. 159, 161.

20 *Ibidem*, p. 172.

21 Tomasz Stanko, 2010, *Desperado: Autobiografia*. Krakow: Wydawnictwo Literackie, p. 25.

22 Andrea Cossu and Matteo Bortolini, 2013, 'The Spider and the Fly: Authenticity, Dualism, and the Rolling Stones', in Helmut Staubmann (ed.), *The Rolling Stones. Sociological Perspectives*. Lanham: Lexington Books, pp. 21–39.

23 Richards, *Ibidem*, pp. 79–80.

24 Stanley Crouch, 2013, *Kansas City Lightning. The Rise and Times of Charlie Parker*. New York: Harper Collins, pp. 194–5.

25 Richards, *Ibidem*, p. 105.

26 Gary Calamar and Phil Gallo, 2009, *Record Store Days: From Vinyl to Digital and Back Again*. New York: Sterling, p. xv.

27 Glenn Gould, 1968, *Glenn Gould: Concert Drop Out*. Glenn Gould in conversation with John McClure. Track B4 'Electronic Music is the Future'. Columbia Records Masterworks, Vinyl LP, BS 15.

28 John Szwed, 2004, *So What. The Life of Miles Davis*. New York: Simon & Schuster, p. 446.

29 Christian Marclay and Yasunao Tone, 2004, 'Record, CD, Analog, Digital', in Christopher Cox and Daniel Warner (eds), *Audio Culture. Readings in Modern Music*. New York: Continuum, p. 345.

30 Peter Hook, 2013, *Unknown Pleasures: Inside Joy Division*. New York: itbooks, p. 85.

31 Hook, *ibidem*, p. 88.

32 Consulted on 30 April 2014 at: http://www.allmusic.com/album/bop-till-you-drop-mw0000189511

33 Jonathan Sterne, 2003, *The Audible Past. Cultural Origins of Sound Reproduction*. Durham, NH and London: Duke University Press, p. 11.

34 Hook, *ibidem*, p. 139.

35 See: Coleman, 2003; Millard, 2005; Patmore, 2009.

36 Jack White in *New Musical Express*, consulted on 14 June 2014 at: http://www.nme.com/news/jack-white/68853

37 Georg Simmel, 1900, 'A chapter in the Philosophy of Value', in Simmel, Georg, 2008, "Englischsprachige Veröffentlichingen 1893–1910", Frankfurt am Main: Suhrkamp, p. 149.

38 Madlib in conversation with Thomas Fehlmann, *Electronic Beats Magazine*, no. 32, p. 76.

39 Richard Kostelanetz, 1968, John Cage, *An Anthology*, New York: Allen Lane.

40 John Cage quoted by Peter Shapiro, 2002, 'Deck Wreckers: The Turntable as Instrument', in R. Young (ed.), *Undercurrents. The Hidden Wiring of Modern Music*. London and New York: Continuum, p. 164.

41 Peter Shapiro, *ibidem*.

42 Hendrik Weber in Michael Jäger, Christine Käppelert, 2013, 'Techno ist wie ein Puls,' *Der Freitag Magazine*. Viewed 20 June 2014: http://www.freitag.de/autoren/christine-kaeppeler/techno-ist-wie-ein-puls

43 Sam Jones, 2011, 'UK music sales decline for seventh successive year despite downloads', *Guardian*, 2 January. Viewed 3 May 2013: http://www.guardian.co.uk/music/2012/jan/02/uk-music-sales-decline-2011.

44 M. Perpetua, 2011, 'Vinyl sales increase despite industry slump', *Rolling Stone*, 6 January. Available at: http://www.rollingstone.com/music/news/vinyl-sales-increase-despiteindustry-slump-20110106

45 Eric Felten, 2012, 'It's alive! Vinyl makes a comeback', *The Wall Street Journal*, 27 January. Available at: http://online.wsj.com/article/SB10001424052970204573704577184973290800632.html#articleTabs%3Darticle (accessed 3 May 2013);

46 Viewed 20 June 2014: http://www.cbsnews.com/videos/vinyls-resurrection-sales-at-a-record-high/

47 G. W. F. Hegel, 1975, *Aesthetics. Lectures on Fine Art.* Volume II. Oxford, Clarendon Press, pp. 889–90.

48 *Ibidem*, p. 909.

49 Andreas Rekwitz, 2002, 'The Status of the *Material* in Theories of Culture: From Social Structure to Artefacts', *Journal for the Theory of Social Behavior*, 2002: vol. 32, no. 2, p. 210.

50 Christine Van Assche, 2010, 'Sonic Process. A New Geography of Sounds', in Mela Davila (ed.), *Sonic Process*. MACBA: Barcelona, p. 10.

51 Jacques Rancière, 2010, 'Metamorphosis of the Muses', in Mela Davila (ed.), *Sonic Process*. MACBA: Barcelona, p. 27.

MEDIUM: HANDLING AND HEARING

1 Marshall McLuhan and Quentin Fiore, 1967, *The Medium is the Message*. New York: Touchstone, p. 8.

2 Daniel Miller, 1987, *Material Culture and Mass Consumption*: Oxford: Blackwell, p. 117.

3 Roger Silverstone, 1993, 'Television ontological security and the transitional object', *Media Culture and Society*, vol. 15, no. 4, pp. 573–98.

4 Terence E. McDonnell, 2010, 'Cultural objects as objects: materiality, urban space, and the interpretation of AIDS campaigns in Accra, Ghana', *American Journal of Sociology*, vol. 115, no. 6, p. 1806.

5 See Karin Knorr-Cetina and Urs Bruegger, 2002, 'Global microstructures: the virtual societies of financial markets', *American Journal of Sociology*, vol. 107, no. 4, pp. 905–50.

6 Tim Ingold, 2004, 'Culture on the ground: the world perceived through the feet', *Journal of Material Culture*, vol. 9, no. 3, pp. 315–40.

7 George Lakoff and Mark Johnson, 2003, *Metaphors We Live By*. Chicago, IL: University of Chicago Press.

8 Ian Hodder, 2012, *Entangled. An Archaeology of the Relationships Between Humans and Things*. Malden, MA: John Wiley and Sons, p. 94.

9 Regis Debray, 2000, *Transmitting Culture*. New York: Columbia University Press, p. 3.

10 Chris Rojek, 2009, *The Labour of Leisure. The Culture of Free Time*. London: Sage.

11 Shuker, Roy, 2010, *Wax Trash and Vinyl Junkies: Record Collecting as a Social Practice*. Aldershot: Ashgate, p. 112.

12 The full title of the original 1996 release is '*Endtroducing .....*', with five periods or full stops after the title. The Discogs website notes that the deluxe reissue of the LP was titled '*Endtroducing ...*', with only three periods after the title. Throughout this chapter, to avoid any grammatical confusion we omit use of the periods after the main title.

13 Stephen Robert Morse, 'DJ Shadow's Killer App, Can This Hip-Hop Sample Artist End-Run iTunes?', Mother Jones, http://www.motherjones.com/media/2009/11dj-shadows-killer-app, Last accessed 16 September 2014.

14 Viewed 22 May 2014, 'Records', http://www.rare-records.net/

15 DJ Shadow, quoted in Eliot Wilder, 2005, *DJ Shadow's Endtroducing*, London: Continuum: pp. 40–1.

16 *Spacehall* is one of the largest and most renowned vinyl record stores in Berlin. It is situated on Zossener Strasse in Kreuzberg. It was featured in an article titled '27 Breathtaking Record Stores You Have to Shop at Before you Die', http://www.buzzfeed.com/mariasherm/best-record-stores-around-the-world

17 Björk, 2011, 'In conversation with Hans Ulrich Obrist', *Electronic Beats Magazine*, vol. 27, p. 46.

18 Mary Douglas and Baron C. Isherwood, 1979, *The World of Goods. Towards an Anthropology of Consumption.* New York: Basic Books, p. 50.

19 Bill Brown, 2001, 'Thing theory', *Critical Inquiry*, vol. 28, no. 1, pp. 16.

20 Jane Bennett, 2010, *Vibrant Matter: A Political Ecology of Things.* Durham, NH and London: Duke University Press.

21 Jonathan Sterne, 2003, *The Audible Past. Cultural Origins of Sound Reproduction.* Durham, NH and London, Duke University Press, p. 13.

22 Peter Hook, 2013, *Unknown Pleasures. Inside Joy Division.* New York: itbooks, p. 168.

23 Brian Eno, 2001, 'In conversation with Max Dax', *Electronic Beats Magazine*, Fall, no. 3, p. 60.

24 Paolo Maguadda, 2011, 'When materiality bites back. Digital music practice in the age of dematerialisation', *Journal of Consumer Culture*, vol. 11, no. 1, pp. 15–36.

25 Daniel Miller, 1998, *A Theory of Shopping.* New York: Cornell University Press.

THING: QUALITIES AND ENTANGLEMENTS

1 Morrissey, 2013, *Autobiography*. London: Penguin Classics, p. 79.

2 P. Magguada, 2011, 'When materiality "bites back": digital music consumption practices in the age of dematerialization', *Journal of Consumer Culture*, vol. 11, no. 1, pp. 15–36.

3 H. White, 1990, *The Content of the Form. Narrative Discourse and Historical Representation.* Baltimore, NJ: Johns Hopkins University Press.

4 W. Welsch, 1998, 'Immaterialization vs. Rematerialization', *Localizer 1.3* (Icons), Berlin: Gestalten.

5 Morrissey, *ibidem*, p. 79.

6 M. Emmison and P. Smith, 2000, *Researching the Visual. Images, Objects, Contexts and Interactions in Social and Cultural Inquiry.* London: Sage, p. 111.

7 See Webb Keane, 2005, 'Signs are not the Garb of Meaning: On the Social Analysis of Material Things', in D. Miller (ed.), 2005, *Materiality*. Durham, NH: Duke University Press, p. 186.

8 M. Merleau-Ponty, 2012, *Phenomenology of Perception*. London: Routledge, p. 352.

9 I. Hodder, 2012, *Entangled. An Archaeology of the Relationships Between Humans and Things*. Oxford: Wiley-Blackwell, p. 94.

10 See D. Miller, 2010, *Stuff*. Cambridge: Polity, pp. 12–41.

11 M. Merleau-Ponty, 2012, *Phenomenology of Perception*. London: Routledge, p. 334.

12 M. Heidegger, 1962, *Being and Time*. New York: Harper & Row, pp. 96–8.

13 *Ibidem*, p. 27.

14 *Ibidem*, pp. 97–8.

15 *Ibidem*, p. 102.

16 *Ibidem*, p. 103.

17 Emile Durkheim, 1995, *Elementary Forms of Religious Life*. New York: Free Press, p. 421.

18 Peter Hook, 2013, *Unknown Pleasures. Inside Joy Division*. New York: itbooks, p. 15.

19 S. Daynes, 2010, *Time and Memory in Reggae Music: The Politics of Hope*. Manchester: University of Manchester Press, p. 33.

20 G. Early, 2008, 'The Last King of America: How Miles Davis Invented Modernity', in *Miles Davis's Special Edition Album Kind of Blue. The 50th Anniversary*. New York: Columbia Records, p. 32.

21 *Ibidem*, p. 30.

22 Robert Haagsma, 2013, *Passion for Vinyl. A Tribute to All Who Dig the Groove*. Haarlem: Record Industry, p. 17.

23 In the 1950s different companies developed such a stereo cut, for example Neumann that offered its technology in 1956 and by the end of the decade was the only one delivering complete tape-to-disc transfer technology.

24 See Walter Moser and Klaus Albrecht Schröder (eds), *Blow-Up. Antonioni's Classic Film and Photography*. Ostfilern and Vienna: Hatje Cantz and Albertina, p. 256.

25 Morrissey, *ibidem*, p. 211.

26 Ross Jackson, 'Under the covers: Stefan Marx', *Resident Adviser*. Viewed 21 June 2014, http://www.residentadvisor.net/feature.aspx?1332

27 Daniel Miller, 1987, *Material Culture and Mass Consumption*. Oxford: Blackwell, p. 116.

28 Antoine Hennion, 2001, 'Music lovers: taste as performance', *Theory, Culture & Society*, vol. 18, no. 1, p. 4.

29 Peter Shapiro, 2002, 'Deck Wreckers: The Turntable as Instrument,' in R. Young (ed.), *Undercurrents. The Hidden Wiring of Modern Music*. London and New York: Continuum.

30 Viewed 12 April 2014, http://www.change.org/en-AU/petitions/panasonic-company-re-introduction-of-legendary-technics-turntables

31 Hans Belting, 2012, 'Body and Image', in Jeffrey Alexander, Dominik Bartmanski and Bernhard Giesen (eds), *Iconic Power: Materiality and Meaning in Social Life*. New York: Palgrave, p. 190.

32 From the track 'Anonymous Collective', *Emperor Tomato Ketchup*, LP by Stereolab, 1996.

COMMODITY: VALUE AND MARKETS

1 David Howes, 2005, 'Hyperesthesia, or, The Sensual Logic of Late Capitalism', in David Howes (ed.), *Empire of the Senses. The Sensual Culture Reader*. Oxford: Berg, p. 284.

2 All prices and notes referred to below are accessed from the *Rare Record Price Guide* online, February 2013, from http://www.rarerecordpriceguide.com/

3 'Rare Sex Pistols 'God Save the Queen' single sells for almost $20,000 at auction', *New Musical Express*. Viewed, http://www.nme.com/news/sex-pistols/64239

4 Ian Woodward, 2011, 'Towards an object-relations theory of consumerism. The aesthetics of desire and the unfolding materiality of social life', *Journal of Consumer Culture*, vol. 11, pp. 366–84.

5 See the website for Analogue Productions. Viewed 12 April 2014, http://analogueproductions.com/index.cfm

6 David Harvey, 1989, *The Condition of Postmodernity*. Oxford: Blackwell.

7 Henry Rollins, 'The Column! Are You Collector Scum?', *LA Weekly*, January 19, 2012. Viewed 30 May 2014, http://www.laweekly.com/westcoastsound/2012/01/19/henry-rollins-the-column-are-you-collector-scum

8 Keith Richards, 2011, *Life*. London, Phoenix, p. 141.

9 Jeffrey Alexander, 2004, 'From the depths of despair: performance, counterperformance, and "September 11"', *Sociological Theory*, vol. 22, no. 1, p. 92.

10 Jeffrey Alexander, 2011, *Performance and Power*. London: Polity, p. 85.

11 The process of making the accompanying artworks and packaging for Brian Eno's *Small Craft on a Milk Sea* is photographically documented on the website http://www.thefoxisblack.com. See http://www.thefoxisblack.com/2010/11/01/limited-edition-small-craft-on-a-milk-sea-by-brian-eno/ (accessed 16 September 2014)

12 No Anchor, 'Real Pain Supernova (Vinyl Release)', http://noanchor.bandcamp.com/album/real-pain-supernova-vinyl-edition (accessed 13 March 2012)

13 In a review of 'Real Pain Supernova' on the website Messandnoise.com, See the review at http://messandnoise.com/releases/2000882 (accessed 16 September 2014)

14 'Peter Saville Wins London Design Medal 2013', *Dezeen Magazine*, 16 September 2013. Viewed 22 June 2014, http://www.dezeen.com/2013/09/16/peter-saville-wins-london-design-medal-2013/

15 *Ibidem*.

16 For an excellent online resource that documents the sleeves, packages and covers of Peter Saville, see, http://www.petersaville.info/sleeves/ (accessed 16 September 2014)

17 Nick Compton 2013, Peter Saville, *Wallpaper*.

18 Yochim and Biddinger, 2008.

19 See The Vinyl Factory's website at: http://www.thevinylfactory.com/ (accessed 16 September 2014)

20 The Vinyl Record Collector Blog, 22/01/14 (accessed 22 January 2014)

21 See the Kickstarter project page: https://www.kickstarter.com/projects/watmmofficial/cat023-caustic-window-own-the-legendary-record-by (accessed 16 September 2014)

22 Regis Debray, 2000, *Transmitting Culture*. New York: Columbia University Press, p. 84.

23 David Graeber, 2007, *Possibilities: Essays on Hierarchy, Rebellion and Desire*, Oakland, CA: AK Press.

24 Jeffrey Alexander, 2008, 'The material feeling of meaning', *Environment and Planning D*, p. 782.

25 Thomas Selig and Urs Stahel (eds), 2004, *The Ecstasy of Things: From the Functional Object to the Fetish in 20th Century Photographs*. Winterthur: Steidl Verlag.

TOTEM: SCENE-MAKING IN URBAN SPACES

1 Eric Felten, 2012, 'It's alive! Vinyl makes a comeback', *The Wall Street Journal*, 27 January. Viewed 3 May 2013, http://online.wsj.com/article/SB10001424052970204573704577184973290800632.html#articleTabs%3Darticle; M. Perpetua, 2011, 'Vinyl sales increase despite industry slump', *Rolling Stone*, 6 January. Available at: http://www.rollingstone.com/music/news/vinyl-sales-increase-despite-industry-slump-20110106

2 Wendy Griswold, Gemma Mangione and Terence E. McDonnell (2013), 'Objects, words, and bodies in space: bringing materiality into cultural analysis', *Qualitative Sociology*, 36(4): pp. 343–64.

3 Martina Löw, 2013, 'The city as experiential space. The repoduction of shared meaning', *International Journal of Urban and Regional Research*, vol. 37, no. 3, pp. 894–908.

4 Dominik Bartmanski, 2012, 'The Liminal Cityscape: Post-communist Warsaw as Collective Representation', in Monika Grubbauer and Joanna Kusiak (eds), *Chasing Warsaw: Socio-material Dynamics of Urban Change Since 1990*. Frankfurt and New York: Campus, p. 140.

5 Ian Hodder, 2012, *Entangled. An Archaeology of Relationships Between Humans and Things*. Malden, MA: Wiley-Blackwell, p. 137.

6 See Margaret Borschke, 2011, 'Disco edits and their discontents: the persistence of the analog in a digital age', *New Media & Society*, vol. 13, no. 6, pp. 929–44; Roy Shuker, 2004, 'Beyond the "high fidelity" stereotype: defining the contemporary record collector', *Popular Music*, vol. 23, no. 3, pp. 311–30; Roy Shuker, 2010, *Wax Trash and Vinyl Junkies: Record Collecting as a Social Practice*. Aldershot: Ashgate.

7 Mark D. Jacobs and Lynn Spillman, 2005, 'Cultural sociology at the crossroads of the discipline', *Poetics*, vol. 33, pp. 1–14.

8 Terrence McDonnell, 2010, 'Cultural objects as objects: materiality, urban space, and the interpretation of AIDS campaigns in Accra, Ghana', *American Journal of Sociology*, vol. 115, no. 6, pp. 1800–52.

9 David Simpson, 2002, *Situatedness, or Why We Keep Saying Where We're Coming From*. Durham, NH and London: Duke University Press.

10 Martina Löw, 2008, 'A City's Own Logic. The Perspective of Spatial Sociology on Urban Theory', in Jolanta Bielanska *et al.* (eds), *Urban Potentials: Ideas and Practice*, Jovis, Berlin, pp. 280–5; Martina Löw, 2001, *Raumsoziologie*. Frankfurt: Suhrkamp; Ian Hodder, 2012, *Entangled. An Archaeology of the Relationships Between Humans and Things*. London: Wiley-Blackwell.

11 Jorge Fontdevila, 2010, 'Indexes, power, and netdoms: a multidimensional model of language in social action', *Poetics*, vol. 38, pp. 587–609.

12 I. Hodder, *ibidem*, p. 48.

13 Antoine Hennion, 2007, 'Those things that hold us together: taste & sociology', *Cultural Sociology*, vol. 1, no. 1, pp. 97–114.

14 Martina Löw, 2008. 'The constitution of space: the structuration of spaces through the simultaneity of effect and perception', *European Journal of Social Theory*, vol. 11, no. 25, pp. 25–49.

15 Ulf Hannerz, 1992, *Cultural Complexity. Studies in the Social Organization of Meaning*. New York: Columbia University Press, p. 6.

16 Will Straw, 2000. 'Exhausted Commodities: The Material Culture of Music', *Canadian Journal of Communication*, North America, 25 January. Viewed 9 November 2013. http://cjc-online.ca/index.php/journal/article/view/1148/1067

17 Sonia Bookman, 2013 'Branded cosmopolitanisms: "global" coffee brands and the co-creation of "cosmopolitan cool"', *Cultural Sociology*, vol. 7, no. 1, pp. 56–72.

18 Arjun Appadurai, 1996, *Modernity at Large: Cultural Dimensions of Globalisation*. Minneapolis, MN: University of Minnesota Press.

19 Bill Brewster, 2012, 'We Breathe Rhythm', in Ata Macias and Christoph Keller (eds), *Come on in my Kitchen. The Robert Johnson Book*. Frankfurt am Main: Ata Macias/ Christoph Keller Editions, p. 210.

20 Philip Smith, 1999, 'The elementary forms of place and their transformations: a Durkheimian model', *Qualitative Sociology*, vol. 22, no. 1, pp. 13–36.

21 Bill Brewster and Frank Broughton, 2010, *The Record Players: DJ Revolutionaries*. London: DJhistory.

22 Gary Calamar and Phil Gallo, 2009, *Record Store Days: From Vinyl to Digital and Back Again*. New York: Sterling, p. x.

23 Sarah Hegenbart and Sven Mündner (eds), 2012, *Mythos Berlin: A London Perspective*. London: The White Review.

24 Ingo Bader and Albert Scharenberg, 2013, 'The Sound of Berlin. Subculture and Global Music Industry', in Matthias Bernt, Britta Grell and Andrej Holm (eds), *The Berlin Reader. A Compendium on Urban Change and Activism*. Bielefeld: Transcript, pp. 239–58.

25 Felix Denk and Sven von Thülen, 2012, *Der Kland der Familie: Berlin, Techno und die Wende*. Berlin: Suhrkamp, p. 10.

26 Witold Rybczynski, 1995, *City Life. Urban Expectations in a New World*. New York: Scribner.

27 Matthias Bernt, Britta Grell and Andrej Holm (eds), 2013, *The Berlin Reader. A Compendium on Urban Change and Activism*. Bielefeld: Transcript, p. 14.

28 Brian Ladd, 1997, *Ghosts of Berlin. Confronting German History in the Urban Landscape*. Chicago, IL and London: University of Chicago Press, p. 3.

29 Gary Calamar and Phil Gallo, 2009, *Record Store Days: From Vinyl to Digital and Back Again*. New York: Sterling, p. xv.

30 *Ibidem*.

31 Florian Sievers, 2013, 'Es ist schwierig, es klein zu halten. Interview with Michael Hain and Torsten Pröfrock', *Groove*, September/October: 65.

32 Denk and von Thülen, *ibidem*, p. 10

33 Dimitri Hegemann, 2013, 'The alphabet according to Dimitri Hegemann', *Electronic Beats: Conversations on Essential Issues*, vol. 35, pp. 30–3.

34 Tobias Rapp, 2010, *Lost and Sound. Berlin, Techno and the Easyjet Set*. Berlin: Innervisions, p. 133.

35 *Ibidem*.

36 Merleau-Ponty, 2012, p. xxxiv.

37 Hennion, 2001, p. 1.

38 Steven Feld, 2005, 'Places Sensed, Senses Placed. Toward a Sensuous Epistemology of Environments', in David Howes (ed.), *Empire of the Senses. The Sensual Culture Reader*. Oxford and New York: Berg, p. 179.

EPILOGUE: MODERN ICON

1 Michael Bull, 2007, *Sound Moves. iPod culture and urban experience*. London: Routledge, p. 5.

2 David Shenk, 2007, *Data Smog: Surviving the Information Glut*. New York: HarperOne.

3 Deborah Curtis, cited by Laura Barton in a *Guardian* article, 'I was just besotted'. Viewed 8 June 2014, http://www.theguardian.com/music/2005/apr/11/popandrock.joydivision

4 Jane Bennett, 2010, *Vibrant Matter: A political ecology of things*. Durham, NH and London: Duke University Press.

5 Michael Bull, *ibidem*.

6 Hans Belting, 2012, 'Body and Image', in Jeffrey Alexander, Dominik Bartmanski and Bernhard Giesen, *Iconic Power: Materiality and Meaning in Social Life*. New York: Palgrave, p. 190.

7 Russell W. Belk, 1995, *Collecting in a Consumer Society*. New York, Routledge.

8 Gary Calamar and Phil Gallo, 2009, *Record Store Days: From Vinyl to Digital and Back Again*. New York: Sterling.

9 Pierre Bourdieu, 1984, *Distinction: A Social Critique of the Judgment of Taste*. Cambridge, MA: Harvard University Press, p. 100.

10 *Ibidem*, p. 101.

11 Jane Bennett, 2010, *Vibrant Matter: A Political Ecology of Things*. Durham, NH and London: Duke University Press.

12 Jeffrey Alexander, Dominik Bartmanski and Bernhard Giesen, *Iconic Power: Materiality and Meaning in Social Life*. New York: Palgrave.

13 Bennett, *ibidem*, p. 5.

14 Constance Classen, 2012, *The Deepest Sense. A Cultural History of Touch*. Urbana, Chicago, Springfield, IL: University of Illinois Press, p. xii.

15 *Ibidem*, p. 9.

16 Ian Woodward, 2007, *Understanding Material Culture*. London: Sage, p. 29.

17 Ralf Burmeister, Alexander Klee and Annelie Lütgens, 'Introduction', in *Vienna-Berlin: The Art of Two Cities*. Munich, London, New York: Prestel, p. 16.

18 See Jordan Rothlein, 2013, 'Borderland: Inside the Electric Garden. Conversation with Moritz von Oswald & Juan Atkins'. Viewed 8 June 2014, http://www.residentadvisor.net/feature.aspx?1894

19 See Isaac Reed, 2009, 'Culture as Object and Approach in Sociology', in Jeffrey Alexander and Isaac Reed (eds), *Meaning and Method: The Cultural Approach to Sociology*. p. 3. He writes: 'One has to involve oneself in the messy work of studying subjectivity and its manifestation in, and molding by, discourse.'

20 See for example, Nick Osbaldiston, 2013, *Culture of the Slow, Social Deceleration in an Accelerated World*. London: Palgrave Macmillan.

21 Regis Debray, 2000, *Transmitting Culture*. New York: Columbia University Press, p. 92.

22 Dominik Bartmanski and Jeffrey Alexander, 2012, 'Materiality and Meaning in Social Life: Toward an Iconic Turn in Cultural Sociology', in Jeffrey Alexander, Dominik Bartmanski and Bernhard Giesen (eds), *Iconic Power: Materiality and Meaning in Social Life*. New York: Palgrave, pp. 1–12.

23 Gottfried Boehm, 2012, 'Representation, Presentation, Presence: Tracing the Homo Pictor', in Jeffrey Alexander, Dominik Bartmanski and Bernhard Giesen, *Iconic Power: Materiality and Meaning in Social Life*. New York: Palgrave, p. 21.

24 Nigel Thrift, 2005, 'Beyond Mediation: Three New Material Registers and their Consequences', in Daniel Miller (ed.), *Materiality*. Durham, NH and London: Duke University Press, pp. 231–55.

25 Dominik Bartmanski, 2011, 'Successful icons of failed time. Rethinking postcommunist nostalgia', *Acta Sociologica*, vol. 54, no. 3, pp. 213–33.

26 Bruno Latour, 2010, *On the Modern Cult of the Factish Gods*. Durham, NH and London: Duke University Press, p. 43.

27 P. Virno, 2008, 'Three Remarks Regarding the Multitude's Subjectivity and Its Aesthetic Component', in D. Birnbaum and I. Graw (eds), *Under Pressure. Pictures, Subjects, and the New Spirit of Capitalism*. Berlin: Sternberg Press, pp. 31–45.

BIBLIOGRAPHY

Alexander, Jeffrey C., 2004, 'From the depths of despair: performance, counterperformance, and "September 11"', *Sociological Theory*, vol. 22, no. 1, pp. 88–105.

—2008, 'Iconic consciousness: the material feeling of meaning', *Environment and Planning D: Society and Space*, vol. 26, no. 5, pp. 782–94.

—2011, *Performance and Power*. London: Polity.

Alexander, Jeffrey C., Bartmanski, Dominik and Giesen, Bernhard, 2012, *Iconic Power: Materiality and Meaning in Social Life*. New York: Palgrave.

Analogue Productions, viewed 12 April 2014, http://analogueproductions.com/index.cfm

Appadurai, Arjun, 1990, *Modernity at Large: Cultural Dimensions of Globalization*. Minneapolis, MN: University of Minnesota Press.

Bader, Ingo and Scharenberg, Albert, 2013, 'The Sound of Berlin: Subculture and Global Music Industry', in Matthias Bernt, Britta Grell and Andrej Holm (eds), *The Berlin Reader: A Compendium on Urban Change and Activism*. Bielefeld: Transcript.

Bartmanski, Dominik, 2011, 'Successful icons of failed time: rethinking postcommunist nostalgia', *Acta Sociologica*, vol. 54, no. 3, pp. 213–33.

—2012, 'The Liminal Cityscape: Post-communist Warsaw as Collective Representation', in Monika Grubbauer and Joanna Kusiak (eds), *Chasing Warsaw: Socio-material Dynamics of Urban Change Since 1990*. Frankfurt and New York: Campus.

—2014, 'The word/image dualism revisited: towards an iconic conception of visual culture', *Journal of Sociology*, vol. 50, no. 2, pp. 164–81.

Bartmanski, Dominik and Alexander, Jeffrey, C., 2012, 'Materiality and Meaning in Social Life: Toward an Iconic Turn in Cultural Sociology', in Jeffrey Alexander, Dominik Bartmanski and Bernhard Giesen, *Iconic Power: Materiality and Meaning in Social Life*. New York: Palgrave.

Bartmanski, Dominik and Woodward, Ian, 2013, 'The vinyl: the analogue medium in the age of digital reproduction', *Journal of Consumer Culture*, published online before print 31 May 2013.

Barton, Laura, 2005, 'I was just besotted', *Guardian*, 11 April, viewed 8 June 2014, http://www.theguardian.com/music/2005/apr/11/popandrock.joydivision

Bataille, Georges, 2012, *Eroticism*. London: Penguin.

Belk, Russell W., 1995, *Collecting in a Consumer Society*. New York: Routledge.

Belting, Hans, 2012, 'Body and Image', in Jeffrey Alexander, Dominik Bartmanski and Bernhard Giesen, *Iconic Power: Materiality and Meaning in Social Life*. New York: Palgrave.

Bennett, Jane, 2010, *Vibrant Matter: A Political Ecology of Things*. Durham, NC and London: Duke University Press.

Bernt, Matthias, Grell, Britta and Holm, Andrej (eds), 2013, *The Berlin Reader: A Compendium on Urban Change and Activism*. Bielefeld: Transcript.

Boehm, Gottfried, 2012, 'Representation, Presentation, Presence: Tracing the Homo Pictor', in Jeffrey Alexander, Dominik Bartmanski and Bernhard Giesen, *Iconic Power: Materiality and Meaning in Social Life*. New York: Palgrave.

Bookman, Sonia, 2013, 'Branded cosmopolitanisms: "global" coffee brands and the co-creation of "cosmopolitan cool"', *Cultural Sociology*, vol. 7, no. 1, pp. 56–72.

Borschke, Margaret, 2011, 'Disco edits and their discontents: the persistence of the analog in a digital age', *New Media & Society*, vol. 13, no. 6, pp. 929–44.

Bourdieu, Pierre, 1984, *Distinction: A Social Critique of the Judgment of Taste*. Cambridge, MA: Harvard University Press.

Brewster, Bill, 2012, 'We Breathe Rhythm', in Ata Macias and Christoph Keller (eds), *Come on in my Kitchen. The Robert Johnson Book*. Frankfurt am Main: Ata Macias/ Christoph Keller Editions.

Brewster, Bill and Broughton, Frank, 2006, *Last Night a DJ Saved my Life. The History of the Disc Jockey*. London: Headline.

—2010, *The Record Players: DJ Revolutionaries*. London: DJhistory.

Brown, Bill, 2001, 'Thing theory', *Critical Inquiry*, vol. 28, no. 1, pp. 1–22.

Bull, Michael, 2007, *Sound Moves: iPod Culture and Urban Experience*. London and New York: Routledge.

Bull, Michael and Back, Les (eds), 2005, *The Auditory Culture Reader*. Oxford: Berg.

Burmeister, Ralf, Klee, Alexander and Lütgens, Annelie, 2013, 'Introduction', in *Vienna-Berlin: The Art of Two Cities*. Munich, London, New York: Prestel.

Calamar, Gary and Gallo, Phil, 2009, *Record Store Days: From Vinyl to Digital and Back Again*. New York: Sterling.

Classen, Constance, 2012, *The Deepest Sense: A Cultural History of Touch*. Urbana, Chicago and Springfield, IL: University of Illinois Press.

Coleman, Mark, 2003, *Playback: From the Victrola to MP3, 100 Years of Music, Machines, and Money*. Cambridge, MA: Da Capo Press.

Compton, Nick, 2013, '6 degrees of Peter Saville', *Wallpaper**.

Cossu, Andrea and Bortolini, Matteo, 2013, 'The Spider and the Fly: Authenticity, Dualism, and the Rolling Stones', in Helmut Staubmann (ed.), *The Rolling Stones: Sociological Perspectives*, Lanham, MD: Lexington Books.

Crouch, Stanley, 2013, *Kansas City Lightning: The Rise and Times of Charlie Parker*. New York: HarperCollins.

Daniel, Moni, u.d., *Re-introduction of Legendary Technics Turntables*, petition, viewed 12 April 2014, http://www.change.org/en-AU/petitions/panasonic-company-re-introduction-of-legendary-technics-turntables

Davis, Clive, with Anthony DeCurtis, 2013, *The Soundtrack of My Life*. New York: Simon and Schuster.

Dax, Max, 2011, '"I was swimming in an ocean of time": Max Dax interviews Brian Eno', interview with Brian Eno, *Electronic Beats*, vol. 27, pp. 56–61.

Daynes, Sarah, 2010, *Time and Memory in Reggae Music: The Politics of Hope*. Manchester: University of Manchester Press.

Debray, Regis, 2000, *Transmitting Culture*. New York: Columbia University Press.

Denk, Felix and von Thülen, Sven, 2012, *Der Kland der Familie: Berlin, Techno und die Wende*. Berlin: Suhrkamp.

Douglas, Mary and Isherwood, Baron C., 1979, *The World of Goods: Towards an Anthropology of Consumption*. New York: Basic Books.

Du Gay, Paul, Hall, Stuart, Janes, Linda, Mackay, Hugh and Negus, Keith, 1997, *Doing Cultural Studies: The Story of the Sony Walkman*. London: Sage.

Duneier, Mitchell, 1999, *Sidewalk*. New York: Farrar, Strauss and Giroux.

Durkheim, Emile, 1995, *Elementary Forms of Religious Life*. New York: Free Press.

Early, Gerald, 2008, 'The Last King of America: How Miles Davis Invented Modernity', in *Kind of Blue: 50th Anniversary Collector's Edition*, vinyl box set. New York: Columbia Records.

Emmison, Michael and Smith, Philip, 2000, *Researching the Visual: Images, Objects, Contexts and Interactions in Social and Cultural Inquiry*. London: Sage.

Etherington, Rose, 2013, 'Peter Saville wins London Design Medal 2013', *dezeen magazine*, viewed 17 June 2014, http://www.dezeen.com/2013/09/16/peter-saville-wins-london-design-medal-2013/

Fehlmann, Thomas and Madlib, '"You've got to pay your dues": Madlib talks to Thomas Fehlmann', conversation between Madlib and Thomas Fehlmann, *Electronic Beats*, no. 32, Winter 2012/13, pp. 72–6.

Feld, Steven, 2005, 'Places Sensed, Senses Placed: Toward a Sensuous Epistemology of Environments', in David Howes (ed.), *Empire of the Senses: The Sensual Culture Reader*. Oxford: Berg.

Felten, Eric, 2012, 'It's alive! Vinyl makes a comeback', *The Wall Street Journal*, 27 January, viewed 3 May 2013, http://online.wsj.com/article/SB10001424052970204573704577184973290800632.html#articleTabs%3Darticle

Fischer, Hartwig, 2005, *Covering the Real: Art and the Press Picture from Warhol to Tillmans*. Köln: DuMont Literatur und Kunst Verlag & Kunstmuseum Basel.

Fontdevila, Jorge, 2010, 'Indexes, power, and netdoms: a multidimensional model of language in social action', *Poetics*, vol. 38, no. 6, pp. 587–609.

Graeber, David, 2007, *Possibilities: Essays on Hierarchy, Rebellion and Desire*. Oakland, CA: AK Press.

Griswold, Wendy, Gemma Mangione and Terence E. McDonnell, 2013, 'Objects, words and bodies in space: bringing materiality into cultural analysis', *Qualitative Sociology*, 36(4): pp. 343–64.

Haagsma, Robert, 2013, *Passion for Vinyl: A Tribute to all who Dig the Groove*. Haarlem, NY: Record Industry.

Hannerz, Ulf, 1992, *Cultural Complexity: Studies in the Social Organization of Meaning*. New York: Columbia University Press.

Hartenbach, Brett, u.d., review of *Bop Till you Drop,* viewed 30 April 2014, http://www.allmusic.com/album/bop-till-you-drop-mw0000189511

Harvey, David, 1989, *The Condition of Postmodernity*. Oxford: Blackwell.

Hegel, G. W. F., 1975, *Aesthetics. Lectures on Fine Art*, Volume II. Oxford: Clarendon Press.

Hegemann, Dimitri, 2013 'The alphabet according to Dimitri Hegemann', *Electronic Beats*, vol. 35, pp. 30–3.

Hegenbart, Sarah and Mündner, Sven (eds), 2012, *Mythos Berlin: A London Perspective*. London: The White Review.

Heidegger, Martin, 1962, *Being and Time*. New York: Harper & Row.

Henke, Robert, 2008, *Mastering*, interview with Rashad Becker, 15 July, http://www.monolake.de/interviews/mastering.html (accessed 16 September 2014)

Hennion, Antoine, 2007, 'Those things that hold us together: taste & sociology', *Cultural Sociology*, vol. 1, no. 1, pp. 97–114.

—'Music lovers: taste as performance', *Theory, Culture & Society*, vol. 18, no. 1, pp. 1–22.

Hertzman, Marc, 2013, *Making Samba: A New History of Race and Music in Brazil*. Durham, NC and London: Duke University Press.

Hodder, Ian, 2012, *Entangled. An Archaeology of the Relationships Between Humans and Things*. Malden, MA: John Wiley and Sons.

Holland, Rich, 2012, 'Steven Levy skypes with Rick Holland', *Electronic Beats Magazine*, no. 29, pp. 71–4, Spring 2012, viewed 20 June 2014, http://www.electronicbeats.net/en/features/conversations/steven-levy-skypes-with-rick-holland/

Hook, Peter, 2013, *Unknown Pleasures: Inside Joy Division*. New York: itbooks.

Howes, David, 2005, 'Hyperesthesia, or, the Sensual Logic of Late Capitalism', in David Howes (ed.), *Empire of the Senses: The Sensual Culture Reader*. Oxford: Berg.

Ingold, Tim, 2004, 'Culture on the ground: the world perceived through the feet', *Journal of Material Culture*, vol. 9, no 3, pp. 315–40.

Jackson, Ross, 2011, 'Under the covers: Stefan Marx', *Resident Advisor*, interview with Stefan Marx, viewed 21 June 2014, http://www.residentadvisor.net/feature.aspx?1332

Jacobs, Mark D. and Spillman, Lynn, 2005, 'Cultural sociology at the crossroads of the discipline', *Poetics*, vol. 33, no. 1, pp. 1–14.

Jäger, Michael and Käppelert, Christine, 2013, '"Techno ist wie ein Puls"', *Der Freitag Magazine*, 8 January, viewed 20 June 2014, http://www.freitag.de/autoren/christine-kaeppeler/techno-ist-wie-ein-puls

Jones, Sam, 2011, 'UK music sales decline for seventh successive year despite downloads', *Guardian*, 2 January. Available at: http://www.guardian.co.uk/music/2012/jan/02/uk-music-sales-decline-2011 (accessed 16 September 2014)

Keane, Webb, 2005, 'Signs are not the Garb of Meaning: On the Social Analysis of Material Things', in Daniel Miller (ed.), *Materiality*. Durham, NC: Duke University Press.

Knorr-Cetina, Karin and Bruegger, Urs, 2002, 'Global microstructures: the virtual societies of financial markets', *American Journal of Sociology*, vol. 107, no. 4, pp. 905–50.

Ladd, Brian, 1997, *The Ghosts of Berlin: Confronting German History in the Urban Landscape*. Chicago, IL: University of Chicago Press.

Lakoff, George and Johnson, Mark, 2003, *Metaphors We Live By*. Chicago, IL: University of Chicago Press.

Latour, Bruno, 2010, *On the Modern Cult of the Factish Gods*. Durham, NC and London: Duke University Press.

Löw, Martina, 2001, *Raumsoziologie*, Suhrkamp, Frankfurt.

—2008a, 'The constitution of space: the structuration of spaces through the simultaneity of effect and perception', *European Journal of Social Theory*, vol. 11, no. 25, pp. 25–49.

—2008b, 'A city's own logic: the perspective of spatial sociology on urban theory', in Jolanta Bielanska and Torsten Birne (eds), *(Urban potentials): Ideas and Practice*. Berlin: Jovis.

—2013, 'The city as experiential space. the reproduction of shared meaning', *International Journal of Urban and Regional Research*, vol. 37, no. 3, pp. 894–908.

McDonnell, Terrence, 2010, 'Cultural objects as objects: materiality, urban space, and the interpretation of AIDS campaigns in Accra, Ghana', *American Journal of Sociology*, vol. 115, no. 6, pp. 1800–52.

McLuhan, Marshall and Fiore, Quentin, 1967, *The Medium is the Message*. New York: Touchstone.

Maguadda, Paolo, 2011, 'When materiality bites back. Digital music practice in the age of dematerialisation', *Journal of Consumer Culture*, vol. 11, no. 1, pp. 15–36.

Marclay, Christian and Tone, Yasunao, 2004, 'Record, CD, Analog, Digital', in Christopher Cox and Daniel Warner (eds), *Audio Culture: Readings in Modern Music*. New York: Continuum.

Merleau-Ponty, Maurice, 2012, *Phenomenology of Perception*. London: Routledge.

Millard, Andre, 2005, *America On Record: A History of Recorded Sound*. Cambridge: Cambridge University Press.

Miller, Daniel, (ed.), 1987, *Material Culture and Mass Consumption*. Oxford: Blackwell.

—1998, *A Theory of Shopping*. New York: Cornell University Press.

—2005, *Materiality*. Durham, NC: Duke University Press.

—2010, *Stuff*. Cambridge: Polity.

Moorhouse, Roger, 2010, *Berlin at War*. New York: Basic Books.

Morrissey, 2013, *Autobiography*. London: Penguin Classics.

Moser, Walter and Schröder, Klaus Albrecht, 2014, *Blow-Up: Antonioni's Classic Film and Photography*. Ostfildern and Vienna: Hatje Cantz & Albertina.

No Anchor, *Real Pain Supernova*, vinyl release, http://noanchor.bandcamp.com/album/real-pain-supernova-vinyl-edition (accessed 13 March 2012).

Obrist, Hans Ulrich, 2011, '"Pythagoras saw the cosmos similarly": Hans Ulrich Obrist talks to Björk', interview with Björk Guðmundsdóttir, *Electronic Beats*, vol. 27, pp. 38–47.

Osbaldiston, Nick, 2013, *Culture of the Slow: Social Deceleration in an Accelerated World*. London: Palgrave Macmillan.

Patmore, David, 2009, 'Selling Sounds: Recordings and the Record Business', in Nicholas Cook, Eric Clarke, Daniel Leech-Wilkinson and John Rink (eds), *The Cambridge Companion to Recorded Music*. Cambridge: Cambridge University Press.

Perpetua, Matthew, 2011, 'Vinyl sales increase despite industry slump', *Rolling Stone*, 6 January, viewed 17 June 2014, http://www.rollingstone.com/music/news/vinyl-sales-increase-despite-industry-slump-20110106

Rancière, Jacques, 2010, 'Metamorphosis of the Muses', in Mela Davila (ed.) *Sonic Process*. Barcelona: MACBA.

Rapp, Tobias, 2010, *Lost and Sound: Berlin, Techno and the Easyjet Set*. Berlin: Innervisions.

Rare Record Price Guide, February 2013, viewed 17 June 2014, http://www.rarerecordpriceguide.com/

Rare Records, n.d., Homepage, Rare Records, viewed 22 May 2014, http://www.rare-records.net/

'Rare Sex Pistols "God Save the Queen" single sells for almost $20,000 at auction',

New Musical Express, viewed 13 February 2014, http://www.nme.com/news/sex-pistols/64239 (accessed 11 June 2012)

Reckwitz, Andreas, 2002, 'Toward a theory of social practices: a development in culturalist theorizing', *European Journal of Social Theory*, vol. 5, no. 2., pp. 243–63.

'Record Store Day ambassador Jack White: "There's no romance in a mouse click"', *New Musical Express*, viewed 14 June 2014, http://www.nme.com/news/jack-white/68853 (accessed 22 February 2013)

Reed, Isaac, 2009, 'Culture as Object and Approach in Sociology', in Jeffrey Alexander and Isaac Reed (eds), *Meaning and Method: The Cultural Approach to Sociology*. Boulder, CO: Paradigm Publishers.

Richards, Keith and Fox, James, 2010, *Life*. London: Phoenix.

Rojek, Chris, 2009, *The Labour of Leisure: The Culture of Free Time*. London: Sage.

Rollins, Henry, 2012, 'The column! Are you collector scum?', *LA Weekly*, 19 January 2012, viewed 9 May 2014, http://www.laweekly.com/westcoastsound/2012/01/19/henry-rollins-the-column-are-you-collector-scum

Rothlein, Jordan, 2013, 'Borderland: Inside the Electric Garden', conversation with Moritz von Oswald and Juan Atkins, *Resident Advisor*, viewed 8 June 2014, http://www.residentadvisor.net/feature.aspx?1894

Rybczynski, Witold, 1995, *City Life: Urban Expectations in a New World*. New York: Scribner.

Selig, Thomas and Stahel, Urs (eds), 2004, *The Ecstasy of Things: From the Functional Object to the Fetish in 20th Century Photographs*. Winterthur: Steidl Verlag.

Shapiro, Peter, 2002, 'Deck Wreckers: The Turntable as Instrument', in Rob Young (ed.), *Undercurrents: The Hidden Wiring of Modern Music*. London and New York: Continuum.

Shenk, David, 2007, *Data Smog: Surviving the Information Glut*. New York: HarperOne.

Sherman, Maria, 2013, '27 Breathtaking Record Stores you have to Shop at Before you Die', http://www.buzzfeed.com/mariasherm/best-record-stores-around-the-world (accessed 16 September 2014)

Shuker, Roy, 2004, 'Beyond the "high fidelity" stereotype: defining the contemporary record collector', *Popular Music*, vol. 23, no. 3, pp. 311–30.

—2010, *Wax Trash and Vinyl Junkies: Record Collecting as a Social Practice*. Aldershot: Ashgate.

Sievers, Florian, 2013, 'Es ist schwierig, es klein zu halten', interview with Michael Hain and Torsten Pröfrock, *Groove*, September/October 2013, p. 65.

Silverstone, Roger, 1993, 'Television, ontological security and the transitional object', *Media Culture and Society*, vol. 15, no. 4, pp. 573–98.

Simmel, Georg, 2008, *Englischsprachige Veröffentlichungen 1893–1910*. Frankfurt: Suhrkamp.

Simpson, David, 2002, *Situatedness, or, Why we Keep Saying Where we're Coming from*. Durham, NC and London: Duke University Press.

'Sleeve designed by Peter Saville: "Sleeves" pages', online database, viewed 17 June 2014, http://www.petersaville.info/sleeves/

Smith, Philip, 1999, 'The elementary forms of place and their transformations: a Durkheimian model', *Qualitative Sociology*, vol. 22, no. 1, pp. 13–36.

Solomon, Bobby, 2010, 'Limited edition "Small craft on a milk sea" by Brian Eno', viewed 17 June 2014, http://www.thefoxisblack.com/2010/11/01/limited-edition-small-craft-on-a-milk-sea-by-brian-eno/

Sterne, Jonathan, 2003, *The Audible Past: Cultural Origins of Sound Reproduction*. Durham, NH and London: Duke University Press.

Straw, Will, 2000, 'Exhausted commodities: the material culture of music', *Canadian Journal of Communication*, North America, vol. 25, no. 1, viewed 9 November 2013, http://cjc-online.ca/index.php/journal/article/view/1148/1067

Swidler, Ann, 2001, *Talk of Love: How Culture Matters*. Chicago, IL and London: University of Chicago Press.

Taussig, Michael, 1993, *Mimesis and Alterity: A Particular History of the Senses*. New York and London: Routledge.

The Vinyl Factory, n.d., homepage, The Vinyl Factory Limited, viewed 17 June 2014, http://www.thevinylfactory.com/

The Vinyl Record Collector blog, n.d., homepage, The Vinyl Record Collector, viewed 23 June 2014, http://www.vinylrecordcollector.net/

Thomas, James E., u.d., 'CAT023 caustic window – own the legendary record by RDJ!', Kickstarter, viewed 17 June 2014, https://www.kickstarter.com/projects/watmmofficial/cat023-caustic-window-own-the-legendary-record-by

Thrift, Nigel, 2005, 'Beyond Mediation: Three New Material Registers and their Consequences', in Daniel Miller (ed.), *Materiality*. Durham, NC and London: Duke University Press.

True, Everett, 2011, 'No Anchor: Real pain supernova', review of *Real pain supernova*, *Mess+Noise*, viewed 17 June 2014, http://messandnoise.com/releases/2000882

Van Assche, Christine, 2010, 'Sonic Process. A new Geography of Sounds', in Mela Davila (ed.), *Sonic Orocess*. Barcelona: MACBA.

Virno, Paolo, 2008, 'Three Remarks Regarding the Multitude's Subjectivity and its Aesthetic Component', in Daniel Birnbaum and Isabelle Graw (eds), *Under Pressure: Pictures, Subjects, and the New Spirit of Capitalism*. Berlin: Sternberg Press.

Welsch, Wolfgang, 1998, 'Immaterialization vs. Rematerialization', in Birgit Richard, Robert Klanten and Stefan Heidenreich, *Icons: Localizer 1.3*. Berlin: Gestalten.

White, Hayden, 1990, *The Content of the Form. Narrative Discourse and Historical Representation*. Baltimore, MD: Johns Hopkins University Press.

Wilde, Oscar, 2008, *The Picture of Dorian Gray*. London: Penguin Classics.

Wilder, Eliot, 2005, *DJ Shadow's Endtroducing*. London: Continuum.

Woodward, Ian, 2007, *Understanding Material Culture*. London: Sage.

—2011, 'Towards an object-relations theory of consumerism: the aesthetics of desire and the unfolding materiality of social life', *Journal of Consumer Culture*, vol. 11, no. 3, pp. 366–84.

Yale University Library, u.d., 'The history of 78 RPM recordings: A brief guide to aid in cataloging', viewed 9 June 2014, http://www.library.yale.edu/cataloging/music/historyof78rpms.htm

Yochim, Emily C. and Biddinger, Megan, 2008 '"It kind of gives you that vintage feel": vinyl records and the trope of death', *Media, Culture, and Society*, vol. 30, no. 2, pp. 183–95.

INDEX